SILCOX MOTOR COACH Co Ltd

PEMBROKE DOCK

SOUTH WALES

By Vernon Morgan

Silcox Motor Coach Company Ltd

Published by Vernon Morgan

October 2017

ISBN: 978-0-9574045-4-0

© Copyright Vernon Morgan (2017)

All photographs are from the author's collection unless otherwise stated.

Other titles published by the same author:

James of Ammanford   (A history of J James & Sons Ltd, Ammanford).

SWT 100   (The South Wales Transport Company Ltd 100th Anniversary).

Images of Old Llanelli & District   (Historical views of Llanelli & District).

Saml Eynon & Sons 'The HERO' (A history of S Eynon & Sons, Trimsaran).

<u>Cover Picture:</u> In the period from 1948 to 1954, Silcox built their own bus and coach bodies owing to the long waiting time of two to three years quoted by coachbuilders. This particular vehicle **SDE 450**, built on a new Bristol K6G chassis was the last of eleven bodies built by Silcox at their fully equipped workshops in Pembroke Dock. Designed by Leonard Silcox himself and built with assistance from his team of skilled craftsmen, it was very modern for the time with a front entrance and staircase, concealed radiator and a full front. Five years later they rebuilt it to rear entrance layout due to problems experienced with the electrically operated entrance doors. The near side windscreen glass was removed during its rebuild for safety reasons, it was continuously misting up on the inside. This photograph was coloured by Paul Banbury.

<u>Rear Cover:</u> New to Silcox in February 2005, ready for the new 'Silcox Coach Holiday' season, carrying a personalised registration mark **CU54 KWS** (Keith William Silcox) was this Volvo B12B with Caetano 'Enigma' C53FT coachwork. There were many styles of liveries in the Silcox fleet but the attractive lines of this coach presented the livery superbly.

<u>Title Page:</u> This excellent view of former Potteries Motor Transport, **LEH 759** was very kindly donated by Jim Saunders of Manchester for inclusion in this publication. The picture captures bus no 68, **LEH 759** a 1948 Leyland 'Titan' PD2/1 with NCME L27/26R body negotiating the notorious 'Bubbleston Bridge' on the B4139 road between Tenby and Lydstep, with only 12ft 6inch headroom, driven here by the late Hubert Williams in 1965. The local authority painted a series of white 'dots' on the road (visible in the photograph) which the driver would use as a guide, aligning the front wheels of the bus with the 'dots' to safely pass beneath the bridge. Obviously, only low-bridge type double-deckers could negotiate the arch, which had another complication – it was situated on a double bend. Silcox's predecessor on the route, D J Morrison of Tenby used a Leyland 'Titanic' on this service during W W II, due to the large Military presence in the area. On a Saturday night, the 'Titanic' would carry massive loads of up to 100 servicemen into Tenby for a night out.

AUTHOR'S ACKNOWLEDGEMENTS

The task of compiling this publication has been an enormous challenge and a pleasure. The extensive research and production of the final product has taken over six years and I'm indebted to numerous people for their sincere help and assistance in compiling it. The photograph collection however has taken a lifetime to collect – beginning in 1960 when I first started visiting the Silcox establishment at Waterloo, Pembroke Dock.

First of all I would like to tender my grateful thanks to my wife Kath, and Katie my daughter for their understanding, co-operation and tolerance over the years, sitting patiently in the car whilst I photographed vehicles at numerous locations. As a child, Katie's 'reward' for her patience would be a visit to her favourite castle – the medieval Pembroke Castle, birthplace of Henry Tudor, later Henry VII of England. Our return home would include a visit to Tenby with more photography and another 'reward' for Katie, a delicious ice cream at Fecci's Ice Cream Parlour.

Special thanks are due to the late Alan Mills of The Omnibus Society Library and Archive at Walsall, for allowing access to their extensive collections, in particular the Notices & Proceedings of the Traffic Commissioners. Access to the photographic collection was provided by Photo Archivist, Alan Oxley. I would also like to thank Dick Picton, former garage foreman at Silcox's Waterloo Garage. Dick had spent his entire working career of fifty years with the company, and has assisted me with additional information, answered several queries and corrected numerous details.

Thanks also to Alan Broughall, Alan Cross, Chris Carter, Chris Mann, Jason Feeley, Jim Saunders, John Bennett, Robert Edworthy and Stephen Powell, for the use of their photographs, not forgetting the late Arnold Richardson, Chris Taylor, D S Giles, Geoffrey Morant, Hubert Williams, John Fielder, Robert Mack, Roy Marshall, R H G Simpson and S E Letts. Thank you also to fellow enthusiasts Andrew Porter, Clive Thomas, John Jones, Meirion Jones (Carmarthenshire C C, Passenger Transport Unit), Mike Hayward, Paul Fox and Richard Evans, for individual contributions and encouragement and to Paul Banbury for colouring the cover photograph.

Most other photographs are views taken by myself or views from my large collection. It has not always been possible to identify the photographer. No discourtesy is intended through lack of acknowledgement, in view of which I trust they will accept my sincere thanks.

Much valuable information has also come from material in the care of Pembrokeshire County Council Cultural Services Department; Carmarthenshire County Council Passenger Transport Unit; The PSV Circle; The Omnibus Society and the archives of Andrew Porter.

CONTENTS

INTRODUCTION

Silcox Motor Coach Company Ltd, were for many years Pembrokeshire's largest passenger vehicle operator, at their peak operating no less than 74 vehicles on local services, contract services, private hire, tours, excursions and holidays, the latter extending to all parts of Great Britain and Europe.

The humble beginnings of this well renowned family concern began in 1882 when William Luther Silcox migrated from Trowbridge, Wiltshire to open a saddlery business at the new military town of Pembroke Dock. The business at Water Street slowly expanded to occupy adjoining buildings when he became a cycle agent and later a motor cycle agent.

W L Silcox's eldest son Luther John Watts Silcox joined the thriving business and qualified as a cycle repairer after training at the BSA cycle factory in Birmingham. The business steadily expanded to include a taxi service, car hire, and a motor car agency, with car sales and vehicle repairs in 1911.

When W L Silcox passed away in 1911, his fourth son William Howard Silcox joined his brother Luther J W Silcox to run the family business which continued to expand taking over a local bus company previously owned by John Rowline Ford of Pembroke in September 1933. This was an ambitious step taken by the Silcox family during the economic depression of the 1930s, with an exceptionally high number of unemployed in the area after the R N Dockyard's closure.

However, the business prospered during World War 2 due to a large military presence in the area, and in the early post-war period there was an acute shortage of new vehicles. This prompted the company to build their own *unique* bus and coach bodies, most of them on Bristol chassis – the General Managers preference.

Expansion continued, absorbing the businesses of E C James, Pembroke in 1948, G B Rees, Angle in 1949, D J Morrison and Grey Garages, Tenby in 1958, combined with additional contract work arriving from the construction of the oil refineries and oil terminals in the area during the 1960's. There was additional contract work in later years with the construction of two L N G terminals and Pembroke power station.

The limited company – Silcox Motor Coach Company Ltd, was formed in December 1960.

Throughout their existence Silcox had gained a tremendous reputation, having reliably served the travelling public of south Pembrokeshire with an excellent transport network for almost a century. However, the much loved company with a name that had become a household word in south-west Wales, suffered serious financial difficulties which culminated as the directors attempted to source a buyer for the business. Their attempt failed, resulting in the company's sad demise, being placed into administration on 6th June 2016.

The Silcox business was split between five operators, the largest part passing to Edwards Coaches of Llantwit Fardre, with First Group subsidiary - First Cymru Buses taking a share along with Taf Valley Coaches of Whitland (D Clive Edwards), Edwards Bros of Tiers Cross and A Phillips of Trecwn, Fishguard.

It must be noted that the spelling of place names referred to in this story are taken from authenticated records of that period, as several welsh place names were changed to the true welsh spelling from around 1960 onwards.

HOW THE BUISNESS STARTED

William Luther Silcox, founder of the Silcox 'empire' was born at Trowbridge, Wiltshire in 1858, where he became a saddle and harness maker by the age of 13.

Seeking better prospects in 1882, William L Silcox and his wife Ellen (nee Watts) migrated from the quiet Wiltshire town, and moved with their infant daughter to the prosperous new military town of Pembroke Dock, which had greatly expanded following the construction of a Royal Naval Dockyard there in 1814. This distinguished dockyard built numerous famous battleships for the admiralty, together with five Royal Yachts during its comparatively short operational period.

Here at Pembroke Dock, William Luther Silcox opened his own saddlery business, and contracted to the Military from his premises at Water Street, which soon expanded to occupy adjoining properties when he began hiring out a pony and trap in 1887. He employed his own groom/coachman, and became a general dealer selling hay, corn, straw and fancy goods. By 1898, he became an agent for Rudge-Whitworth bicycles and soon expanded the business to include a motorcycle dealership. As the business expanded, so did the family, having ten children by 1904, five sons and five daughters. However, not all the family worked in the business but the eldest son, Luther John Watts Silcox joined his father as a saddler, and after completing a training course at the BSA (Birmingham Small Arms Co) cycle factory, Small Heath, Birmingham, he qualified as a cycle repairer by 1900.

W. L. SILCOX

17 & 19 Water Street,
Pembroke Dock

**General Saddler,
Harness Maker,**

and Army Contractor

**GOOD HAY, CORN,
and STRAW**

Always kept in stock

**FANCY DEALER &
WATERPROOF
WAREHOUSE**

Pony and Trap let on hire at
Moderate terms.

Left: This very early advertisement for W L Silcox's extremely diverse business was found in the Pembroke & Pembroke Dock Gazette dated February 1889.

Below: Another interesting advertisement was found in the 'small ads' section of the Western Mail newspaper dated 27th July 1892.

WANTED, Situation as Groom-Coachman; thoroughly up to his duties; ride and drive well.—Apply to Mr. Silcox. Saddler. Pembroke Dock.

The business steadily expanded in subsequent years to include car hire and a taxi service in 1914. Car sales and repairs commenced in 1911 with an agency for Ford and Oldsmobile motor cars. Some of the early hire fleet were Ford model 'T' cars locally registered as DE 464/787/844, together with a Daimler Landaulette DE 1304, Briscoe Tourer DE 1953 and a second-hand 1914 Overland 20hp registered BX 439, which had previously operated with a Hackney Carriage owner at Pontyates.

However, W L Silcox & Son were not the first car hire business in the community, as that can be credited to J & A Stephens of East Back Works, Pembroke, who also operated the first motor omnibus in the community when they bought a second-hand double decker called 'The Dreadnought' in May 1910. Additionally, J & A Stephens were cycle dealers, competing against Silcox's cycle agency.

Left: The first motor omnibus to enter service at Pembroke in 1910 was this 1906 ABC (All British Car Company Ltd) double deck bus which had an un-laden weight of 2 tons 11 cwt and seated around 34. Registered **DE 243**, it was called 'The Dreadnought' after the famous 1906 battleship of the same name. It was purchased second-hand by Pembroke's first omnibus proprietor, J & A Stephens Pembroke in May 1910. Manufacturers of ABC vehicles were at Bridgeton, Glasgow and were known to have built only ten buses.

W L Silcox sadly passed away on 1st July 1911 at the age of 53. After his death, his fourth son William Howard Silcox by then aged 18, relinquished his position as a student teacher to join his elder brother L J W Silcox to run the family business.

The business survived the four long years of World War I (1914-8) reasonably well considering there was a severe petrol shortage, coupled with competitors setting up transport businesses in car hire, haulage and passenger services. The Great Western Railway Company had also made their presence known in Pembrokeshire, operating bus services as feeder services to the railway stations, not leaving much scope for other transport operators in the rural communities of Pembrokeshire.

Left: Another early bus operator in Pembroke was haulier, John Ford of Quay Street, Pembroke. One of Ford's charabancs **DE 3789** seen here on an outing, was a 'Karrier' 20 seater with detachable body, dating from 1921. The other vehicle is probably DE 4650, a 39hp 'Bean' of Grey Garages Ltd, Water St, Pembroke Dock, later moving to Tenby. It's likely that both vehicles had detachable bodies, common-place in those far gone days. Charabanc bodies could be interchanged with platform lorry bodies, to allow the carriage of goods.

A short while later in 1925 came the devastating news of the Dockyard's closure, which took place in the year of the 'General Strike' 1926, followed by the economic depression. Unemployment became very high in the area making it extremely difficult for the Silcox business to survive until the Royal Air Force 210 Squadron arrived at Pembroke Dock in 1931 with their 'Flying Boats'. Pembroke Dock later became the largest operational base for flying boats in the world.

Despite all their difficulties, the next major event in the company's history was to purchase the passenger services and buses owned by John Rowline Ford, of The Stores, Quay Street, Pembroke. Formerly a miller, John Ford was a local haulier and bus operator, and at the age of 52 decided to slim down his business and sell the bus services to the Silcox family, continuing with the haulage business until he passed away six years later. Ford's bus services passed into Silcox ownership in September 1933 together with the nine Road Service Licences (RSLs) and a mixed fleet of eight Dennis, Guy, and Thornycroft buses.

This was the beginning of the company's bus operation, but expansion to that side of the business was slow at first due to the economic depression. The fleet name 'Ford & Silcox' was used for a short while together with 'John Ford's Bus Service' on all their time tables – simply as a good will gesture. The company at this time were still trading as W L Silcox & Son, of 15/17/19 Water Street, Pembroke Dock, and applied to the Ministry of Transport Traffic Commissioners on 27th September 1933 for the licences previously held by J R Ford. The licences were all granted in November 1933 as follows:-

TGR 1847/1: **Pembroke Dock (Hobbs Point) to Pembroke (East End)**
via: Water St, Laws St, Pembroke St, High St, The Green, Pembroke (Main St).

TGR 1847/2: **Pembroke Dock to Wallaston Cross**, via: Pembroke, Monkton and Hundleton.
Note: this service was extended to reach Angle in December 1935.

TGR 1847/3: **Pembroke Dock to Merrion**,
via: Monkton, Hundleton and Castlemartin, returning via Loveston, Chapel Hill, Maidenwells, St Daniels Grove and East End Square.

TGR 1847/4: **Pembroke Dock to Tenby**,
via: Pembroke, Bosherston, Milton, Sageston, St Florence and Gumfreston (with modification to run 2 journeys on Fri/Sat only & divert via Redberth on return).

TGR 1847/5: **Pembroke Dock to Freshwater East**, via: Pembroke & Lamphey.

TGR 1847/6: **Excursions & Tours** starting from Pembroke Dock.

TGR 1847/7: **Pembroke Dock to Stackpole**, via: Pembroke, Monkton, Hundleton & Castle-martin, return via Merrion, Sampsons Cross, Stackpole, Kingsfold & Pembroke.

TGR 1847/8: **Pembroke Dock (Star Corner) to Pennar**, via: Laws Street, Bush Street, Pembroke Street, Bellevue Terrace, Bethany, Tre-Owen Rd and Military Road.

TGR 1847/9: **Pembroke Dock to Manorbier**,
via: Pembroke, Lamphey, Hodgeston, Jameston and Roblin Cross.
Note: extended to the Military Camp at Skrinkle near Manorbier in 6/1937.

Two years later in October 1935, another Road Service Licence was applied for to provide a 'new' service of stage carriage. This was granted as follows in January 1936:-

TGR 1847/10:   **Pembroke Dock   to   Bosherston**,
via: Pembroke, Kingsfold, St Petrox, Sampson Cross, Bosherston alternatively via Stackpole and Cheriton. (To operate Mon to Fri only, when the Elementary Schools are open). *Note: In 4/1937, this service was modified and extended to reach Flimstone, via Monkton, Hundleton and Maidenwells, returning via Bosherston, Stackpole, Cheriton & Pembroke (operating Monday – Saturday).*

Acquiring John Ford's business created another problem for the company, the question of housing and maintaining the bus fleet. This brought about the construction of a completely new garage for the buses in 1939. The new garage was built on a former rubbish tip at London Road, Pembroke Dock, in a district known as 'Waterloo', and equipped with full workshop facilities. After WW II ended the workshop was hugely extended and equipped with facilities for motor car maintenance and repair, integrating their well-established motor car business with the buses, all under one roof. Simultaneously, the car sales department for Austin, Morris and Standard cars continued to operate from the original premises at 15-19 Water Street, controlled by W H Silcox, son of the founder.

JOHN FORD'S BUS SERVICE.
Tenby Summer Time Table.

Pembroke Dock. Dept.	Pembroke. Dept.	Tenby. Dept.
7.30 a.m.	7.45 a.m.	8.40 a.m.
9.45 a.m.	10.0 a.m.	10.35 a.m.
12.30 p.m.	12.45 p.m.	1.30 p.m.
2.0 p.m.	2.15 p.m.	3.0 p.m.
3.55 p.m.	4.10 p.m.	4.45 p.m.
6.10 p.m.	6 25 p.m.	7.10 p.m.
7.15 p.m.	7.30 p.m.	8.15 p.m.
9.30 p.m.❖	9.45 p.m.❖	10.30 p.m.❖

❖ Wednesday and Saturdays Only.

FRESHWATER EAST SUMMER TIME TABLE.

Pembroke Dock. Dept.	Pembroke. Dept.	Freshwater East. Dept.
7.30 a.m.	7.45 a.m.	8.0 a.m.
10.30 a.m.	10.45 a,m.	11.10 a.m.
1.0 p.m.	1.15 p.m.	1.30 p.m.
2.15 p.m.	2.30 p.m.	3.5 p.m.
5.0 p.m.	5.15 p.m.	5.35 p.m.
7.0 p.m.	7.15 p.m.	7.30 p.m.
8.30 p.m. Cinema.	8.45 p.m.	9.0 p.m.

Press of News in a Nutshell.

Left: One of John Ford's timetables dating from 1933.
(The Omnibus Society collection).

Above: One of the eight vehicles Silcox acquired from J R Ford, Pembroke with his PSV business in September 1933 was **DE 7985** which received fleet no 1. **DE 7985** was a 1930 normal control Guy BB with a Guy 31 seat dual entrance body, and was captured here at South Parade, Tenby in 1935, looking slightly battered and about to depart on its return journey to Pembroke Dock. This bus was withdrawn and scrapped in 1936.   *(The Omnibus Society collection, John H Fielder).*

Above: This strange looking little coach was the first 'new' vehicle purchased by Silcox in January 1936. Registered as **BDE 96**, (f/n 9) its Thornycroft 'Dainty' DF cassis priced at £360, was fitted with fully fronted coachwork by Grose – described as C24F layout (front entrance). I would have thought that this was a centre entrance.   *(The Omnibus Society collection).*

JOHN FORD'S BUS SERVICE

Proprietors: W. L. SILCOX & SON, PEMBROKE DOCK

From— SATURDAY, MAY 25th, 1935 UNTIL FURTHER NOTICE. (PHONE 43).

PEMBROKE DOCK and PEMBROKE

SUMMER TIME TABLE.

MONDAY TO THURSDAY.				FRIDAYS.				SATURDAYS.			
HOBBS POINT.	STAR CORNER.	E. END.	TOWN CLOCK.	HOBBS POINT.	STAR CORNER.	E. END.	TOWN CLOCK	HOBBS POINT.	STAR CORNER.	E. END.	TOWN CLOCK.
a.m.	a.m.	a.m.	a.m.	a.m.	a.m.	a.m.	a.m.	a.m.	a.m.	a.m.	a.m.
	6.55	7.5	7.10		6.55	7.5	7.10		6.55	7.5	7.10
7.25	7.30	8.5	8.15	7.25	7.30	8.5	8.15		6.55	7.5	7.10
	7.55	8.40	8.45		7.55	8.40	8.45	7.25	7.30	8.5	8.15
	8.30	8.55	9.0		8.30	8.55	9.0		7.55	8.40	8.45
8.40	8.45	9.50	10.0	8.40	8.45	9.20	9.30		8.30	8.55	9.0
	9.30	10.50	11.0		9.0	9.50	10.0	8.40	8.45	9.50	10.0
	9.45	11.55	12.0		9.30	10.20	10.30		9.30	10.50	11.0
	10.30	p.m.	p.m.	9.50	10.0	10.50	11.0		9.45	11.55	12.0
10.50	11.0	12.55	1.5		10.30	11.20	11.30		10.30	p.m.	p.m.
	11.30	1.50	2.0	10.50	11.0	11.55	12.0	10.50	11.0	12.55	1.5
11.55	12.0	2.50	3.0		11.30	12.20	p.m.		11.30	1.50	2.0
	12.20C	p.m.	p.m.	11.55	12.0	12.55	12.30	11.55	12.0	2.20	2.30
p.m.	12.30	3.30	3.35		12.20C	1.20	1.5		p.m.	2.50	3.0
12.50	1.0	3.55	4.0	p.m.	12.30	2.20	1.30	p.m.	12.30	3.20	3.30
	1.30	4.30	4.35	12.50	1.0	2.50	2.0	12.50	1.0	3.55	4.0
1.50	2.0	4.55	5.0		1.30	3.20	2.30		1.30	4.20	4.30
	2.30	5.20	5.25	1.50	2.0	3.55	3.0	1.50	2.0	4.55	5.0
	3.5	5.43	5.50		2.30	4.20	3.30		2.30	5.20	5.30
	3.30	5.50	6.0	2.50	3.0	4.55	4.0	2.50	3.0	5.50	6.0
	3.50C	6.30	6.35		3.30	5.20	4.30		3.30	6.20	6.30
	4.30	6.50	7.0		3.50C	5.55	5.0	3.50	4.0	6.50	7.0
5.0W	5.0	7.40	7.45	3.50	4.0	6.20	6.30		4.30	7.20	7.30
	5.25	8.20	8.30		4.30	6.50	7.0		5.0	7.50	8.0
5.45	5.50	8.30	9.0	5.0W	5.0	7.20	7.30		5.25	8.20	8.30
	6.25	9.30	9.35		5.25	7.50	8.0	5.45	6.0	8.50	9.0
7.10	7.15	9.50	10.0x	5.45	6.0	8.20	8.30		6.30	9.20	9.30
7.50	8.0	10.20	10.30		6.30	8.50	9.0		7.0	9.50	10.0
	8.30Cin				7.0	9.20	9.30		7.30	10.20	10.30
8.55	9.10				7.30	9.50	10.0	7.45	8.0		
9.45	10.0			7.45	8.0	10.20	10.30		8.30Cin		
	11.0Cin				8.30Cin				9.0		
					9.0			9.45	9.30		
				9.45	9.30				10.0		
					10.0				11.0Cin		
					11.0Cin						

X Pembroke Cinema.
C County School Buses and will not run when Elementary Schools are closed.
W Carries Workmen and is always full.
Cin Runs from Pembroke Dock Cinema.

PEMBROKE DOCK, PEMBROKE, MONKTON, HUNDLETON, & WALLASTON CROSS.

		FRIDAYS ONLY.			SATS. ONLY.					FRIDAYS ONLY.			SATS. ONLY.	
		a.m.	p.m.	p.m.	p.m.	p.m.				a.m.	p.m.	p.m.	p.m.	p.m.
PEMBROKE DOCK	Dept.	8.45	2.30	5.0	5.0	8.30	WALLASTON CROSS	Dept.	9.30	3.5	—	5.30	9.10
PEMBROKE ...	Arr.	9.0	2.45	5.10	5.10	8.45	HUNDLETON ...	Arr.	9.40	3.15	5.25	5.40	9.20
MONKTON	Arr.	9.5	2.50	5.15	5.15	8.50	MONKTON ...	Arr.	9.50	3.20	5.35	5.50	9.30
HUNDLETON .	Arr.	9.15	2.55	5.20	5.15	8.55	PEMBROKE ...	Arr.	10.0	3.25	5.40	5.55	9.35
WALLASTON CROSS	Arr.	9.25	3.0	—	5.20	9.5	PEMBROKE DOCK ...	Arr.	10.15	3.40	5.55	6.5	9.50
					5.30								

The Silcox bus timetable reproduced above was dated 25th May 1935, and it can be seen that Silcox were still using the title 'John Ford's Bus Service' as a good-will gesture. The second half of this comprehensive timetable is reproduced opposite.

(The Omnibus Society collection).

12

PEMBROKE DOCK, PEMBROKE, CAREW CROSS ROADS, ST. FLORENCE & TENBY

With Extension to REDBERTH Fridays and Saturdays.

		a.m.	a.m.	p.m.	p.m.	p.m.	p.m.	p.m.	p.m.
Pem. Dk	Dep.	7.30	9.45	12.30	2.0	3.55	6.10	7.15	9.30a
Pembroke	Arr.	7.40	9.55	12.40	2.15	4.10	6.25	7.30	9.45a
Carew X	Arr.	7.55	10.10	12.55	2.30	4.25	6.40	7.50	10.0a
Minerton X	Arr.	8.0	10.20	1.0	2.35	4.30	6.45	7.55	10.15a
S Florence	Arr.	8.10		1.10			6.55b		
Tenby	Arr.	8.25	10.30	1.25	2.50	4.40	7.5	8.10	10.25a

		a.m.	a.m.	p.m.	p.m.	p.m.	p.m.	p.m.	p.m.
Tenby	Dept.	8.40	10.35	1.30	3.0	4.45	7.10	8.15	10.30a
S Florence	Arr.		1.45		5.0	7.25			10.45b
Minerton X	Arr.	8.50	10.45	1.50	3.10	5.5	7.30	8.25	10.50a
Carew X	Arr.	9.0	10.55	2.0	3.20	5.15	7.40	8.40	11.0a
Pembroke	Arr.	9.15	11.10	2.15	3.35	5.25	8.0	8.55	11.15a
Pem. Dk	Arr.	9.30	11.20	2.25	3.50	5.45	8.15	9.10	11.30a

a—Wednesday and Saturdays only. But will run nightly from July 31st to September 30th.   b.—Saturdays only.

SUBSTITUTED TABLE FOR FRIDAYS & SATURDAYS ONLY TO REDBERTH.

		a.m.	p.m.	p.m.			a.m.	p.m.	p.m.
Pembroke Dock	Dept.	9.45	12.30	3.55	Tenby	Dept.	10.45	1.30	5.10
Pembroke	Arr.	9.55	12.40	4.10	St. Florence	Arr.	10.55	1.45	5.25
Carew Cross	Arr.	10.10	12.55	4.25	Redberth	Arr.	11.10	2.0	
Redberth	Arr.	10.20		4.35	Carew Cross	Arr.	11.20	2.10	5.40
St. Florence	Arr.	10.30	1.10	4.50	Pembroke	Arr.	11.35	2.25	5.55
Tenby	Arr.	10.40	1.25	5.5	Pembroke Dock	Arr.	11.50	2.40	6.5

A 'Bus will run from SADGESTON during time Schools are Open.

		a.m.							
Sadgeston	Dept.	8.5	Carew Cross ... Arr. 8.10	Pembroke	Arr. 8.30	Pembroke Dock	Arr.	8.40

SUNDAY SERVICES.

		p.m.	p.m.	p.m.			p.m.	p.m.	p.m.
Pembroke Dock	Dept.	2.15	5.20	9.30	Tenby	Dept.	3.10	8.30	10.30
Pembroke	Arr.	2.25	5.35	9.40	Carew Cross	Arr.	3.35	8.50	10.50
Carew Cross	Arr.	2.45	5.50	9.55	Pembroke	Arr.	3.45	9.5	11.5
Tenby	Arr.	3.5	6.15	10.20	Pembroke Dock	Arr.	4.0	9.20	11.20

SERVICE TO BE RUN BETWEEN MAY 23th and SEPTEMBER 30th.

PEMBROKE DOCK, PEMBROKE, LAMPHEY, & FRESHWATER EAST.

		a.m.	a.m.	p.m.	j.m.	p.m.	p.m.	p.m.
Pem. Dock	Dept.	7.30	10.30	1.0	2.15	5.0	7.0	8.30Cin
Pembroke	Arr.	7.45	10.40	1.10	2.25	5.10	7.10	8.45
Lamphey	Arr.	7.50	10.50	1.20	2.35	5.20	7.20	8.50
Freshwater East	Arr.	7.55	11.0	1.25	2.45	5.30	7.25	8.55

Cin—This Bus runs from Pembroke Dock Cinema.

		a.m.	a.m.	p.m.	p.m.	p.m.	p.m.	p.m.
Freshwater East	Dept.	8.0	11.10	1.30	3.5	5.35	7.30	9.0
Lamphey	Arr.	8.10	11.20	1.40	3.15	5.45	7.35	9.10
Pembroke	Arr.	8.20	11.25	1.50	3.25	5.50	7.45	9.20
Pem. Dock	Arr.	8.35	11.40	2.0	3.45	6.10	8.0	9.30

SUNDAY SERVICE.

		p.m.			p.m.
P'BROKE DOCK	Dept.	2.15	FRESHWATER E.	Dept.	8.30
PEMBROKE	Arr.	2.25	PEMBROKE	Arr.	8.40
FRESHWATER E.	Arr.	2.40	P'BROKE DOCK	Arr.	8.50

PEMBROKE DOCK & PENNAR
FRIDAYS ONLY.

Leave Pennar	...	...	10 a.m. and 11.50 a.m.
Leave Star Corner	...	...	11.35 a.m.

PEMBROKE DOCK, PEMBROKE, LAMPHEY, HODGESTON, JAMESTON & MANORBIER

COMMENCING JULY 1st

SUMMER TIME-TABLE.
MONDAY TO SATURDAY.   (First Week in July to End of August).

		a.m.	a.m.	p.m.	p.m.	p.m.			a.m.	a.m.	p.m.	p.m.	p.m.
Pem. Dock	Dept.	8.45b	11.0c	3.0	4.30s	8.30Cin	Manorbier	Dept.	9.35b	11.50c	3.40	5.10s	9.20
Pembroke	Arr.	9.0b	11.15c	3.15	4.45s	8.50	Jameston	Arr.	9.40b	11.55c	3.45	5.15s	9.25
Lamphey	Arr.	9.5b	11.50c	3.20	4.50s	8.55	Hodgeston	Arr.	9.45b	12.0n nc	3.50	5.20s	9.30
Hodgeston	Arr.	9.10b	11.55c	3.25	4.55s	9.0	Lamphey	Arr.	9.50b	12.5c	3.55	5.25s	9.35
Jameston	Arr.	9.15b	11.50c	3.30	5.0s	9.5	Pembroke	Arr.	9.55b	12.10c	4.0	5.30s	9.40
Manorbier	Arr.	9.20b	11.55c	3.35	5.5s	9.10	Pembroke Dock	Arr.	10.10b	12.40c	4.15	5.50s	9.55

b—Fridays Only.   c—Will not run on Fridays.   Cin—From Cinema.   s—Mons. & Sats. Only

"WEST WALES GUARDIAN" OFFICE, 63, BUSH STREET, PEMBROKE DOCK.

A very interesting report appeared in the 'Commercial Motor' magazine dated 9th March 1937, regarding an illegal brake test carried out by Police officers on one of Silcox's vehicles. The Police knowingly overloaded the bus and allegidly without authority tested its brakes on a long gradient. The handbrake was satisfactory but the footbrake was said to be inadequate, which resulted in a fine of 10 shillings to the company, for permitting the use of a defective bus, and a fine of 10 shillings to the driver for using the defective bus.

Above: Pictured here at Leyland Motors premises before delivery in April 1936 is bus No 10. Registered **BDE 238**, it was a Leyland 'Tiger' TS7 with Leyland B32F bodywork fitted with a sliding roof, and was the first full size vehicle purchased. Its bodywork was extensively rebuilt by Silcox incorporating a concealed radiator as shown below. *(M A Sutcliffe MBE, collection).*

Above: Silcox had some fine craftsmen working for them in the 1940s and 1950s, men that had built ships at the local Hancock's Dockyard. Under supervision of partner Leonard Silcox, (with an engineering degree), this 1936 Leyland 'Tiger' TS7 **(BDE 238)** had its Leyland bodywork extensively rebuilt in 1950 receiving a concealed radiator, new headlights, sliding cab door, removal of its sliding roof, new rubber mounted windows and re-panelled to include the famous 'Silcox' fish tail side flash. *(G. Morant).*

Above: The second Leyland in the Silcox fleet was another 'Tiger' TS7 with Leyland bodywork and a diesel engine. Registered **CDE 259**, this one differed slightly, having a rear entrance and 36 seats. However, at some point after W W II ended, Silcox rebuilt the bodywork to front entrance layout with 35 coach seats, and added the Silcox fish tail side flash. *(Alan B Cross).*

Above: DDE 963 was one of six Bedford WTBs operated by the company, It was new to Silcox in August 1938 fitted with a 25seat coach body built locally by Thomas & Thomas of Carmarthen. After W W II ended, Silcox took preference to heavyweight chassis and sold off all their lightweight Bedfords, this ended its days with T M Daniel of Cardigan where it's seen here in 1950 outside Cardigan Town Hall working a service to Gwbert-on-Sea, a pretty little seaside village near Cardigan. *(Alan B Cross).*

W. L. SILCOX & SON

Motor Engineers & Bus Proprietors

WATER STREET, PEMBROKE DOCKS

Private Cars for Hire   'Phone 43

Agents for Austin, Morris & Standard Cars
- -   Any make of Car supplied   - -
Good selection of Used Cars always in stock
- -   Cash or deferred payments   - -

HIRE OUR LUXURY COACHES FOR YOUR PRIVATE OUTINGS

Quotations on request

Company advertisement dated 1938.

Above: Captured here on the forecourt of Silcox's depot at 'Waterloo' Pembroke Dock in 1950 was this very rare vehicle, a Leyland 'Cub' KPZ4 with a C26F body by Thomas & Thomas of Carmarthen. Registered **EDE 735**, it was one of three identical vehicles delivered in 1940, and were the last Cubs built for the British market. In the backdrop is Bristol L5G, JDE 431. *(Alan B Cross)*.

THE DARK DAYS OF WORLD WAR II

World War II brought much extra business to the thriving company from the intense Military activity in south Pembrokeshire. The fleet more than doubled during the war years, brought about by the increased workload transporting personnel to the numerous Military establishments in the area. To provide these extra services during the war, additional licences had to be applied for as usual, but were now only authorised by the Ministry of Defence (Ministry of War Transport), as were all other operating licences issued during the hostilities. Licences to operate Excursions and Tours were suspended in order to conserve fuel and rubber, as were the licences for Express Carriage services three years later. It appears that no less than ten Defence Permits which replaced Road Service Licences were granted to Silcox by the Regional Transport Commissioner to operate services of special need during the hostilities. Records of these services have not been kept – maybe for security reasons, but were known to be numbered TGR 1847/11 to 1847/20. Only five of those licences have been traced and are listed below:-

TGR 1847/11   TGR 1847/12   TGR1847/13   TGR 1847/15   TGR 1847/16   - No record.

TGR 1847/14   **Pembroke Dock to Loveston,** via: Slade Cross, Sadgeston and Redberth.

TGR 1847/17   **Pembroke Dock to Manorbier.** *(Workmen's stage carriage service Mon-Sat)* via: Pembroke, Lamphey, Freshwater East, Hodgeston, Jameston & Manorbier.

TGR 1847/18   **Pembroke Dock (RN Repair depot & Hancock's Shipyard) to Monkton,** via: Bethany, High Street, Bish Lodge, The Green, Lion Hotel, Westgate Hill, Monkton and Salutation Inn.   *(Workmen's stage carriage service Mon-Sat).*

TGR 1847/19   **Pembroke Dock to Cosheston,** *later* **Mount Pleasant Cross** *(Fri & Sat only).*

TGR 1847/20   **Pembroke Dock to Tenby**, via: Cresswell Quay, Cresselly and Kilgetty. *(Abandoned by Greens Motors, Haverfordwest in September 1939).*

At the beginning of World War II the supply of new buses was hardly affected with three new Leyland 'Cubs' arriving between July and September 1940, followed by two second-hand Bedford WTBs and a Dennis Arrow Minor. Soon afterwards the government (Ministry of War Transport) imposed a complete stoppage on all bus chassis production and the movement of second-hand vehicles, which took effect in February 1941, when the stock of new buses already built were 'frozen'.

By December 1941, Silcox were desperate to have extra buses to cover their massive workload. With assistance from the MOWT they were able to hire three AEC Regent double deck buses with open staircases from London Transport (ST910/21/33). These were the first double-deckers operated by the company, which returned to London in February 1943 after the arrival of new buses.

The stock of 'frozen' buses that were under control of the MOWT were eventually released in 1941/2 to companies that desperately needed them, and in April 1942 Silcox acquired one of these vehicles through the authority. Registered FDE 215, it was a Bristol K5G with 'standard' Duple L30/26R bodywork (not utility type), and was a marque that was well received by the partnership.

In late 1942, the above regulations were relaxed allowing new buses to be built once again but to strict utility specifications. The only PSV chassis built during this period were Bedford, Bristol, Daimler and Guy with Karrier and Sunbeam trolleybuses, all built in limited numbers and controlled by the MOWT. Purchase of new vehicles and the movement of second-hand vehicles were all under control of the MOWT and sanctioned only in special circumstances. Silcox were granted a total of 16 new vehicles by the MOWT to cover their huge commitment of military establishment work, 1 Bristol K5G, 10 Bedford OWBs and 5 Guy Arabs, which increased the fleet in size to 30 vehicles by 1945.

Receiving these Guy Arabs and the solitary Bristol K5G was a new beginning for the Silcox management. They took a tremendous liking to the Bristol chassis *and* the Gardner engine marques, resulting in the Bristol/Gardner combination becoming standard for the post war fleet.

Ten Bedford OWBs with Duple utility bodies arrived between August 1942 and February 1943, but all were disposed of by 1950 as they were superseded by more luxurious vehicles. The five Gardner engine Guy Arabs (28-32) FDE 517/609/733, GDE 124/235 bodied with Strachan low-bridge utility bodies lasted a while longer, as they were extensively rebuilt by the company. FDE 517 (28) was rebuilt beyond recognition with a full-front layout, designed by Leonard Silcox, grandson of the founder. More information and a photograph of this vehicle can be found on page 32.

Interesting to note at this point is the fact that Silcox were using fleet numbers on all their vehicles, but confusingly re-used old fleet numbers on replacement vehicles. The fleet number 13 however was never used – that number was regarded as unlucky by many operators including Silcox, and some operators never used fleet number 113.

Above: Pictured here before delivery in April 1942 is bus No 20 **FDE 215**, a Bristol K5G with handsome Duple L30/26R bodywork of the same style fitted to pre-war Red & White Albions. It was an 'unfrozen' vehicle (as mentioned on page 17) and was the first vehicle to arrive at Pembroke Dock under the Ministry of War Transport regulations. Note the wartime headlights fitted, and the lifeguard rail and front mudguards painted white, all part of the wartime specifications. Fifteen more wartime vehicles were sanctioned later, Guy Arabs and Bedford OWBs which were all built to the government's utility specification.

Right: Captured here at Pembroke Dock, working a local service to the nearby district of Pennar is **FDE 609** (29) a 1943 Guy Arab I (6LW) fitted with Strachan utility body of low-bridge layout. It was later rebuilt with rubber mounted sliding windows at 'The Works' the company's workshops and refurbished with new 'dunlopillo' seats.

These advertisements above could be found printed on the reverse side of Silcox's 'Bell Punch' bus tickets for many years, until the change to 'Setright Speed' TIM's c1960.

Right: This 1944 Guy Arab II (6LW) with Strachan utility low-bridge body, **FDE 733** fleet no 29 appears to be in exceptionally good original condition when captured here at the depot in 1950.
It appears to have been freshly painted here looking at the shine on its panelling. It was withdrawn in 1955 and scrapped.
(Alan B Cross).

Above: An excellent view of **GDE 124** (No 31) a 1945 Guy Arab II (5LW) with Strachan low-bridge 'utility' body. It's seen here at Pembroke Dock on its return from Tenby via Cresselly, a route withdrawn by Green's Motors of Haverfordwest in 1939.

Above: This was the last utility vehicle delivered to Silcox in September 1945. Numbered 32, and registered **GDE 235** it was another Guy Arab II with a Gardner 5LW unit and Strachan low-bridge bodywork. This body was completely rebuilt by Silcox c1954, giving it a completely different look. A picture of it in its new guise can be seen on page 33. **GDE 235** is seen here trundling on through the south Pembrokeshire countryside to Pembroke Dock from Tenby, on a slightly different route via Redberth.

THE POST WAR YEARS

Soon after World War II ended, several changes took place within the business. Firstly, in 1947 the depot at 'Waterloo' was greatly extended and became known as 'The Works' a fully equipped workshop with facilities for motor car and commercial repairs, integrating the complete workforce. Senior partner, Luther John Watts Silcox retired from the business in 1947 and Leonard William Silcox, grandson of the founder, joined his father W H Silcox to run the family business.

The immediate post war period however, suffered an acute shortage of new buses, as most of those built were for the export market. Nevertheless, Silcox were looking to replacing the ten Bedford OWBs acquired during the hostilities with new diesel engine vehicles, but experienced problems with the supply of bodywork.

Their fondness of the Bristol K5G supplied during the war coupled with the reliability of the Gardner engine led Silcox to the Bristol marque, making a deal to purchase six Bristol L5G's in 1947 and a separate deal with Strachan Coachworks to body them. The first two arrived very quickly, before the year had ended, the others in April 1948, all built as dual purpose 35 seaters, and registered JDE 426-431. The company's long association with Bristol Commercial Vehicles had begun.

Nevertheless, they did manage to buy one new Leyland double decker at this difficult time, a Leyland 'Titan' PD1 with the 7.4 litre diesel engine and Leyland 53 seat low-bridge bodywork. This arrived in September 1947 registered as JDE 43, but was replaced 6 years later by a Bristol K6G.

At around the same time in 1947-8 there were several changes made to the services operated, time tables and routes were modified, and six 'new' stage carriage licences applied for as follows:-

TGR 1847/21 **Pennar to Kingswood,**   (Mon – Sat).
via: Tre-Owen Road, Bellevue, Victoria Road, The Avenue, Melville Street, Albion Square, Bush Street, Laws Street, Water Street, and London Road.

TGR 1847/22 **Kingswood to Pembroke (Main St),**   (Mon – Sat).
via: London Rd, Ferry Lane, Bush Hill, The Darlane and Pembroke (Main St).

TGR 1847/23 **Pembroke Dock to Narberth,**   (Thurs & Fri only).
via: Pisgah, Lawrenny, Martletwy, Northill Cross, Templeton and Washfield Cross

TGR 1847/24 **Lawrenny to Pembroke Dock,**   (Sat only).
via; Martletwy, Reynalton, Jeffreyston, Cross Inn, Redberth, Carew Cross, Slade Cross and Pembroke Dock.

TGR 1847/25 **Tenby to Angle,**   (Mon – Sat).
via: St Florence, Redberth, Carew Cross, Pembroke Dock, Pembroke, Stackpole, Bosherston, Castlemartin, Freshwater West, Angle, Wallaston Cross, Hundleton.

TGR 1847/26 **Monkton to Pembroke Dock,**   (Mon – Sat).
via: Monkton Bridge, Westgate Hill, Main Street (Pembroke), East End Square, Lion Hotel, The Green, Bush Lodge, Red Roses, High Street, Bethany, Albion Square, Bush Street, Laws Street, Star Corner and Water Street.
Note: This licence superseded TGR 1847/18 (Workmen's stage carriage service).

All six licences were granted but TGR 1847/25 & 26 were not taken up.

Amongst all this activity, on 3rd March 1948, Leonard William Silcox applied for the licences previously held by competitor Ernest Caleb James (t/a: Pioneer Bus Service) of 57 Queen Street, Pembroke Dock. E C James' two Bedford buses were purchased with his business (see fleet list), and the licences transferred to L W Silcox (t/a: Pioneer Bus Service) 17 Water St, Pembroke Dock, on 14th April 1948, with a new application number TGR 3809.

This was a separate entity to the main W L Silcox & Son's business yet certain vehicles belonging to the main Silcox fleet became licenced to L W Silcox (t/a Pioneer Bus Service).

The Road Service Licences granted to L W Silcox (t/a: Pioneer Bus Service) were:-

TGR 3809/1 **Pembroke Dock** to **Freshwater East**,
via; Pembroke and Lamphey.   *(Mon/Tue/Wed during July & August only)*.

TGR 3809/2 **Pembroke Dock (Hobbs Point)** to **Pembroke (Town)**,
via; Bush Street, Pembroke Street, High Street and Pembroke (Main St), with revised timetable to run jointly with W L Silcox & Son.

TGR 3809/3 **Excursions & Tours** starting from Pembroke Dock (Star Corner).

Above: **ADE 903** is the neat little Bedford WTL, Duple 20 seat bus that Leonard Silcox acquired by with the Pioneer Bus Service business in 1948. It's seen here at Hobbs Point, Pembroke Dock working E C James's service to Pembroke town. There is some doubt whether L W Silcox ever operated this vehicle after James' takeover, as it was sold off very quickly.   *(Chris Carter).*

On 28th April 1948, the main Silcox company applied for renewal of all W L Silcox & Son licences (RSLs) in the name of William Howard, Leonard William and Doreen Ellen Silcox (t/a: W L Silcox & Son). It was a new family partnership made between W H Silcox, his son Leonard and daughter Doreen Ellen Silcox. D E Silcox later became Mrs D E Miller.

Renewal of these licences was granted on 23rd June 1948, with a <u>new</u> application number:-

TGR 3836/1	Previously	TGR 1847/1	Pembroke Dock (Hobbs Point) to Pembroke (East End).
TGR 3836/2	"	TGR 1847/2	Pembroke Dock (Star Corner) to Angle.
TGR 3836/3	"	TGR 1847/3	Pembroke Dock (Star Corner) to Merrion.
TGR 3836/4	"	TGR 1847/4	Pembroke Dock to Tenby via Pembroke & Gumfreston.
TGR 3836/5	"	TGR 1847/5	Pembroke Dock (Star Corner) to Freshwater East.
TGR 3836/6	"	TGR 1847/7	Pembroke Dock (Star Corner) to Stackpole.
TGR 3836/7	"	TGR 1847/8	Pembroke Dock (Star Corner) to Pennar.
TGR 3836/8	"	TGR 1847/9	Pembroke Dock (Star Corner) to Manorbier.
TGR 3836/9	"	TGR 1847/14	Pembroke Dock to Loveston.
TGR 3836/10	"	TGR 1847/17	Pembroke Dock (Hobbs Point) to Manorbier.
TGR 3836/11	"	TGR 1847/19	Pembroke Dock (Albion Square) to Mount Pleasant.
TGR 3836/12	"	TGR 1847/20	Pembroke Dock to Tenby via Cresselly & Kilgetty.
TGR 3836/13	"	TGR 1847/21	Pennar Barracks to Kingswood.
TGR 3836/14	"	TGR 1847/22	Kingswood to Pembroke (East End).
TGR 3836/15	"	TGR 1847/23	Pembroke Dock (Albion Square) to Narberth.
TGR 3836/16	"	TGR 1847/24	Lawrenny to Pembroke Dock.
TGR 3836/17	"	TGR 1847/25	Angle to Tenby.
TGR 3836/18	"	TGR 1847/26	Monkton to Pembroke Dock (Star Corner)
TGR 3836/19	"	TGR 1847/6	Excursions & Tours starting Pembroke Dock (Star Corner)

Note: All the RSL's held under TGR 1847 were surrendered upon receipt of TGR 3836 in June 1948. Most of the above services departing from Star Corner were modified to start from Hobbs Point in 1950/1, and in May 1949 a joint service arrangement was introduced between W L Silcox & Son and their associate company Pioneer Bus Services.

In addition to the services listed above, they applied for another RSL on 9th June 1948, to operate a 'new' stage carriage service between Pembroke Dock & Tenby:-

TGR 3836/20   **Pembroke Dock** to **Tenby**   *(Saturdays only).*
via: Pembroke (Main Street), Carew Cross, Redberth, East Williamston, Temple Bar, Wooden and New Hedges.
Note: *After objections from competitors Green's Motors of Haverfordwest and D J Morrison of Tenby, the application was withdrawn on 6th January 1949.*

On 13th April 1949, the expanding company applied for another 'new' licence:-

TGR 3836/21   **Excursions and Tours** starting from Merrion Camp.
This was granted on 20th July 1949.   Surrendered 1/9/1954.

Meanwhile, there was a long standing competitor running between the village of Angle and Pembroke Dock, operating a daily stage carriage service combined with a mail contract. George Barger Rees & Sons of the Hibernia Inn, Angle, had operated this service since the days of WW I, latterly with a former War Department Fordson 7V lorry re-registered JDE 890, and converted into a 20 seat bus. In 1949, Rees lost the mail contract and offered the service to Silcox, surrendering his Road Service Licence TGR 1968/1 and operator licence in July 1949, he continued with his haulage business.

Throughout the years, numerous modifications were made to the services operated by the company, many of which are regarded as unimportant. Consequently, only noteworthy changes to services are recorded in this publication.

Above: The immediate post war period suffered an acute shortage of new vehicles, but after a long wait this Leyland Titan PD1 registered **JDE 43** was first to arrive in September 1947, fitted with a Leyland L27/26R low-height body. The preferred choice of vehicle soon changed, making this superb decker redundant and sold off in 1953. This picture was taken sometime afterwards.

Above: Experiencing difficulties in obtaining new buses in the immediate post war period, coupled to the company's penchant for the Bristol chassis and Gardner engine marques, steered the partnership into purchasing seventeen new Bristol chassis by the time Bristol Tramways & Carriage Company Ltd were nationalised. **JDE 431** (38) pictured here was numerically the last one delivered from an initial order of six Bristol L5Gs fitted with Strachan DP35F bodies, delivered in 1947/8. They were all rebuilt by Silcox with rubber mounted windows, and JDE 426/9 were converted for one person operation with driver operated doors. When JDE 429 was taken out of service in 1961 (last of the batch), it was converted into a breakdown lorry which saw another 10 years' service. A photograph of this breakdown lorry can be found on page 285. *(The Omnibus Society collection).*

THE WEIRD & WONDERFUL CREATIONS OF L W SILCOX

Leonard William Silcox joined his father William Howard Silcox in the family business at the age of 24 in 1947, after qualifying with a BSc in Mechanical Engineering. He brought with him a wealth of engineering knowledge, and his arrival into the business came during the early post war period when there was an acute shortage of new buses.

The partnership had already bought six new Bristol L5Gs and a Leyland PD1 (as mentioned on page 21) but were experiencing problems – long delays in obtaining new vehicles. Delivery of new chassis was very slow coupled with the problem of finding coachbuilders to body them.

With his confidence and ingenuity, Leonard Silcox decided he couldn't wait for these coachbuilders so designed his own bodies and set about building them 'in house' at 'The Works' using some of his finest craftsmen. Some of these men had previously worked at the local Hancock's Shipbuilding yard, building ships – a remarkable change from ship building, but these buses were a credit to all involved.

First off the Silcox production line in May 1949 was a Crossley SD42/7, built as a 35 seat coach and registered LDE 340, followed two months later by LDE 630 a Leyland 'Tiger' PS1/1 with 35 coach seats. A further nine bodies were built between 1950-4, two on Leyland 'Comet' CPO1 chassis, one Leyland 'Tiger' PS1/1 and, on what became the company's favourite chassis, the Bristol marque, three Bristol L5Gs, two Bristol LL5Gs and one Bristol K6G along with several rebuilt bodies. Added to the list are the two 'new' Bristol K6G chassis which were fitted with 12 year old bodies removed from former Birmingham Corporation trolleybuses in 1952. The company's bodybuilding activities came to an end in 1954, when mass produced bodies became more readily available and at reasonable cost. The Silcox 'rebuilds' however continued in one form or another until the company's demise.

Above: The first example of Silcox bodywork was built on **LDE340** (8) a new Crossley SD42/7 chassis. Registered in May 1949 it had 35 coach seats, and was sold to Harper Bros, Heath Hayes, Staffordshire, in 1953, where it's seen here. Harper Brothers retro-fitted it with a Leyland 8.6 litre engine and re-bodied it in 1959 with a body built by themselves. *(D S Giles).*

Above: This was the second body built by Silcox, fitted to a new Leyland 'Tiger' PS1/1 chassis in 1949. Registered **LDE 630**, (9) it seems to have an identical body style to the earlier Crossley SD42/7, (LDE 340) with panoramic seating rising toward the rear end of the coach. In fact, quite a pleasing looking vehicle, lettered 'Silcox Radio Coach' – a feature of the day - having a radio fitted in a coach. This 'dual purpose' coach was licenced to associate licence holder, L W Silcox (Pioneer Bus Service). *(Chris Taylor).*

Above: Numerically the third Silcox bodied vehicle was this rare Leyland 'Comet' CPO1 registered **MDE 530** (No 1) in June 1950. Here again the design is attractive, a distinctive style with sliding ventilator windows, ramped floor towards the rear giving passengers a panoramic view and of course the famous Silcox side flash which became standard practice. The 'Comet' was not a popular passenger vehicle chassis, this particular one was fitted with a 90 bhp Leyland 0.350 diesel engine and 5 speed gearbox. Passing to Daniels of Cardigan in July 1953, its front entrance body seated 32. (The Omnibus Society/CF Klapper).

Above: This was Silcox's last Leyland 'Comet' which they bodied as a <u>33 seat</u> dual purpose coach, entering service in June 1950 as **MDE 531** (No 2) registered to L W Silcox (Pioneer Bus Service). It differed slightly in design from its sister by having 33 seats, and a higher mounted windscreen with curved waist-rail near the bulkhead. This coach also left the fleet in 1953, due to the company's modernisation plan. *(Alan B Cross).*

Above: Silcox also built the coachwork on this Leyland 'Tiger' PS1/1 registered **MDE 532** in June 1950. This was allocated fleet number 7, fitted with 35 coach seats, and a ramped floor towards the rear (identical to its sisters) for panoramic views of the countryside. This vehicles bodywork however differed slightly from the earlier PS1/1, in that the cab side window and waistrail sloped downwards, altering its appearance to look much neater. **MDE 532** was sold in March 1953. *(Chris Taylor).*

Above: More vehicles of the Bristol marque arrived in March 1951 with the arrival of Bristol L5Gs, NDE 330/1 which were both bodied by the company as dual purpose 39 seaters. **NDE 330** is seen here at the depot in 1963 shortly after being fitted with driver operated doors and conversion to one person operation (note the modification to the bulkhead cab window). *(R H G Simpson).*

Above: **NDE 331** was numerically the second Bristol L5G to enter service in March 1951 fitted with a Silcox DP39F body, featuring again the full width canopy and ramped floor towards the rear, as seen from the seating. Unlike any previous Silcox bodies, the drivers cab was fitted with a sliding door. It looks absolutely stunning in appearance and belied the fact that they were 'home built' bodies. **NDE 331** had fleet no 4 and was converted to B39F (bus seats fitted) in May 1964, remaining in service until 1967, when it was sold to Wm Way scrap dealer at Cardiff Docks in October 1967. *(The Omnibus Society collection – C F Klapper).*

Above: Although an identical chassis to its sisters NDE 330/1 opposite, Silcox bodied this Bristol L5G registered **NDE 332** to a different layout, entering service in June 1951 with a full width cab, retaining its exposed radiator. The unique Silcox side flash is still evident together with the curved down waistrail at the rear end of the body, and was fitted with a sliding cab door. In June 1961 however, **NDE 332** received a new 'full front' body built by Marshall to FDP39F layout. See photo on page 67.

Above: The ninth body built by Silcox was fitted to a Bristol LL5G (a longer version of L5G chassis) registered **NDE 616** in June 1951. Due to its increased length (30 feet) it accommodated 41 dual purpose seats, and in July 1959 was converted to one person operation with driver operated door and modification of the bulkhead cab window to take fares. It's captured here circa 1962 operating a workers contract for the contractor 'Baxter' to the Texaco Oil Refinery at Rhoscrowther near the village of Angle.

29

Above: Another true classic built by Silcox in 1952 was **ODE 600,** a 7ft 6inch wide Bristol LL5G chassis fitted with their own 8ft wide coachwork. Licenced in July 1952, this also had 41 dual purpose seats and a ramped floor towards the rear. By September 1959 it was converted by the company to half-cab layout and fitted for one person operation with a driver operated door – pictured below. *(D S Giles).*

Above: This later view of Bristol LL5G, **ODE 600** shows it in its final guise in 1959, converted to half-cab layout for one person operation. It was taken out of service in 1965 and scrapped. Parked alongside is Strachan bodied Bristol L5G, JDE 429 which was converted into a breakdown tender/lorry by the company in 1963, and pictured on page 285. *(Alan Broughall).*

Above & Below: The chassis of this Bristol K6G was built in 1950, delivered to Silcox in 1951 and stored. It was eventually bodied by Silcox themselves in 1953 with this peculiar looking fully-fronted, low height body seating 32/28. Completed in November 1953 it entered service in June 1954 registered **SDE 450** (f/n 39). The appearance of this double decker was most unusual at the time, with front entrance and staircase, concealed radiator, 60 dual purpose seats, upper deck emergency window at the front and a glazed near side windscreen, let alone the tiny windows on the lower deck. Five years later due to problems with the electrically operated front doors jamming, it was rebuilt to rear entrance and rear staircase layout, **as seen below,** fitted with new windows, near side windscreen glass removed for safety reasons and re-seated to 32/27. It was finally withdrawn in 1969 and sold for scrap.

Above: An off-side view of the 'weird' Silcox bodied Bristol K6G, **SDE 450** No 39 mentioned on the previous page. It looked a heavy body but was quite compatible to other marques of vehicles having an un-laden weight of 7 tons 11 cwt.

Above: This was a re-built body by Silcox in late 1954. **FDE 517** (28) was a Guy Arab I (5LW) new to Silcox in February 1943 with a Strachan utility body. Strachan's utility bodies were some of the poorest bodies built, often framed with inferior quality timber which deteriorated. However, this Silcox re-build was quite similar to the Bristol K6G above (SDE 450) built to FL32/27R layout. This one also had a glazed near side windscreen which was eventually removed for safety reasons. Its upper deck emergency window remained at the rear end, and the upper deck side windows are slightly larger than GDE 235 opposite.

Above: This 1945 Guy Arab II, **GDE 235** (32) was new to Silcox in September 1945 with Strachan utility L27/28R body. Its body was completely rebuilt by Silcox in the mid-1950s, incorporating a sliding cab door, new rubber mounted windows and new seating. A picture of this in its original form can be seen on page 16. Note the size of the upper deck side windows. *(R H G Simpson).*

Above: Silcox's body shop was so busy in 1949 bodying their own coaches, their first three Bristol K6G chassis purchased in 1949 had to be sent to outside coachbuilders for bodying. **LDE 850** (21) seen above was one of them. It received this low-bridge type body built by Barnard Ltd of Norwich to L27/26R layout, and entered service in November 1949. By the time this picture was taken in the early 1960s alongside the ancient 'Town Wall' at Tenby, it had been fitted with new rubber mounted windows – but the upper deck windows are unique, the sliding vents are located in the centre of the pane. This bus survived a hard life of 20 years at Silcox.

Above: As mentioned on the previous page, three new Bristol K6G chassis were sent to outside coachbuilders for bodying in 1949 due to the heavy workload at Silcox's own body department. **LDE 949** (22) seen here outside Pembroke Dock Co-operative was bodied by D J Davies of Merthyr in October 1949 together with LDE 950 opposite. Their high-bridge bodies can not have been of good quality, as both were rebodied in 1961 with *older* secondhand bodies built in 1948 (see below). *(R H G Simpson).*

Right: This second view of Bristol K6G, **LDE 949** (22) was taken at Pembroke in 1962, after it had been re-bodied with a second-hand Willowbrook low-height body up-seated to L31/28R and dating from 1948.

The body fitted in 1961 had been donated by Silcox's RC 4627 (41), a 1937 AEC Regent previously operated by Trent Motor Traction, (1331).

In its new guise, this Bristol K6G worked hard until 1969 when it was withdrawn and used as a source of useful spare parts. Its Gardner 6LW engine give another three years' service after being retro-fitted into a 1955 Bristol LD6B Lodekka RFM457 (91) in late 1969.

LDE 949 (22) opposite and (23) **LDE 950 above** were 'identical twins' both bodied by D J Davies of Merthyr in October 1949 on identical Bristol K6G chassis, with consecutive chassis numbers 76108/9. It's even pictured at the same location outside Pembroke Dock Co-operative shop, working the same service, No 1 to Pembroke town. Like its twin opposite, this K6G also received a second-hand up-seated Willowbrook L31/28R body in 1961, which is pictured on next page.   *(R H G Simpson)*.

Above: A nearside view of bus No 23, **LDE 950** the D J Davies bodied Bristol K6G seen here leaving Waterloo Garage to operate a school contract in 1957.   *(The Omnibus Society collection)*.

Left: In 1961, the company decided to re-body three of their Bristol K6Gs with second-hand low-bridge type Willowbrook bodies retrieved from three of their AEC Regents.

After the body transfers were completed it was a legal requirement to have all three re-bodied vehicles tilt tested. This photograph taken in 1961 captured **LDE 950** going through that procedure at Silcox's 'Works' Waterloo Garage, using very primitive home-made equipment.

(Hubert Williams).

Above: bus No23, **LDE 950** is seen here at Pembroke Dock after it's re-bodying with a second-hand up-seated Willowbrook L31/28R body dating from 1948. The body was donated from (47) RC 4633 another former Trent Motor Traction (1335), AEC Regent of 1937 vintage. This bus was finally withdrawn in 1971, the chassis having seen 21 years' of service and the body 23 years.

Above: Seen here at 'The Works' in Pembroke Dock is **ODE 401 (24)**, another Bristol K6G. It was one of three chassis purchased in 1951 and stored, finally emerging in June 1952 bodied as shown, with a second-hand MCCW body of 1940 vintage, removed from a former Birmingham Corporation, Leyland trolleybus (90) FOK 90, pictured below.   *(Coloured by Paul Banbury).*

Above: Seen here in service at Birmingham shortly before its withdrawal in 1951 is Birmingham Corporation Leyland trolleybus (90) FOK 90, with MCCW H30/24R body. It was sold to a scrap dealer who in turn sold the body to Silcox. The coachbuilders at Silcox did a neat job modifying the front end to suit the Bristol chassis of **ODE 401** (shown above) and re-seated it to H32/28R.

Right: After removal of its trolleybus body in 1961, **ODE 401** became the third Bristol K6G in the fleet to receive a second-hand low-bridge Willowbrook body. The body dating from 1948 had been removed from their last remaining 1937 AEC Regent (42) RC 4630, which had arrived along with RC 4627/33 from Trent Motor Traction (1334) in 1959. It's captured here at 'The Works' in August 1965, with Roe bodied AEC Regal IV, ODE 1 parked up behind it - withdrawn.
(Vernon Morgan).

Above: **ODE 402** (25) was the second Bristol K6G chassis that had been stored for a year before receiving a body. The body it received was another second-hand MCCW trolleybus body dating from 1940, acquired from the same source as its twin ODE 401 opposite; a Birmingham Corporation trolleybus (83) FOK 83. This body received the same cosmetic work to the front end to incorporate the radiator, and was similarly re-seated to H32/28R. It remained in service with this body throughout its working life, until it was withdrawn in 1967. Note the modern headlight on the nearside, probably too expensive to replace both, the second one of the pair was fitted to ODE 401 (see picture on page 37).

I recall having a ride aboard this interesting vehicle in April 1964, when a group of bus enthusiasts hired it for a private tour from Waterloo Garage, Pembroke Dock to Tenby, via Carew, Sadgeston (later Sageston) and Gumfreston. This was a route from Pembroke Dock to Tenby which avoided low bridges. *(R H G Simpson).*

Above: In 1951, Silcox bought five Birmingham Corporation, Guy Arab IIs with Weymann H30/26R bodies, registered FOP 349/53/66/80/403. Pictured here on the forecourt of Waterloo Garage in 1959 is **FOP 403** (27) which was the last one in service. It was sold to the dealer Frank Cowley in April 1960. To its left is GHN 189 (32) a 1942 Bristol K5G (1949 ECW) ex United Automobile Services in 1959. *(Alan B Cross).*

Above: **FOP 349** (42) was the eldest of five Birmingham Corporation, Guy Arab IIs acquired in 1951. This one dating from 1943 was fitted with a Gardner 5LW engine and Weymann H30/26R body, which Silcox re-built with rubber mounted windows. It gave the company seven years' service – withdrawn in 1959. *(The Omnibus Society collection).*

In addition to the two trolleybus bodies acquired from Birmingham Corporation in 1951 for the new Bristol K6G chassis in store (ODE 401/2), the company purchased five Guy Arab IIs with Weymann H30/26R bodies from Birmingham in 1951. These were registered FOP 349/53/66/80/403.

However, it has been suggested that Silcox bought new body shells from Portsmouth Aviation or Bruce Coachworks for construction of their own bodies. This is certainly not true, evidence has proven that Leonard Silcox drew up his own blueprints, and designed his own bodies which were built from scratch at 'The Works' buying in components such as seats, windows, lights, panels etc. Confirmation of this can be found on page 300.

The fascinating story of Leonard Silcox's creations nevertheless did not end in 1954 when new bodies were becoming more readily available, and at reasonable cost. Silcox's coachbuilding activities continued on a smaller scale, carrying out numerous body modifications and rebuilds from entrance layout to re-designed front ends continuing, besides body repairs and re-paints for other companies. Some of these Silcox 'rebuilds' are pictured at relevant points throughout this publication.

In the early 1950s, the business continued to prosper, with Leonard Silcox taking over responsibility of running the buses whilst his father W H Silcox ran the car side of the business. New stage and express carriage services continued to be added to the increasing list of RSLs, as listed below:-

TGR 3836/22   **Excursions & Tours** starting from **Cresswell Quay**, picking up at Cresselly, Jeffreyston and Cross Inn.   *Granted 7/6/1950.*

TGR 3836/23   **Excursions & Tours** starting from **Pennar (The Royal Oak),** picking up at Pennar (Cross Park).   *Granted 7/6/1950.*

TGR 3836/24   **Excursions & Tours** starting from **Monkton**, picking up at Hundleton (The Green).   *Granted 7/6/1950.*

On 3rd September, 1952 the following licence was applied for:-

TGR 3836/25   **Pembroke Dock** to **Carmarthen (Express Carriage)** Wednesdays only, all year. via: Carew Cross, Creswell Quay, Cresselly, Jeffreyston, Reynalton, Templeton, Cold Blow, Princes Gate, Tavernspite (last pick up), Red Roses & St Clears. Objectors: Railway Executive & Ebsworth Bros. *Application withdrawn 15/10/52.*

The licences applied for in 1953 were:-

TGR 3836/26   **Extended Excursions & Tours** starting **Pembroke Dock** (Waterloo Bus Station) Picking up at Star Corner, Albion Sq, Pennar, The Green, Pembroke, Monkton, East End, Lamphey, Manorbier, Sadgeston, Cresswell Quay & Jeffreyston. To operate throughout year, including continental tours.   *Refused 27/5/1953.*

TGR 3836/27   **Pembroke Dock (RAF Station)** to **Cardiff (Museum Ave, Cathays Park).** **(Express Carriage)** limited to RAF personnel only, from Pembroke Dock. Objectors: Railway Executive and Ebsworth Bros Laugharne. *Refused 16/9/1953.* **Note:** *Silcox appealed directly to the Transport Minister who over ruled his inspectors recommendation and allowed the appeal against the South Wales T A licensing authority's refusal of the licence. The main objector British Railways had allegedly made an arrangement with Ebsworth Bros.*   *Granted 3/3/1954.*

TGR 3836/28   **Neyland (Rees' Garage) to Kete (RNAS) Express Carriage** Mon – Fri all year
Picking up at Waterston, Milford Haven, Hubberston, Rickeston Bridge and St
Ishmaels, for conveyance of Admiralty employees only.   *Granted 17/2/1954.*

In 1954, a total of nine 'new' licences were applied for:-

TGR 3836/29   Was an application for stage carriage service between any two points on existing
stage carriage licences held by W L Silcox & Son. The services were to operate
after cessation of normal services, as required, and to cater for late dances and other
special events.   *Granted 26/5/1954.*

TGR 3836/30   **Excursions & Tours** starting from **Angle (The Globe Hotel).**
Picking up at Castlemartin, Axton Hill, Wallaston Cross, Speculation Inn,
Hundleton and Monkton.   *Granted 9/6/1954.*

TGR 3836/31   **Excursions & Tours** starting from **Cosheston**.
Picking up at Slade Cross, Milton, Carew Cross, Redberth, Sadgeston and
Pembroke Dock (Waterloo Garage).   *Granted 9/6/1954.*

TGR 3836/32   **Excursions & Tours** starting from **Freshwater East**.
Picking up at Hodgeston, Lamphey, St Florence, Sadgeston and Pembroke Dock
(Waterloo Garage).   *Granted 9/6/1954.*

TGR 3836/33   **Excursions & Tours** starting from **Stackpole (Post Office)**.
Picking up at Bosherston (Post Office), Merrion Cross, St Twynnells, Chapel Hill,
Maidenwells, Hundleton and Monkton.   *Granted 9/6/1954.*

TGR 3836/34   **Manorbier (School of A A Artillery) to Birmingham (Express Carriage)**.
Only Military personnel from the School of A A Artillery to be carried.
                                                       Application withdrawn 23/6/1954.

TGR 3836/35   **Pembroke Dock (RAF Station)** to **Birmingham   (Express Carriage)**.
Only RAF personnel from Pembroke Dock to be carried.   *Granted 23/6/1954.*

TGR 3836/36   **Pembroke Dock (RAF Station)** to **Manchester (Express Carriage)**.
Only RAF personnel from Pembroke Dock to be carried.   *Granted 23/6/1954.*

TGR 3836/37   **Manorbier (School of A A Artillery) to Manchester (Express Carriage)**.
Only Military personnel from the School of A A Artillery to be carried.
                                                       Application withdrawn 23/6/1954.

In 1955, only one 'new' stage carriage licence was applied for on 16th February:-

TGR 3836/38   **Golden Hill Avenue (Junc. Golden Hill Rd) to Pembroke (East End Square)**.
via: Golden Hill Rd, St Anne's Cres, Windsor Rd, Beaufort Rd, Woodbine Terr,
Dark Lane and Main St.   Mon - Fri during school term only.   *Granted 6/7/1955.*

Applications TGR 3836/27, 28, 34-7 above were made to cater for the large Military presence in
south Pembrokeshire, conveying servicemen going on leave. That express carriage work came to an
end when National Service was abolished after November 1960, phased out to May 1963. The British
Army left the area and the Royal Air Force drastically reduced their presence at Pembroke Dock.

Above: Silcox purchased this very rare Beccols C35F bodied Leyland 'Royal Tiger' registered **LYL 725** (f/n 18) in late 1952 at just over a year old. It had been new to Blue Cars, London WC1 in June 1951, and was closely followed by its sister - LYL 722.

Above: Purchased second-hand in 1954 for the company's extended tours programme was **KWW 541** (f/n 7) another 1951 Leyland 'Royal Tiger' PSU1/15, fitted with a rather unusual looking centre entrance body built by Plaxton, called the 'Venturer'. Seating 41, it replaced a 35 seat Silcox bodied Leyland 'Tiger' PS1/1 (old No 7) MDE 532 under a fleet modernisation plan. It looked unusual due to its centrally mounted fog lamp, which became a characteristic feature of the Plaxton 'Venturer' coachwork. In 1961, when only 10 years old, it was downgraded to DP45C specification by fitting 45 bus seats, and two years later Silcox converted it to a front entrance layout. (See picture opposite). *(R H G Simpson)*.

42

Above: The coachbuilders at Silcox did a splendid conversion job to the Plaxton 'Venturer' bodywork of this 1951 Leyland 'Royal Tiger' (No 7) **KWW 541** in 1963. The entrance steps and doorway were moved from the centre to the front, with both sides repanelled and new lifeguard rails fitted. The seating had been changed to 45 bus seats two years earlier (view it as original on opposite page). The Leyland 'Royal Tiger' PSU1/15 chassis featured an underfloor horizontal 9.8 litre Leyland 0.600 unit coupled to a four speed synchromesh gearbox and vacuum brakes.

Above: Another Leyland 'Royal Tiger' PSU1/15 in the fleet arrived at Pembroke Dock in December 1952 from W D Smith, of Fernhill Heath, Worcestershire. **KAB 338** was new in June 1951 to M & M Coaches, Kidderminster and was fitted with this stylish Burlingham 'Seagull' C37C coachwork. KAB 338 was given fleet number 19 a number previously carried by a 1939 Bedford WTB, registered FXT 824. *(R H G Simpson)*.

Above: **MRH 226** was another identical Leyland 'Royal Tiger' PSU1/15 with attractive Burlingham 'Seagull' C37C coachwork. New in February 1952 to Bluebird Coaches of Hull, **MRH 226** had replaced a 1950 Silcox bodied Leyland 'Comet' CPO1 (MDE 530) in January 1954. It was given the fleet number previously carried by the sold Leyland 'Comet' No 1, but was re-numbered 41 in May 1965 and withdrawn in 1967. The Burlingham 'Seagull' was by far the most successful type of coach body built for the early underfloor engine chassis.

Above: An absolute 'Classic'. Silcox purchased this magnificent vehicle **SDE 400** (9) brand new in April 1954. It had the same identical Burlingham 'Seagull' coachwork as the coach pictured above, but seated 33, and its chassis was different – the newly introduced Leyland 'Tiger Cub' PSUC1/2 fitted with horizontal 5.7 litre Leyland O.350 underfloor engine, coupled to a constant mesh gearbox and air brakes. In April 1964 it was re-seated to C41F for a further ten years' service. It's seen here in 1955 passing through Orchard St, Neath, the main thoroughfare to Cardiff in those far gone days. The Queens Hotel is now The Canterbury Arms.

Above: New to the company in May 1956 was **WDE 343** another 'Seagull' coach built by H V Burlingham of Blackpool, with just a slight difference outwardly – positioning of the headlights and seating 41. On the other hand the chassis was something completely new to Silcox, a Guy Arab LUF, with the Gardner 6HLW engine. They were obviously influenced by the availability of a chassis with their preferred Gardner engine. **WDE 343** (46) is pictured here at Upper Park Road, Tenby sometime in the 1960s before the construction of the town's multi-story car park. This coach was withdrawn and scrapped in 1969 – only thirteen years old!

Above: ACK 871 (44) was one of two 1945 Guy Arab IIs acquired from Ribble Motor Services in 1956, with 7 litre Gardner 5LW engines which developed 84 bhp at 1700 rpm, and fitted with Roe L27/26R bodywork. It's captured here in late 1959 early 1960 on layover between school duties, shortly before withdrawal in 1960. Its partner was registered ACK 875. *(R H G Simpson).*

Above: This very interesting view of 'Silcox' bodied Bristol L5G NDE 332 (5) was taken by an unidentified photographer at the Port of Dover in the mid - 1950s. The coach was being loaded on to the cross channel ferry 'Prinses Josephine Charlotte' for its crossing to Ostend on what may have been Silcox's first visit to the continent. Their first licence for continental tours came in 1954.
(The Omnibus Society collection).

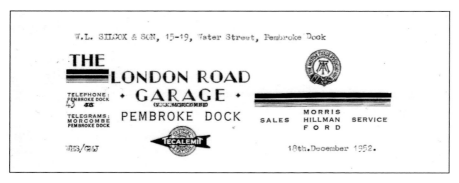

Above is a letterhead with the name and address of a 'Motor Garage' business absorbed by W L Silcox & Son in 1952.

Despite the company's increased activity in the mid–1950s it is interesting to note that the purchase of new vehicles virtually came to a standstill after 1954. From 1955 to 1961 only *one* 'new' vehicle arrived, a Guy Arab LUF (with Gardner engine) registered WDE 343, which was amongst an assortment of twenty nine second-hand buses and coaches acquired during the same period.

On 21st December 1956, Luther John Watts Silcox, eldest son of the founder and retired manager of the business passed away aged 71. L J W Silcox was a widower with no children. Probate was granted to his nephew Leonard William Silcox, M D of the business.

Above: After a little detective work, this undated view of Waterloo Garage, Pembroke Dock, was in the mid-1950s, before the road improvement took place. Running left to right of the picture is London Road (A477) close to the garage forecourt, and in the immediate foreground is Ferry Lane (A4139) with finger post road sign placed at the junction. *(The Omnibus Society collection).*

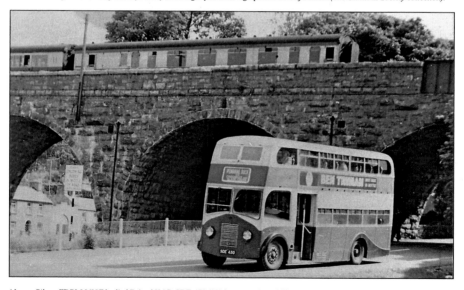

Above: Silcox FDPL32/28F bodied Bristol K6G, **SDE 450** (39) is seen at Greenhill Road, Tenby working service No12 from Tenby to Pembroke Dock. The railway arches in the background with a headroom of 15ft 9inches, form the rail approach into Tenby Railway Station. Service 12 to Pembroke Dock warranted a low-bridge decker due to a low railway bridge at Kilgetty. *(S E Letts).*

47

Call and see why
owners, drivers and
owner-drivers all say

AUSTIN

—that's my truck !

AUSTIN A40 PICK-UP
Stylish. Fast-moving. A hard worker with a 42 b.h.p. O.H.V. engine and 3-seater cab. Takes a 10 cwt. load easily.

—you'll be welcome at

W. L. SILCOX & SON
WATER STREET :: PEMBROKE DOCK
Phone : 343, 344 PEMBROKE DOCK

Above: This advertisement for Silcox's Austin dealership dates from 1955.

48

EXPANSION

An interesting development in March 1958 was an application made by W L Silcox & Son, for all the Road Service Licences held by D J Morrison Ltd, (Douglas Jerrold Morrison) of Deer Park Garage, Tenby Pembrokeshire. Negotiations with D J Morrison had taken place, resulting in the following Morrison licences being applied for on 12th March:-

TGR 3836/39   **Tenby (South Parade)** to **Amroth**, via: Twy Cross, Bethesda, Pentlepoir Hill, Begelly Cross, Stepaside, Cambrian Cross and Summer Hill.

TGR 3836/40   **Tenby (South Parade)** to **Whitland**, via: Kilgetty, Sardis, Amroth, Longstone, Princes Gate and Narberth.

TGR 3836/41   **Tenby (South Parade)** to **Jameston**, via: Penally and Lydstep.

TGR 3836/42   **Tenby (South Parade)** to **Lawrenny**, via: Begelly Cross, Templeton, Reynalton, Loveston, Yerbeston and Martletwy.

TGR 3836/43   Between any two points on existing services (as TGR 3836/29 on page 41).

TGR 3836/44   **Manorbier (School of A A Artillery)** to **Manchester (Express Carriage)**.

TGR 3836/45   **Manorbier (School of A A Artillery)** to **Birmingham (Express Carriage)**.

TGR 3836/46   **Excursions & Tours** starting from **Tenby.**

TGR 3836/47   **Excursions & Tours** starting from **Saundersfoot.**

TGR 3836/48   **Excursions & Tours** starting from **St Florence.**

TGR 3836/49   **Tenby (Grey Garages door South Parade)** to **Tenby (Heywood Lane Football Ground)**.

TGR 3836/50   **Tenby (South Parade)** to **Tenby (Serpentine Rd)**, via: Maudlins and Heywood Court.

TGR 3836/51   **Whitland** to **Lampeter Velfry**, via: Penparc.

However, the above applications were all withdrawn on 30th July 1958 as negotiations with Morrison had broken down. After further negotiations, W L Silcox & Son re-applied for the same licences on 10th November 1958, resulting in the immediate issue of special short term licences to operate *all* the services from 10/11/1958 to 4/1/1959 inclusive and later 5/1/1959 to 1/3/1959, until the full term licences were granted on 1/3/1959. The official date of take-over was given as 5th December 1958.

D J Morrison's subsidiary coach company, Grey Garages Ltd, Frog Street, Tenby was also absorbed along with Grey Garages' one coach and Morrison's thirteen vehicles. The only licence held in the name of Grey Garages, TGR 500/3 (Excursions and Tours starting from Tenby) was absorbed by Pioneer Bus Services (LW Silcox T/A). Only four Morrison vehicles all AECs - MDE 333, ODE 1, UDE 111, YDE 444 were operated by Silcox together with the solitary Grey Garages coach, OHA 298. The remaining nine vehicles were sold off unused. Consequently, Silcox opened an outstation at the Pembrokeshire C C owned North Beach Coach Park, Tenby with very basic facilities, and leased a tours booking office/enquiry office initially at No1 Trafalgar Road, Tenby.

The Grey Garages' licence which transferred to Pioneer Bus Service (L W Silcox T/A) became:-

TGR 3809/4 **Excursions & Tours** starting from **Tenby (South Parade)**.

Above: Seen here in June 1950 is **MDE 333** an AEC Regal III with a Burlingham B35F body, which was new to Morrison, Tenby in April 1950. It passed to Silcox with Morrison's business in December 1958. Note the incorrect spelling of Manorbier.

Above: ODE 1 was a 1952 Roe B44F bodied AEC Regal IV which also came from Morrison, Tenby with the 'transfer of undertaking' in December 1958. It was withdrawn in 1965 and passed to Arlington Motors (dealer) who sold it off for scrap.

(R H G Simpson).

Above: Captured here working a local excursion to Stack Rocks in south Pembrokeshire is another former D J Morrison of Tenby vehicle, **UDE 111**. New to Morrison in May 1955, this AEC Reliance MU3RV had very stylish Plaxton 'Venturer' III coachwork seating 39 passengers. This coach was sold in September 1970. *(R H G Simpson).*

Above: Pictured here at Gas Lane, Tenby is bus number 43, **YDE 444** a 1957 AEC Reliance MU3RA with Burlingham B45F bodywork. It was the newest of the vehicles acquired with the Morrison business and remained with Silcox until 1970 when it was sold to a dealer with no further trace. D J Morrison usually booked registration numbers with all three numerals identical.

Above: Another coach with attractive lines was this 1950 AEC Regal III with Harrington C37F coachwork. **OHA 298** (34) was new to Gliderways Coaches, Smethwick, passing to Grey Garages, Tenby in 1951 (a subsidiary of D J Morrison Tenby). This coach was transferred to Silcox with the Morrison/Grey Garages business in December 1958, but was licenced to Silcox's subsidiary company 'Pioneer Bus Service' (L W Silcox T/A).

Immediately after the Morrison take over there was a fleet re-shuffle. Several Morrison vehicles were not acceptable - having petrol engines or being of non-standard marques, i.e: Sentinel, TSM and Bedford. These were quickly exchanged for second-hand Bristol L5Gs and Leyland Tigers.

Above: One of the first vehicles acquired to replace the unwanted Morrison fleet in December 1958 was **DDB 269** above, a former North Western R C C (269) Bristol L5G with Windover C32F bodywork. DDB 268/9 (15/6) were both acquired in December 1958 for the Morrison work and were withdrawn in 1962, eventually used as a source of spare parts. *(R H G Simpson).*

On 4th March 1959, W L Silcox & Son applied for a 'new' Saturday only stage carriage service:-

TGR 3836/52 **Pembroke Dock** to **Tenby** via: Carew Cross, Cresswell Quay, Lawrenny, Martletwy, Cross Hands, Loveston Cross, Templeton, Reynalton, Jeffreyston, Cross Inn, East Williamston and Moreton. *Granted for Sats only, 10/6/1959.*

Two months later they applied for an Express Carriage licence to convey workers to the first 'Oil Refinery' in Pembrokeshire owned by 'Esso Petroleum Co Ltd'. The site was in the heart of Western Welsh Omnibus Co territory, and of course they objected to the application. Furthermore, Western Welsh operated all the transportation services to the refinery site during its construction. The Esso refinery became operational in 1960, employing hundreds of local people from a region that had been classified as a 'distressed area'.

TGR 3836/53 **Pembroke Dock (Waterloo Garage)** to **Herbrandston (Esso Refinery)**, via: Pembroke, Carew Cross, Cresselly, Cannaston Bridge, Haverfordwest, Ratford Bridge and Tiers Cross. *To operate Mon-Fri throughout the year and Sats/Suns when required. This application was withdrawn on 30/9/1959.*

On 14th October 1959, another local schools stage carriage licence was applied for:-

TGR 3836/54 **Maidenwells** to **Pembroke Dock (Hobbs Point)**, via: St Daniels Hill, East End Square, Main St, Bush Hill, Belle Vue, Pembroke Street, Bush Street, and Water St. *To run on schooldays only. Granted 23/12/1959.*

Note: *TGR 3836/43 – withdrawn by 27/9/1961, TGR 3836/51 – surrendered 10/6/1959.*

Right: Acquired in April 1959 from Western National (242), was this 1937 Bristol GO5G registered **ETA 967**. The Eastern Coach Works L27/28R low-bridge body was new in 1949. ETA 967 was given f/n 37 by Silcox and was withdrawn in 1968 with no further trace – believed to have been the last Bristol G type in regular passenger service in Britain.

(Vernon Morgan).

53

Above: The chassis of this AEC Regent dated from 1937 and its Willowbrook L27/28R body from 1948. Silcox bought three of these re-bodied Regents from Trent Motor Traction (1331/4/5) RC 4627/30/33 in 1959, but took them all out of service after only a year. Their bodies however were transferred to other Silcox vehicles (see pages 34/6/8) this particular one **RC 4630** (42) was fitted to ODE 401 (24) a 1952 Bristol K6G which had previously carried a MCCW trolleybus body dating from 1940. *(Alan Broughall).*

Above: **RC 4627** (41) was another 1937 AEC Regent 0661 acquired from Trent Motor Transport (1331) in 1959. Its Willowbrook L27/28R body (new in1948) was up-seated and donated to LDE 949 (22) a 1949 Bristol K6G in 1960/1 (picture on page 34). Visible in the background is a Silcox bodied Bristol L5G, NDE 330 (3) dating from 1951.

(The Omnibus Society collection, D S Giles).

Above: A splendid 'Old Lady' **GNO 693** (28) captured here at the depot freshly painted in July 1959. This was a 1938 Bristol K5G with 'original' Eastern Coach Works L27/28R body, new to Eastern National O C (3749), to United Counties (628) in 5/52, returning to Eastern National (1016) in 11/1955, passing to Silcox in 1959. Withdrawn in 1960 it passed to a showman by 1961.

Above: Nearest the camera is **GHN 189** a 1942 Bristol K5G fitted with a second-hand 1949 ECW L27/26R body in 1954 by its previous owners United Automobile Services. It arrived at Silcox in April 1959 and is seen here at South Parade, Tenby working service 11 to Pembroke Dock in 1960. Behind is former West Wales Motors of Tycroes, **NBX 310** a 1956 Guy Arab LUF with Burlingham B44F body, which Silcox purchased in April 1960. **NBX 310** is working service 10, Tenby to Manorbier Camp.

Above: **DDB 279** was acquired from North Western Road Car Co (279) in 1959 to cover the extra work inherited with the Morrison business a few months earlier. DDB 278/9, had Leyland PS2/3 chassis with Windover C32F bodies, and were both acquired in early 1959. This one however was withdrawn in December 1962 and used for spares, the remains were scrapped in 1967.

Above: Former Southdown Motor Services **HUF 299** (1299) was also one of a pair acquired in 1959. This and its twin HUF 300 were 1948 Leyland 'Tiger' PS1s with very pleasing lines of their Park Royal C32R coachwork. **HUF 299** is seen here at the depot in its early days with the company, painted in Silcox's coach livery – later changed to bus livery for contract work. These two by far outlived the 'Tigers' acquired from North Western Road Car Co, as they were not withdrawn until 1970. *(Robert F Mack).*

56

Above: **MUX 794** bus No 8 was a Leyland 'Tiger Cub' PSUC1/2 new in January 1956 to J T Whittle, Highley, West Midlands, fitted with Burlingham 'Seagull' C41F coachwork. The body was rebuilt, repanelled and re-seated with 41 bus seats in March 1965. Re-classified as DP41F, it then received bus livery for use on schools and contract work, as seen here. *(Alan Broughall).*

Right: This was the original PSV licence disc carried by Leyland 'Tiger Cub' **MUX 794** (pictured above) from 5/4/62 to 4/4/63. Renewable annually, it was a legal requirement to display the vehicle's PSV licence disc in the appropriate vehicle's windscreen, displaying the name of the licence holder and the vehicle's identification details. This style of licence was discontinued under the 1980 Road Traffic Act, in favour of the coloured operator licence discs of today, which are now transferable between individual vehicles provided the vehicle carries a current Certificate of Fitness.

Above: Pictured here at the depot in June 1959, just three months after its cab had been rebuilt by the company for one person operation is Bristol L5G, **JDE 426** (33) with Strachan DP35F bodywork. It had been purchased new by Silcox in December 1947. After carrying out the modification to the cab, it was sold a year later to a dealer, and scrapped by December 1960. The little square box cut-away to the right hand of the doorway housed the 'emergency only' door control switch.

Above: Burlingham Coachworks also bodied double decker vehicles - as shown here on **LAL 691** (40) captured at the depot in 1967. LAL 691 was a 1950 Leyland 'Titan' PD1A with Burlingham L27/26R body, acquired from East Midlands Motor Services, Chesterfield in September 1959. East Midlands had acquired this 'Titan' from Wass Brothers of Mansfield in March 1958.

Above: This Leyland 'Titan' PD1A, **GDE 834** (49) with neatly styled Burlingham L27/28R bodywork, had been new to D J Morrison of Tenby (23) in July 1946. It passed to Green's Motors, Haverfordwest in December 1951 and later passed to Western Welsh (987) with Green's Motors 'omnibus business' in January 1957. (Green's continued with their garage business). Silcox acquired GDE 834 from W W O C in June 1959, and sold it ten months later in April 1960.

Above: LDE 600 (50) was a Guy 'Arab' III with Gardner 6LW engine and Barnard L27/26R body. This was also acquired from Western Welsh (382) in April 1960, and had been new to Green's Motors, Haverfordwest in 1949 fitted with Meadows 6DC engine.

Above: This view of **LDE 600** (50) a former Greens Motors Guy Arab III with Barnard L27/26R body was taken at Water St, Pembroke Dock c1965 after a repaint. Alongside the bus is a Ford Thames 402E pick-up truck registered 949 RDE, owned by 'Bechtel' one of the contractors building the Texaco Oil Refinery at Rhoscrowther. Just visible in the gap between the truck and bus is WL Silcox & Son car sales showroom, 15-19 Water St, where the business all started from *(Omnibus Society collection)*.

Above: This view of Bubbleston Bridge on the B4139 between Tenby and Lydstep was kindly supplied by John Bennett of Loughborough who worked as a conductor at Silcox during his summer vacation from College in 1971 and 1972. The local authority painted a series of white dots on the roadway which the driver used as a guide, aligning the front wheels with the dots to safely pass under the bridge. This particular Bristol K6G **(LDE 950)** was one of the most photographed buses in Wales.

(John Bennett).

TIME FOR CHANGE

At this point in time, W L Silcox & Sons had been trading for 78 years – as a private unregistered company. With the business expanding considerably, the time had come when it was essential to register the business as a Limited Company in order to safeguard the family partnership.

On 20th December 1960, **'SILCOX MOTOR COACH COMPANY LTD'** was incorporated as company number 00678372 and the directors were given as W H Silcox, W M Silcox, L W Silcox (Managing Director) and Mrs D E Miller, with the registered office remaining at 17 Water Street, Pembroke Dock and the operating centre Waterloo Garage, London Road, Pembroke Dock.

As previously mentioned, the Managing Director Leonard W Silcox, and Mrs Doreen Ellen Miller were the son and daughter of W H Silcox, and his wife W M Silcox.

A second limited company registered on the same date was W L Silcox & Son Ltd, motor engineers and dealers, from the same shared premises as the buses and coaches - Waterloo Garage.

In 1960, the new £18m 'Esso' refinery opened at Herbrandston across the 'Haven' (Cleddau River) from Pembroke Dock, bringing much needed work to the distressed area, and within a short space of time the Regent Petroleum Co (Texaco) was building a refinery on the south bank of the 'Haven' at Rhoscrowther, situated between Pembroke and the village of Angle – which opened in 1964.

Construction of the Texaco refinery brought much extra work to Silcox, conveying employees to and from the construction site and within the confines of the enormous site. Extra buses were purchased for this work, increasing the fleet to 42, with a variety of interesting vehicles mainly Leyland.

Above: Another former Southdown Motor Services 'Leyland' that migrated west to Pembroke Dock in January 1960 was **GUF 685** (48) a 1946 Leyland 'Titan' PD1 with Park Royal H28/26R high-bridge bodywork. GUF 685 saw continuous service until December 1965, and is pictured here at Pembroke working a school days only (service 3A) from Maidenwells to Hobbs Point, a service that was authorised on 23rd December 1959.   *Note the driver giving hand signals – no indicators in those far gone days.*

Above: Silcox were not a fond user of AEC vehicles, apart from the five acquired with Morrison's business only four others were acquired; three 'Regents' which only ran for a year and this early 'Reliance' **UTB 550** (49) with Plaxton 'Venturer' C41C coachwork in 1960. It was sold for further use in 1966 to J Kelleher, Boherbue, Co Cork and re-registered DZK 494.

Above: LDE 601 (51) was one of two identical Guy Arab IIIs with Barnard L27/26R bodies acquired in 1960 from Western Welsh (382/3) LDE 600/1. They were both new to Green's Motors of Haverfordwest in 1949, and passed to Western Welsh in January 1957 with Green's business. Originally fitted with Meadows 6DC diesel engines, both were retrofitted with second-hand Gardner 6LW units in 1957. **LDE 601** was withdrawn in 1962 and used for spares, whilst LDE 600 soldiered on until August 1967.

Above: This Guy Arab II, fleet no 52, **GNN 134** was new to East Midland Motor Service as D34 in May 1944, and re-bodied by Chas H Roe in April 1954. Fitted with Gardner 5LW engine it arrived at Pembroke Dock with its twin sister GAL 433 below in April 1960, giving excellent service until 1973. *(BVBG).*

Above: (53) **GAL 433** was a 1943 Guy Arab II with Gardner 5LW five cylinder engine, re-bodied in April 1954 by C H Roe to L27/28R layout. This also came from East Midland M S (D33) in April 1960 and spent twelve years working for Silcox. It was captured here at Pembroke Town Hall (Main St) on 29th August 1963. *(V. Morgan).*

Another example of Silcox's rebuilding work is captured here with these two pictures. **SVX 233** (55) was a Leyland 'Royal Tiger'
PSU1/11, bodied to C37C configuration by Windover, and new to Harris of Grays, Essex in 1951. Silcox acquired it in 1960 from
F A Laker (Freddie Laker the airline entrepreneur) Southend on Sea, operating it in its original form as seen above (don't know
about the headlight) for quite a while before reseating it with 41 *bus* seats, rebuilding the front end and repanelling all around. The
entrance doorway of this rebuild surprisingly remained at the centre. However, the driver pictured in the lower view certainly had
no regard for the safety of the school children aboard his bus – travelling along the highway with the entrance door wide open. This
vehicle was withdrawn in 1964 and sold to Arlington Motors, Cardiff in part exchange for a new coach, eventually moving on to its
final resting place, W Way's scrap yard at Cardiff Docks.

Above: **120 LDE** was the first mini-bus operated by the company. Registered in May 1961, it was obviously bought through their own Austin dealership. This type of Austin LDO5AR were available as a chassis/cab or alternatively a complete 14 seat personnel carrier. The body of **120 LDE** (58) is quoted as Austin/Silcox B14F – suggesting that Silcox converted its Austin bodywork to PSV standards. The conversion took two months as it wasn't licenced until July 1961.   *(Alan Broughall).*

Above: The first Leyland 'Leopard' in the fleet arrived January 1962. Registered **50 NDE** (61) it was the L2 model, fitted with Duple 'Britannia' C45F coachwork, which was re-seated with 45 bus seats by September 1978. It passed to the dealer, Martin of Middlewich in April 1981, with no further trace.   *(John Bennett).*

Above: The Leyland 'Royal Tiger' was very appealing to Silcox throughout the years with no less than ten passing through, all second-hand, and carrying bodies built by six different manufacturers. Pictured above is **CRC 512** with coachwork by Leyland, fitted to a Royal Tiger PSU1/15 type chassis, which had been new to Trent Motor Traction (202) in May 1951 built to C41C configuration. It was re-seated with 45 bus seats by Silcox before entering service in April 1962, therefore re-designating it <u>DP45C</u>.

Above: Another Leyland 'Royal Tiger' PSU1/15 in the fleet with Leyland C41C coachwork was **FJA 615** seen here at 'The Works' in August 1968. **FJA 615** was new to North Western (615) in May 1953, and arrived at Pembroke Dock in July 1962. This one retained its coach seating and centre entrance throughout, finally being withdrawn in 1971. Visible on the left is (29) a former Morrison AEC 'Reliance' UDE 111 which had lost its front bumper by 1968 after a rebuild. See original on page 51. *(V. Morgan).*

Above: Bristol L5G, NDE 332 was new to Silcox in 1951, fitted with a Silcox FDP39F body (pictured on page 29). In April 1961 its Silcox body was removed, the chassis overhauled and sent to Marshalls of Cambridge to have this new body fitted. It returned to service in June 1961 with this new Marshall FDP39F body, which saw a further eleven years' service.

Above: Captured here at Upper Park Road, Tenby is another 'Silcox Special' registered **702 RDE**. The chassis of **702 RDE** f/n 65 (later re-numbered 64) was built in 1962 mainly comprising the chassis frame of DDB 270 (14) a 1949 Bristol L5G. The overhauled chassis was dispatched to Marshalls of Cambridge where it was re-bodied to FDP39F configuration, matching NDE 332 above, and using coach seats from a former Trent Motor Traction Leyland 'Royal Tiger' coach. Finally, this vehicle was given a new identity, chassis type Bristol/Silcox LL/SX/5G and chassis number LL/SX/65/1962.

Above: An amendment to the Construction & Use act in 1961 brought about a new maximum permitted length for buses and coaches to 36 feet (11 metre). The first 36 feet long vehicle to enter service with Silcox was **734 PDE** (62) a new Leyland 'Leopard' PSU3/3R with Willowbrook C51F body in October 1962. It's seen here accompanied by Silcox's Plaxton bodied AEC Reliance, UTB 550 operating a 'Private Hire' in the mid-1960s. 734 PDE had its roof dome windows panelled over later in its working life, and was taken out of service in 1983.   *(Hubert Williams).*

Above: One of a large intake of 'pre-used' vehicles in 1963 was **LEH 42** pictured here, a 1947 Leyland 'Tiger' PS1/1 with second-hand 1949 Weymann B39F body. It was one of five Leylands acquired from Potteries Motor Transport, Stoke on Trent in 1963.

Above: Three former Southdown Motor Services Guy Arab IIs were purchased in 1963 primarily for contract work at the new Texaco refinery. Registered **GUF 118/35/58** (418/35/58) and fitted with NCME (Northern Counties) H28/26R bodies they received Silcox fleet numbers 16/4/5 respectively. I captured this view of **GUF 158 (left)** behind 'The Works' in June 1966. It must have taken lots of skill and confidence to reverse this bus up the steep ramp to the pressure washing bay. *(V Morgan).*

Above: Another new Leyland 'Leopard' PSU3/3R arrived in May 1963, fitted with Duple 'Alpine Continental' C51F coachwork. This was registered **635 SDE** (f/n 65) and is seen here at Cardiff working a private hire assignment to the WRU Rugby International, with 614 XDE another Silcox 'Leopard' close behind. *(V Morgan collection).*

The last Road Service Licence applied for in the name of W L Silcox & Sons was made on 28th March 1962, to run a daily stage carriage service including Sundays throughout the summer. It was granted as follows on 20th June 1962:-

TGR 3836/55 **Pembroke Dock (Hobbs Point)** to **Tenby (South Parade)** via Pembroke, Freshwater East, Hodgeston, Jameston, Manorbier, Lydstep and Penally.

Bearing in mind that the business was a limited company from December 1960, the company continued to use RSLs in the name of W L Silcox & Son until October 1962 when they eventually applied for a transfer of all licences held by W L Silcox & Son to Silcox Motor Coach Company Ltd. At the same time there was still one remaining Pioneer Bus Service licence held, TGR 3809/4 which continued as such until February 1968, when it was finally surrendered.

Having said that, Silcox had applied for five Express Carriage licences in the name of Silcox Motor Coach Co Ltd, on 12th April 1961, but withdrew the applications (listed below) on 21st June 1961:-

TGR 4902/1 **Mydrim** to **Pendine (Experimental Establishment)** via St Clears Station, Lon Hafren, and Church Gate, *to run Mon–Fri only when Pendine E E is working.*

TGR 4902/2 **Llanddowror** to **Pendine (Experimental Establishment)** via Llanteg, Folly Cross, Kilanow, Cambrian Cross, Amroth Arms and Beof's Park, *to run Mon-Fri only when Pendine E E is working.*

TGR 4902/3 **Whitland** to **Pendine (Experimental Establishment)** via Tavernspite, Red Roses Cross Roads and Pendine Church, *to run Mon-Fri only when Pendine E E is working*

TGR 4902/4 **Carmarthen (Old Oak)** to **Pendine (Experimental Establishment)** via Elliston Terrace, Water St, Bancyfelin, Chapel Mair, Milford Arms (St Clears) and Blue Boar, *to run Mon-Fri only when Pendine E E is working.*

TGR 4902/5 **Carmarthen (Capitol Cinema)** to **Pendine (Experimental Establishment)** via Milford Arms, Johnstown, Pass By, St Clears (Old P O), Morfa Bach and Cross Inn, *to run Mon-Fri only when Pendine E E is working.*

Fares for the above services would be subsidised by a Travel Assistance Scheme.

On 10th October 1962, Silcox Motor Coach Company Ltd, applied for all the RSLs previously held by W L Silcox & Son, which were granted individually between December 1962 and January 1963:-

TGR 4902/6	Previously TGR 3836/1	Pembroke Dock (Hobbs Point) to Pembroke (East End).
TGR 4902/7	" TGR 3836/2	Pembroke Dock (Hobbs Point) to Angle.
TGR 4902/8	" TGR 3836/3	Pembroke Dock (Hobbs Point) to Merrion.
TGR 4902/9	" TGR 3836/4	Pembroke Dock to Tenby.
TGR 4902/10	" TGR 3836/7	Pembroke Dock to Pennar.
TGR 4902/11	" TGR 3836/8	Pembroke Dock (Hobbs Point) to Manorbier.
TGR 4902/12	" TGR 3836/11	Pembroke Dock to Mount Pleasant.
TGR 4902/13	" TGR 3836/12	Pembroke & Pembroke Dock to Tenby via Cresselly.
TGR 4902/14	" TGR 3836/13	Pennar Barracks to Kingswood.
TGR 4902/15	" TGR 3836/14	Kingswood to Monkton.
TGR 4902/16	" TGR 3836/15	Pembroke Dock to Narberth.

TGR 4902/17	Previously TGR 3836/17	Angle to Tenby.
TGR 4902/18	" TGR 3836/18	Monkton to Pembroke Dock.
TGR 4902/19	" TGR 3836/35	Pembroke Dock (RAF Station) to Birmingham (Express)
TGR 4902/20	" TGR 3836/36	Pembroke Dock (RAF Station) to Manchester (Express)
TGR 4902/21	" TGR 3836/38	Golden Hill Avenue to Pembroke (East End).
TGR 4902/22	" TGR 3836/39	Tenby to Amroth.
TGR 4902/23	" TGR 3836/40	Tenby to Whitland.
TGR 4902/24	" TGR 3836/41	Tenby to Jameston via Lydstep & Manorbier Camp.
TGR 4902/25	" TGR 3836/42	Tenby to Lawrenny.
TGR 4902/26	" TGR 3836/44	Manorbier (School of Artillery) to Manchester (Express)
TGR 4902/27	" TGR 3836/45	Manorbier (School of Artillery) to Birmingham "
TGR 4902/28	" TGR 3836/49	Tenby (Grey Garages) to Tenby (Football Ground).
TGR 4902/29	" TGR 3836/50	Tenby (South Parade) to Tenby (Serpentine Road).
TGR 4902/30	" TGR 3836/55	Pembroke Dock to Tenby via Freshwater East.
TGR 4902/31	" TGR 3836/54	Maidenwells to Pembroke Dock (Hobbs Point).
TGR 4902/32	" TGR 3836/52	Pembroke Dock (Hobbs Point) to Tenby (South Parade).
TGR 4902/33	" TGR 3836/27	Pembroke Dock (RAF Station) to Cardiff (Express)
TGR 4902/34	" TGR 3836/29	Any two points on existing stage carriage service.
TGR 4902/35	" TGR 3836/19	Excursions & Tours starting Pembroke Dock (Star Corner)
TGR 4902/36	" TGR 3836/22	" " " " Cresswell Quay.
TGR 4902/37	" TGR 3836/23	" " " " Pennar (Royal Oak).
TGR 4902/38	" TGR 3836/24	" " " " Monkton & Hundleton.
TGR 4902/39	" TGR 3836/30	" " " " Angle (The Globe Hotel).
TGR 4902/40	" TGR 3836/31	" " " " Cosheston.
TGR 4902/41	" TGR 3836/32	" " " " Freshwater East.
TGR 4902/42	" TGR 3836/33	" " " " Stackpole (Post Office).
TGR 4902/43	" TGR 3836/46	" " " " Tenby.
TGR 4902/44	" TGR 3836/47	" " " " Saundersfoot.
TGR 4902/45	" TGR 3836/48	" " " " St Florence.

Simultaneously on 10th October 1962, another 'new' stage carriage licence was applied for:-

TGR 4902/46 **Pembroke Dock (Bush Estate)** to **Pembroke (East End)**, via St John's Rd, Hawkstone Rd, Laws St, Bush St, Pembroke St, Victoria Rd, Bellvue Terr, High St, Bush Hill, Dark Lane and Main St. *To run on school days only. Granted 12/1962.*

Note: All the RSLs held under TGR 3836 were surrendered upon receipt of new licences TGR 4902.

On 17th July 1963, two more Express Carriage licences were applied for:-

TGR 4902/47 **Pembroke Dock** to **Castlemartin (RAC Ranges)** *Royal Armoured Corps.*
Granted 9th October 1963.

TGR 4902/48 **Sardis** to **Pembroke Dock (Llanion Barracks)**, via Kilgetty, Saundersfoot, Tenby, and Manorbier. *Granted 9th October 1963.*

A modification of TGR 4902/7 was applied for in February 1964, diverting the service at Glebe Cross to include the new Regent Refinery (Texaco) at Rhoscrowther which was scheduled to open in 1964.

When the Texaco refinery opened, Silcox negotiated a contract to maintain the large fleet of Texaco 'Road Tankers' operating from Pembroke. In addition to this, Silcox's extensive workshop facilities carried out commercial vehicle repairs, mechanical and coachwork for several businesses in the west Wales area, in addition to contractor's vehicles working at the refineries. One of these contractors was 'Bechtel' an American based company, who operated the Bristol L5G pictured below.

BJA 414 above was a 1947 Bristol L5G with Weymann B35R bodywork owned by 'Bechtel' an American based construction company, working at the Texaco refinery site, Rhoscrowther, Pembroke in the early 1960s. It was maintained by Silcox and garaged at their yard, hence the view taken at Waterloo Garage in 1964.

Above: Pictured here at London Road, Pembroke Dock in 1963 is bus no 2, **PRE 735** a 1948 Leyland 'Tiger' PS1/1 fitted with a 1949 Weymann B39F body recovered off NEH457 in 1955 by its previous owners Potteries M T. **PRE 735** was withdrawn in 1967.

0226

SILCOX
Coach Tours

8/-

DATE ፲8 7 6ۅ

DEPARTURE TIME
2 ⌐00

Bell Punch Company, London.   J6175

Serial No. 4244

SILCOX MOTOR COACH CO. LTD.

Stack Rocks & Bosherston

Price .... *1·40*

Date *17/6*

Departure time 14.15

Above: Coach tour tickets used by Silcox Motor Coach Co Ltd in the 1960s and 1970s.

Above: Purchased in June 1963 from Ribble Motor Services (2720), was **CRN 219** (f/n 67) a 1949 Leyland 'Titan' PD2/3 with classic Leyland L27/26R low-bridge type bodywork. Leylands were the MDs second choice of vehicle at a time when the Bristol marque were unavailable. CRN 219 had the standard Leyland 0.600 engine, four speed synchromesh gearbox and vacuum brakes, but this double decker was one of several operating for Silcox fitted with incompatible headlights. It gave the company six years' service before withdrawal in June 1969.   *(R H G Simpson).*

73

Above: Seen on layover at South Parade, Tenby is **KRR 70** (66) another Leyland L27/26R bodied Leyland 'Titan' dating from 1950. This one had chassis type PD2/1 (7ft 6ins wide) and arrived from East Midland (D70) in April 1963. KRR 70 was another vehicle fitted with incompatible headlights but gave excellent service until February 1969.

Above: Upper Park Road, Tenby is the backdrop to this photograph of **FUH 412** (17) an integrally built Leyland 'Olympic' HR44, new to Western Welsh (412) in June 1951. It was the only 'Olympic' operated by Silcox, arriving there in February 1964, and is captured working service number 6, Tenby to Lawrenny, a Saturday only service inherited with the Morrison business in 1958.

Above: This 1954 Burlingham 'Seagull' C41C bodied Leyland 'Tiger Cub' PSUC1/2; **PVO 624** (20) is seen here at Pendine working one of the company's excursions in the mid-1960s. Acquired in April 1964 from East Midland (C24) it followed a sister vehicle (PVO 622) to Pembroke Dock, but had an extended life after receiving a new body in 1967 – see photograph below.

Above: In early 1967 the company removed the original Burlingham 'Seagull' body off the chassis of **PVO 624** (seen in upper photograph) overhauled the chassis and converted it to PSUC1/2T specification by fitting a two speed rear axle. After overhaul, it was sent to Plaxton Coachworks where it received this new Plaxton 'Panorama II' C43F body in February 1967. In its new guise pictured here, it saw a further nineteen years' use, taken out of service in July 1986 and scrapped in 1992. But it doesn't end there; its cherished registration number **PVO 624** continued to be used by the company on two newer vehicles - until 2004. *(RHGS)*.

Above: This Leyland 'Leopard' PSU3/3RT was the only new vehicle purchased in 1964 and was exhibited at the Commercial Motor Show, Earls Court, London in September 1964. Registered **614 XDE** (f/n 69) it had Duple 'Commander' C51F coachwork which was converted to DP51F and re-numbered 64 in 1979. It was withdrawn in November 1981. *(RHG Simpson).*

Above: With regard to vehicle intake, 1965 was by far the company's quietest year in post war times. Only three vehicles were purchased throughout the year, all second-hand. **VGT 330** pictured here at Pembroke in 1972, was one of two 1958 Leyland 'Tiger Cub' PSUC1/2 with Harrington 'Wayfarer IV' C41F coachwork, which arrived in January 1965 from George Ewer (Grey-Green) London N16. The pair (**VGT 328/330**) had fleet numbers 70/1 respectively, and were licenced in April. Later that year the third purchase of 1965 arrived, another Leyland 'Tiger Cub', this time from Western Welsh and pictured opposite.

Above: The third and last vehicle acquired in 1965 was (72) **HUH 47**, a 1954 Leyland 'Tiger Cub' PSUC1/2T with Weymann 'Hermes' B44F bodywork from Western Welsh (1047). It was seen here at Waterloo Garage in 1968 accompanied by two other 'Tiger Cubs' OUP 660 / URR 346 formerly operated by Sunderland District and East Midland respectively.   *(V Morgan).*

Above: The second mini-bus purchased by the company **664 WDE** (73) arrived second-hand in June 1966 from a local non-PSV owner. This 1964 Austin LDO5AR had previously worked as a personnel carrier, but was converted to PSV standards by Silcox themselves who also fitted it with 14 seats. In 1974 it was downgraded to non-PSV use and used as a garage breakdown tender.

Above: In 1966 the company took delivery of two new Leyland 'Tiger Cub' PSUC1/12 with Plaxton 'Panorama'C45F coachwork. They were identical vehicles with consecutive chassis numbers but their delivery and registration numbers were far apart. **DDE 950D** (74) pictured above was delivered in February whilst the second one FDE 282D (75) arrived in June.

Above: A superb view of this Leyland 'Leopard' **HCU 962** (77) leaving 'The Works' at Pembroke Dock in September 1972. This L2 'Leopard' with Duple 'Commander' C43F coachwork was new to Hall Brothers of South Shields in June 1963, and was purchased from them in October 1966 and sold to Arlington Motors (dealer) Cardiff in February 1973.

Above: I captured this former East Midland Leyland 'Tiger Cub' **URR 349** at South Parade, Tenby in June 1968 about to depart for Pembroke Dock. Silcox acquired **URR 349** (79) and identical URR 346 (78) from East Midland (R349/6 respectively) in May 1967. They were new in December 1956, and were fitted with B44F bodies built by Metro-Cammell. *(V. Morgan).*

Above: Leaving Upper Park Road, Tenby for Jameston on the daily service numbered 10, via Lydstep, Manorbier Camp and Manorbier is **HDE 903E** (80) the company's first 11 metre service bus. New in July 1967, **HDE 903E** was a Leyland 'Leopard' PSU3/3R with 4 speed manual gearbox and a Plaxton 'Derwent' B62F body (3+2 seating). It was also the company's first high capacity single deck vehicle which saw 21 years' service before being sold on for further use in August 1988.

Above: New to Silcox in May 1968 was this Leyland 'Leopard' PSU3/3RT, (81) **MDE 914F**, fitted with Plaxton 'Panorama I' coachwork which had a seating layout of 3+2 seating 51. This was part exchanged for a new 'Leopard' PSU3C/4R in July 1975.

Above: Former Northern General (1545) **DCN 845** is seen here at the bottom of Ferry Lane, Pembroke Dock, at the junction with London Road (A477). Acquired in April 1968, DCN 845 (f/n 1, later 2) was a 1954 Leyland 'Tiger Cub' PSUC1/1 with B44F body built by Saunders-Roe (Anglesey) Ltd, at Beaumaris, North Wales. Withdrawn in January 1975, it was used as a source of spare parts and broken up in 1976. *(Alan Broughall).*

In October 1968, the company applied to the licensing authority for permission to introduce an 'All Wales Road / Rail Ticket' to the value of £10. The application made on **TGR 4902/C** would allow tickets to be issued on any day, and permit 7 days travel on stage carriage services, and on the services of participating companies: British Railways, Western Welsh, South Wales Transport, United Welsh, Red & White, Rhondda, Thomas Bros, Crosville and Mid-Wales Motorways. The tickets were to be introduced for the Investiture Year 1969, commencing from the Saturday preceding Easter Monday up to and including 31st October. The licence was granted for the season and withdrawn in late 1969.

At this point in time, June 1969 the company were holding 37 RSLs and operated 15 stage carriage services. Directors of the company were Mrs W M Silcox (W H Silcox's widow), L W Silcox (MD), Mrs N Silcox (L W Silcox's wife) and Mrs D E Miller (L W Silcox's sister). The company secretary was Keith W Silcox (L W Silcox's son) who later became Managing Director.

An interesting development came in January 1968 when details of the 1968 Road Traffic Act were announced by the Minister of Transport. The Act which was implemented by Transport Minister Mr Richard Marsh gave stage carriage bus operators financial grants of 25% towards the purchase of new service buses, provided that they complied with certain requirements of the Ministry of Transport, including for example an extreme front entrance doorway under driver supervision, suitable for one-person operation. The intention of the grant scheme was to encourage operators to modernise their fleets and make buses more competitive in terms of comfort with private cars. The scheme applied only to buses used primarily on stage carriage services initially, but by 1970, when the grant was increased to 50% it was agreed that coaches could also qualify for grant if used to a sufficient extent on such bus services, provided that the coach bodies were built with minor essential modifications such as 'jack knife entrance doors' and other features which complied with the bus grant specification. The conditions attached to the 'New Bus Grant' were that operators would have to refund the grant if they sold the vehicle or ceased to use it for stage service within five years of its delivery.

The scheme which came into being on 1st September 1968 and ended in March 1984 was a blessing to most operators, but simultaneously put several operators deep into debt by purchasing vehicles they could ill-afford, a situation that caused the downfall of several operators nationwide. In addition to the bus grant, provision was made to increase the fuel duty rebate introduced in 1965 to 100% from 10d to 1/7d a gallon, paid to operators of rural bus services from 1st January 1969 and also the introduction of 'Rural Bus Grants' – subsidising un-remunerative rural bus services.

Despite having all this financial assistance, the company successfully applied for a fare increase on all services in April 1969, which became a regular feature with Silcox in April each year.

Nine months later another 'new' stage carriage licence was applied for:-

TGR 4902/49   **Britannia Estate (Pembroke Dock)** to **Pennar Infants & Junior Mixed Schools**.

A special short term licence TGR 4902/Sp/10 was issued to operate the above service in the interim period 6/1/1970 to 1/3/1970 until the full term licence was granted in March 1970.

On 18th February 1970 another 'new' Express Carriage licence was applied for as follows:-

TGR 4902/50   **Tenby (Upper Park Road)** to **Pendine (Experimental Establishment)**,
via: Saundersfoot, Begelly Cross, Amroth and Pendine.
A subsidised service for employees of the Establishment, who will make a contribution toward the amount paid by the Ministry of Defence.

Additionally, a special short term licence TGR 4902/Sp/11 was applied for to run the afore-mentioned workers 'Express Carriage' service to Pendine (E E) but was *refused* along with TGR 4902/50 on 1st April 1970. Furthermore, TGR 4902/25 and TGR 4902/30 were surrendered in July 1970.

Above: Silcox were amongst the first handful of Welsh operators to order grant aided buses, immediately placing an order for two Bristol LH6Ls. At this point in time, vehicles of Bristol manufacture had again become available to operators outside the T H C Group. **RDE 659G** pictured here at Waterloo Garage was numerically the first of an identical pair (87/8) RDE 659/60G which were fitted with Plaxton 'Derwent' DP43F bodies and entered service in July 1969.

Above: The economical Leyland 'Tiger Cub' proved to be a popular chassis with Silcox. An assortment of these were acquired throughout the years, with no less than six arriving from North Western Road Car Co (632/7/46/7/8/56) in 1969-72. Fitted with the lightweight Weymann 'Hermes' B44F bodies, two of them **KDB 648/6** (84/105) are seen here on a schools journey layover.

Above: Silcox had a penchant for the Bristol chassis and Gardner engine combination as mentioned previously, and quickly returned to that marque for new and second-hand vehicles from 1969 onwards. **SFM 8** (90) pictured here was a former Crosville Motor Services (DLB719) Bristol Lodekka LD6B (fitted with a Gardner 6LW engine by Crosville) with Eastern Coach Works H33/25R bodywork. **SFM 8** was new in May 1955 and arrived at Pembroke Dock in October 1969, working continuously until withdrawn and sold in 1977.

Above: Another superb view of this Bristol 'Lodekka' **SFM 8** is captured at Hobbs Point, Pembroke Dock in 1974. Hobbs Point was not only the terminus of service No 1, Pembroke Dock to Pembroke town, the service connected with a ferry service crossing the Cleddau Estuary to Neyland. Another 'fine cop' linked to this historical view is the 1971 Austin 1100 police car owned by Dyfed-Powys Police which is registered OBX 575J. These were known as 'Panda Cars'.   *(Jason Feeley collection).*

83

Above: **VFM 587** (89) was another former Crosville Motor Services (DLB722) Bristol 'Lodekka' LD6B acquired in October 1969. This one had also been fitted with a Gardner 6LW unit by Crosville but the Eastern Coach Works 58 seat bodywork was slightly different, it was fitted with platform doors H33/25RD. It's seen here in 1973, alongside Bristol KSW6G, HAP 985 (86) at the Neyland outstation, conveniently located on the slipway of the Neyland-Pembroke Dock car ferry. *(Alan Broughall).*

Above: Captured here at East End, Pembroke is another former Crosville Bristol 'Lodekka' LD6B with ECW H33/25R body. **RFM 457** was acquired from Crosville (DLB712) in late 1969 and retro-fitted with the Gardner 6LW engine removed from Silcox's 1949 Bristol K6G, LDE 949 (22) before entering service in 1970. It was one of only nine 'Lodekkas' operated by Silcox and was given fleet number 91. It only saw 3 years' service at Pembroke Dock before moving on in 1973 for scrap. *(R H G Simpson).*

Above: OHY 984 (96) was a 1953 Bristol KSW6G with ECW H32/28R bodywork acquired from Bristol Omnibus Co (C8127) in September 1970. It's looking superb here at the Neyland outstation, with the famous hostelry named 'London Coffee House' 3 Picton Road in the background. OHY 984 was sold in 1978 to the Eastern Counties Omnibus Society (preservation group) as a source of spare parts for their preserved fleet. *(T S Powell collection).*

Right: Another ECW bodied Bristol KSW6G in the Silcox fleet was **HAP 985** (86). This one was acquired from Southdown Motor Services, Brighton (447) in May 1969, but was not operated by them. It was new to Brighton Hove & District (6447) in July 1953. **HAP 985** is also seen at Neyland outstation, and gave Silcox almost ten years use before being sold for preservation to P Ticehurst & J Shorten of the Brighton Transport Society in 1979. It's now fully restored into its original Brighton Hove & District livery, and owned by the 'Go-Ahead' subsidiary, Brighton & Hove.

Above: A typical rural Pembrokeshire scene. This former Crosville Bristol LD6B (6LW) 'Lodekka' **RFM 457** (91) was photographed here by the conductor – John Bennett in August 1971, outside the Cresselly Arms, Cresswell Quay, on its return journey from Tenby to Pembroke Dock. This service, number 12 was inherited from Green's Motors Ltd, Haverfordwest during W W II. Green's withdrew the service at the outbreak of W W II in September 1939, to conserve fuel.   *(John Bennett).*

Above: The 1970s saw more than 100 Bristol vehicles pass through the gates of Waterloo Garage. I have photographs of each vehicle, but unfortunately have not got sufficient space to reproduce each photograph in this publication. This 1955 Bristol LS5G pictured above, **WHN 122** (94) with ECW B45F body arrived from United Automobile Services, Darlington (2122) in June 1970.

Above: Former Bristol Omnibus (2902) **XHW 418,** a Bristol LS5G is seen here at Hobbs Point waiting for the ferry to arrive from Neyland. Just visible on the opposite side of the river (arrowed to the left of the view) is Silcox's Neyland 'outstation' situated on the slipway to the ferry. Hobbs Point slipway, to the right of the bus was ideally suited for Silcox bus crews, they crossed as foot passengers from Pembroke Dock daily to operate school contracts in the Milford Haven, Neyland and Haverfordwest districts.

(Jason Feeley collection).

Above: Another scene at Hobbs Point circa 1969 shows the ferry from Neyland offloading, and cars for the return crossing are stopping the progress of Leyland 'Tiger Cub' **KDB 647** (83) on its journey to Pembroke town. Just visible on the skyline above the bus roof are the first two assembled sections of the ill-fated Cleddau Bridge, completed in 1975. *(Omnibus Society collection).*

Above: OFM 670 was a Bristol LS6G with Eastern Coach Works C37F body acquired from Crosville Motor Services (CUG298) in 1970 together with a sister vehicle registered OFM 690. They were given fleet numbers 98/9 respectively and withdrawn in 1976. OFM 670 was used as a source of spare parts before passing to a scrap dealer in late 1976.

Above: This Bristol LS5G with ECW B45F body, (100) **XHW 402** was new in November 1956 to Bristol Omnibus Co (2886). It arrived here in September 1970 and was one of seven Bristol Omnibus LSs to find a home at Pembroke Dock. The other six LSs from Bristol Omnibus were: PHW 927/XHW 404/11/8/22/YHY 77 (2837/88/95/2902/6/19). **XHW 402** is seen here at Pembroke, accompanied by Bristol LS6G (98) OFM 670, working a local private hire. It was withdrawn and scrapped in 1977.

Above: The first 'Grant Aided' *coaches* in the fleet arrived in December 1970. They were Plaxton 'Panorama Elite Express II' C53F bodied, Leyland PSU3A/4R type 'Leopards' registered VDE 873/4J (101/2). Conditions applied to the 'New Bus Grant' requested that the operator would have to refund the 50% grant if the vehicle was sold within 5 years. They were both exchanged for further 'grant' vehicles in early 1976, barely over the five year stipulation. **VDE 874J** (102) is seen here at Waterloo Garage when still quite new in 1971.

Above: This 11 metre Leyland 'Leopard' coach **VDE 873J** is seen negotiating a very tight double bend over a narrow bridge on the B4319 road near Freshwater West. This one mile section of single track road through sand dunes, barely wide enough for a bus, is located between Angle and Castlemartin, on Silcox's circular service No 3. Incidentally, when I worked for Davies Bros (Pencader) Ltd, in 1993, I had to negotiate this awkward bridge with a 12 metre Leyland 'Tiger' coach operating a West Wales 'Mystery Tour'. In appreciation my passengers were clapping and cheering after the manoeuvre had been completed safely!

89

Left: XFM 180 (103) was another ECW bodied Bristol 'Lodekka' LD6B acquired from Crosville Motor Services (DLB769) in August 1970. This one had been fitted with a Gardner 6LW engine by Crosville, and entered service in April 1971 with a modified roof. The curved upper deck cove panels on both sides were removed and flat panels fitted – giving it extra clearance to negotiate the arched bridge known as Bubbleston Bridge near Tenby. A photograph of Bubbleston Bridge with its official headroom of 12ft 6ins can be seen on the title page and on page 60.

Above: **LTA 990** (106) was another Bristol LS5G with ECW B41F body, and was new to Southern National, Exeter in 1953. It arrived at Silcox in February 1972 via Western National (1693), and was re-seated to B45F. This was re-numbered 108 by April 1976. Partly visible on the left is the rear off side of VDE 874J a Leyland Leopard PSU3A/4R pictured on page 89.

Above: XHW 411 (117) was another Bristol LS5G acquired from Bristol Omnibus Company (2895) in 1972. Licenced in February the following year it was taken out of service in late 1979 and sold for scrap. It's seen here at Waterloo Garage parked between two other LSs acquired from Bristol Omnibus. *(Alan Broughall)*.

Also new to Southern National (1341) was **LTA 997** (108) **pictured above.** This was another 1953 Bristol LS6G with ECW C39F coachwork, which had two previous owners before finding its way to Pembroke Dock by February 1972. The destination box had been removed by a previous owner, probably Bates of Sale, Manchester, a non PSV operator. LTA 997 and LTA 990 (opposite) exchanged fleet numbers in 1976, when LTA 997 became number 106.

Above: Looking rather knocked about with damage to both wheel arches and centre panel is **OAH 751**, one of six Bristol LSs, OAH 751-3, WVX 445, MAX 111 and SNG 763 received from Eastern Counties Omnibus Company in April 1972. **OAH 751** (111), pictured here at 'The Works' was a 1953 Bristol LS6B with ECW C39F body, which was withdrawn and sold for scrap in 1976.

Above: **SNG 763** (115) was another Bristol LS acquired in a package of six from Eastern Counties, Norwich in April 1972. **SNG 763**, was a 1955 Bristol LS5G with ECW DP39F, and is pictured here at the pressure washing bay to the rear of 'The Works' (Waterloo Garage) in preparation for service in April 1972. It was withdrawn in March 1977 and sold for scrap. *(C D Mann)*.

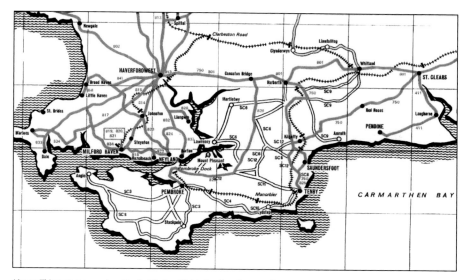

Above: This route map produced by the Western Welsh Omnibus Company in **1969**, also shows the stage carriage routes operated by Silcox Motor Coach Co in south Pembrokeshire. The Silcox routes are marked in plain white and numbered SC1-14. Services marked in red were operated by Western Welsh O C, with yellow indicating Mid-Way Motors of Crymmych.

At this point in time, Silcox were eager to expand their services to the opposite bank of the Cleddau River - Milford Haven, Neyland and Haverfordwest. A box-girder type bridge spanning the river had been under construction between Pembroke Dock and Neyland since 1968, but was delayed after a section collapsed during construction on 2nd June 1970. Building work re-commenced in October 1972, and the bridge finally opened four years late on 20th March 1975, costing £9.7k over budget.

In the meantime, some new school contracts became available at Milford Haven in 1969, and later a 'schools service' which Silcox successfully applied for with an immediate start. The following emergency licences were issued to operate the 'schools stage carriage' service:-

TGR 4902/Sp/12   **Hubberston (Junc Croft Rd/Haven Drive)** to **Milford Haven (Grammar School)** *Granted for period 8th March 1972 to 2nd May 1972.*

TGR 4902/Sp/13   **As above:** *Granted for period 3rd May 1972 to 27th June 1972.*

TGR 4902/Sp/14   **As above:** *Granted for period 28th June 1972 to 22nd August 1972.*

TGR 4902/Sp/15   **As above:** *Granted for period 23rd August 1972 to 22nd October 1972.*

The full term <u>stage carriage</u> licence was eventually applied for on 13th September 1972:-

TGR 4902/51   **Hubberston (Junction Croft Rd/Haven Drive)** to **Milford Haven (Grammar School)** *Service limited to carriage of school children.*   *Granted 6/12/1972.*

The additional school contracts led to an outstation at Neyland ferry slipway. Bus crews caught the ferry twice daily from Pembroke Dock to Neyland to operate the services, avoiding a 56 mile de-tour.

Above: MAX 111 (114) was yet another Bristol LS6G with ECW B45F body acquired from Eastern Counties O C in April 1972. This was new in July 1954 to Red & White, Chepstow (U1154) and passed to Eastern Counties O C (LM 590) in January 1969. After withdrawal by ECOC in February 1972, it passed to Silcox in April 1972 where it ran for a further four years until July 1976.

Above: February 1973 saw the arrival of two more 'Grant Aided' coaches in the fleet. Pictured here at the depot is **GDE 375L** (120), a Bristol LH6L with Plaxton 'Panorama Elite Express III' C45F coachwork which was numerically the second of an identical pair (GDE374/5L) built to full grant specification. Bearing in mind the amount of services Silcox were operating at this point, they would have been entitled to invest in more grant vehicles than they actually did!

Above: No less than six former Western National Bristol LS/ECW from the OTT registration series found a home at Pembroke Dock in 1971-3. Silcox initially received: OTT 63/50 (1709/1696) direct from Western National in 1971/2, purchasing OTT 49/52/56/59 (1695/8/1702/5) from Creamline Services, Tonmawr, West Glam in 1973. **OTT 56** pictured here, was allocated fleet number 122 and was last of the six to be withdrawn in January 1979.

Above: Captured here freshly painted outside Silcox's workshops in May 1973 is **MAX 105** (125) another Bristol LS6G with ECW B45F body which had been new to Red & White Services, Chepstow (U554) in June 1954. It was acquired from Crosville Motor Services (SUG288) in May 1973 and sold for scrap in October 1978.

Above: During the 1970s there was a massive intake of Bristol vehicles, new and second-hand, amongst them was this LS5G with ECW B45F body, **RWW 985** (126), which was new in July 1956 to West Yorkshire Road Car Co (EUG60). It was acquired in Sept 1973 from Simpson (Pennine Motor Service) Gargrave, N Yorkshire, and operated on hire to Pioneer Coaches, Laugharne in May 1978, when they had some major problems. It was eventually sold for scrap in 1979.

Above left: **NDE 803M** (127) was one of those horrible little Austin-Morris 250JU twelve seat minibuses, which Silcox bought new in October 1973 through their own British Leyland (BLMC) agency. It was withdrawn and scrapped in January 1981. On its right is another Bristol LS5G/ECW B45F acquired from Western National Omnibus Company (1693). New in 1953, and registered LTA 990 it received f/n 106 later to 108.

Above: The first Bristol MW in the Silcox stable was this ECW coach registered **OO 9548**, a MW6G which seated 34. **OO 9548** (128) arrived at Pembroke Dock in late 1973 from Tillings Travel, Chelmsford, and is seen here still operating in NBC livery, accompanied by former Brighton Hove & District (447) Bristol KSW6G, HAP 985.

Above right: Former Bristol Omnibus Company (2919) **YHY 77**, a 1957 Bristol LS5G with ECW B45F body was acquired in 1974 from John Lewis Coaches, Morriston, Swansea. YHY 77 was given fleet number 129 and withdrawn in 1979, later sold for scrap. To the left is **KDB 656** (85) another former North Western (656) Leyland 'Tiger Cub' PSUC1/1T with Weymann 'Hermes' B44F body. **KDB 656** was acquired in May 1969 and withdrawn in 1976. Sold for preservation in February 1977, it finally ended up at a Barnsley breakers yard a few months later.

Above: Three more 'Grant Aided' coaches arrived in 1974, the first being **PDE 570M** (130) pictured here. It was a Leyland Leopard PSU3B/4R with Plaxton 'Panorama Elite Express II' C51F coachwork, built in early 1973 to the order of Tillingbourne Bus Co. Cranleigh, Surrey. This 'diverted order' arrived in February 1974, and operated in full Tillingbourne Valley livery for two months.

Above: **RDE 876M** (132) was numerically the second Bristol LHL6L delivered in 1974. The identical pair, RDE 567/876M had Plaxton 'Panorama Elite Express III' C51F coachwork built to full grant specification. Partially visible on the right is **OWT 787M** (7) one of six consecutively registered Bristol LH6Ls with ECW bodies acquired from West Yorkshire (1177-82) in 1981.

After modification of the aforementioned 'New Bus Grant' in 1970, no less than twenty eight new vehicles were delivered to the company in the first decade, nineteen with Leyland chassis and nine Bristol, all except one YBX 608V (Leyland) fitted with bodywork built to grant specification. As a direct result of this the fleet was incredibly modernised and simultaneously the contract fleet was renewed almost entirely with pre-owned Bristol vehicles, KSW, LD, LS, MW, RE and FLF. The exception was a solitary Daimler Fleetline CRG6LX, which was the only Daimler ever owned, three Bedford YRTs, three Leyland Leopards and three Tiger Cubs.

Taking into consideration that Llanion Barracks had been closed for six years, Silcox were still holding an 'Express Carriage' licence in 1973 to operate a service from Sardis to Pembroke Dock (Llanion Barracks) with TGR 4902/48. This licence was not renewed on 15th August 1973.

On 1st April 1974, Pembrokeshire County Council amalgamated with the neighbouring counties of Cardiganshire and Carmarthenshire to form *one county* renamed 'Dyfed', later splitting up and returning to its original identity of Pembrokeshire. During the reorganisation of local government in 1974, the vehicle licensing office at Carmarthen County Hall closed down transferring the old Carmarthenshire registration mark of BX to Haverfordwest Vehicle Registration Office (DVLA), with TH the other Carmarthenshire registration mark passing to Swansea. Concurrently, Haverfordwest retained their original DE registration mark. From that period on, several new vehicles in the Silcox fleet received BX registration marks.

As we have seen, the company directors were eager to expand their services to the northern side of the river Cleddau and patiently waited for the opportunity - the opening of the long awaited 'Cleddau Bridge'. The 820 metre (half mile) controversial bridge eventually opened to traffic on 20th March 1975. Silcox immediately submitted an application to operate a 'new' stage carriage service across the bridge, providing a replacement to the ferry service for foot passengers:-

TGR 4902/52   **Pembroke Dock (Water Street Car Park)**   to   **Neyland (Ferry Approach)**
     via: Water Street, London Road, A477 to Cleddau Bridge, Honeyborough Green and High Street, Neyland.
     To operate daily except Good Friday, Easter Monday, Christmas Day, Boxing Day and New Year's Day.   *Granted 10th September 1975.*

Opening of the Cleddau Bridge brought the communities of Milford Haven, Neyland, Pembroke and Pembroke Dock closer together, ending an alternative trek of twenty-eight miles in each direction for larger vehicles, via Carew, Canaston Bridge, Haverfordwest town centre and Johnston.

Furthermore, the bridge was a godsend to the enterprising company, it opened new doors and gained extra work from the local authority, school contracts and later stage carriage services (local service). As a consequence, an outstation was firstly established at Neyland close to the ferry, later moving to Milford Haven (Docks), transferring to a yard at Station Approach in 1990, and latterly operating from Victoria Depository, Waterston Industrial Estate; Waterston, Milford Haven.

In February 1976, the company's legal address was officially changed from 17 Water Street, Pembroke Dock (where William Luther Silcox; founder of the Silcox empire had originally set up in 1882) to Waterloo Garage, London Road, Pembroke Dock – the operating centre since 1939!

Above: **HBX 190N** (133) seen here at Tenby coach park was another Bristol LHL6L (Leyland 401 engine) and Plaxton 'Panorama Elite Express III' C51F coachwork. Delivered to full grant specification in April 1975, complete with 'Bristol Dome' destination box, it was sold in September 1983 to a local operator – Hawkins, Haverfordwest. HBX was previously a Carmarthenshire issued mark, but had been transferred to Haverfordwest VRO (DVLA) when Carmarthen VRO closed in October 1974.   *(R F Mack).*

Above: This grant aided bus, **HDE 250N** (134) had a Leyland 'Leopard' PSU3C/4R 11 metre chassis, with pneumo-cyclic gearbox and a Duple 'Dominant' B65F body (3 + 2 seating). It was delivered in May 1975 and was 25 years old when it was withdrawn for scrap in March 2000 – quite a lengthy service for a vehicle with this make of bodywork.

Above: Taking full advantage of the government's 'Bus Grant', the company purchased an additional five new vehicles in 1975. **HDE 612N** (136) pictured here in November 1975 was one of four semi-automatic Leyland 'Leopard' PSU3C/4R delivered between May and July that year, this one and 137 below had Plaxton 'Panorama Elite Express III' coachwork seating 53. The other two 'Leopards' (134/5) had Duple coachwork and the Bristol LHL6L opposite (133) had Plaxton 'Panorama Elite Express III' coachwork. HDE 612N was later re-classified as a 'dual purpose' vehicle when it was fitted with 53 bus seats.

Above: HDE 617N (137) a Leyland 'Leopard' PSU3C/4R with Plaxton 'Panorama Elite Express III' C53F coachwork was last of the batch delivered in 1975. It's pictured here on 18th April 1987 in the company's restyled livery which was first introduced in February 1983. Registration numbers HDE 613-6N were used on new cars sold from Silcox's associated car business. *(V.Morgan)*.

Above: In 1976, a five more grant aided vehicles arrived, three Bristol LHL6Ls and two Leyland 'Leopards'. One of the PSU3C/4R 'Leopards' **LDE 163P** (138) new in May 1976 with Duple 'Dominant Express' C53F coachwork is captured here at Carmarthen on 3rd August 1983. The pair LDE 163/4P (138/9) were withdrawn in 1997 and sold for scrap. They were replaced by former Ministry of Defence Plaxton 'Derwent' bodied Leyland Tigers. *(V. Morgan).*

Above: Only three Bristol LH chassis were ever bodied with Duple 'Dominant' bus shells, two of them to the order of Silcox, (140/1) LDE 165/6P, the third to Davies Bros (Pencader) Ltd, as KBX 38P. One of these unique Bristol LH6Ls **LDE 165P** (140) delivered to Silcox in May 1976 with 47 seat Duple 'Dominant' bus bodywork, is seen here at the depot yard on 3rd May 1987, with sister vehicle LDE 166P hiding behind it. They were both withdrawn in May 1997 after twenty-one years' service. *(V Morgan).*

Above: As mentioned earlier there was a huge influx of Bristol vehicles in the 1970s, amongst them was **928 AHY** (6) a 1958 Bristol MW5G with ECW B45F body acquired from Bristol Omnibus Co (2998) in May 1976. Silcox acquired seven MW5Gs from Bristol Omnibus (2933/8/46/9/70/97/8) in 1976, of which 928 AHY was one of the last to survive. *(V. Morgan).*

Above: Pictured here at Hobbs Point, Pembroke Dock is **519 JHU** (f/n 2) another former Bristol Omnibus Co (2933) Bristol MW5G with ECW B45F body dating from 1960. It entered service with Silcox in May 1976 and is seen working service 2 from the former 'Neyland Ferry' terminal (Hobbs Point) to Monkton via Pembroke Dock and Pembroke. The Neyland car ferry service ceased operating when the new 'Cleddau Bridge' opened on 20th March 1975 – hence the lack of passengers.

Above: This Bristol MW5G with ECW B45F body, **HLJ 916D** (12) was new to Hants & Dorset Motor Service (860) in December 1966. It entered service with Silcox in January 1977, and was sold in September 1981 to a scrap dealer at Carlton, Barnsley.

Above: **NDE 86R** (143) was another grant aided Leyland 'Leopard' PSU3C/4R with Duple 'Dominant' B65F body (3+2 seating) delivered in February 1977. In December 2000 it was re-registered 9195 PU, a much used cherished registration number which it carried until withdrawal in March 2004. It was re-registered PWN 807R upon withdrawal but not carried, and eventually broken up at the depot in November 2010. This picture was taken on 24th May 1987. *(V. Morgan).*

Above: Another 'Grant Aided' Leyland 'Leopard' PSU3C/4R in the Silcox stable was **NDE 999R** (145) pictured here at Tenby coach park in 1984. It was added to the fleet in January 1977 together with identical NDE 998R (144) both fitted with Duple 'Dominant Express' C53F coachwork. The pair received this new style of livery in 1984 and were sold to D Coaches, Morriston (Swansea) in September 1986 for use on Dyfed C C tendered services acquired through deregulation.

Above: HEL 391D (10) was yet another Bristol MW5G with Eastern Coach Works B43F body acquired from Hants & Dorset Motor Services (857) in January 1977. Seen here on layover between school workings on 27th September 1980, it was withdrawn in June 1981 and sold in early 1982. *(V. Morgan).*

Above: This very tidy Bristol MW6G/ECW was another example purchased from Hants & Dorset (835) in February 1977. Bus No 14, **EMR 300D** had been new to Wilts & Dorset (725) in June 1966 as DP41F and transferred to H & D in October 1972. It's seen here at Eastern Avenue, Pembroke Dock in June 1980 by which time it had been re-seated to B45F. *(V. Morgan).*

Above: The end of an era – the last 'new' Bristol delivered to Silcox was **RDE 298S** (146) which arrived in January 1978. This Bristol LH6L with Plaxton 'Supreme Express' C45F coachwork was built to full grant specification and is pictured here on 11th March 1983. Knowing about the management's preference towards the Bristol marque, it was quite a surprise in late 1983 to see RDE 298S being exchanged for a second hand Leyland 'Leopard' PSU5 at Arlington Motors, Cardiff. This Bristol eventually passed to Williams, Cwmdu (Brecon) and was later exported to Malta – see photo opposite. *(V. Morgan).*

Above: Captured here on an excursion to Carmarthen on 13th June 1984 is another 'Grant Aided' Leyland 'Leopard' PSU3E/4R with Duple 'Dominant Express II' C53F coachwork. **RDE 772S** (147) was delivered in February 1978, and had received a different style livery in 1983 – similar to that applied on the Leyland 'Tigers' delivered in 1982/3 - again adding a little blue to the livery.

Above: Captured here at Valletta, Malta in its new guise, sporting an AEC motif is former Silcox Bristol LH6L Plaxton 'Supreme Express' **RDE 298S** (see photo opposite). After operating briefly with Williams of Brecon, it passed to Malta Bus Route licence holder Joseph Xuereb of Mellieha in Sept 1986, registered as Y-0611, later re-registered EBY-611 as seen here. *(T S Powell).*

107

In June 1977, a 'new' Express Carriage *'permit'* was issued under section 30 of the RTA 1968:-

TGR 4902/p/1   **Begelly (Thomas Chapel)** to **Tenby (South Parade)**.

At the same time, the following 'Stage Carriage' *special* licence was issued:-

TGR 4902/Sp/16   **Pembroke Dock** to **Pembroke Power Station** for period 23/5/77 – 17/6/77.

In January 1978, the following Sunday only 'Stage Carriage' licence was applied for:-

TGR 4902/53   **Pembroke Dock (Car Park)** to **Carmarthen (Railway Station)**
via: Carew Cross, Sageston, Tenby, Twy Cross, Saundersfoot, Hill, Kilgetty,
Begelly, Narberth, Whitland, St Clears and Bancyfelin.
One journey in each direction.   Single fares only.

In the meantime, the following *special* 'Stage Carriage' licences were issued to operate the above Sunday service for the interim period - awaiting the Traffic Commissioners hearing:-

TGR 4902/Sp/17   **Pembroke Dock** to **Carmarthen** Period of operation 7/1/1978 to 3/3/1978.
TGR 4902/Sp/18   **Pembroke Dock** to **Carmarthen**   "   "   "   4/3/1978 to 28/4/1978.
TGR 4902/Sp/19   **Pembroke Dock** to **Carmarthen**   "   "   "   29/4/1978 to 23/6/1978.
TGR 4902/Sp/20   **Pembroke Dock** to **Carmarthen**   "   "   "   10/9/1978 to 4/11/1978.

The full term licence TGR 4902/53 was granted at the special hearing held in November 1978. This RSL however had been surrendered by February 1983.

Returning to August 1977, the company applied for a new 'Schools Stage Carriage' service listed below under section 53 of the RTA 1968:-

TGR 4902/54   **Sandy Hill/Stammers Road Housing Estate (Saundersfoot)** to **Greenhill Comprehensive School (Heywood Lane, Tenby)**.

With regard to the *'permit'* TGR 4902/p/1 previously issued in June 1977 for 'Express Carriage' Begelly (Thomas Chapel) to Tenby, this special licence was requested once more on 6th February 1980 for a second period of operation, and was granted on 16th April 1980.

Mention should be made here about route numbers. We have seen from the early photograph collection that Silcox did not display route numbers which were allocated and published in their timetables. However, the new local authority Dyfed County Council introduced a co-ordinated route numbering system throughout the county using 3 digits, with the former Pembrokeshire area receiving the 3xx series of route numbers in 1980. It was not a mandatory requirement to have a service/route number at this time, but most operators including Silcox introduced these route numbers on their destination blinds in 1981.

There was an interesting development in November 1979, the announcement of the 1980 Road Traffic Act by the Minister of Transport Mr Norman Fowler. The Act which came into effect on 1st October 1980 was basically the beginning of deregulation, allowing Express Carriage services over 30 miles in distance to be freed from licensing regulations, with Excursions and Tours not requiring licensing at all. The Act also abolished the licensing of bus conductors from 19th May 1980, and reduced the minimum age for PSV (later PCV) drivers from 21 to 18 with a restriction that under 21's may only drive a PSV within a 30 mile radius of their base. The Act also brought about the new 'coloured' operator licence discs indicating National (blue); International (green) and Restricted/Special restricted (orange). At the same time operator identification numbers were changed from TGR xxxx to PG xxxx prefix (in the SWTA), with other traffic areas following suite with their appropriate traffic area letters. The Minister also announced that the 'new bus grant' scheme would cease by 31st March 1984.

However, at the start of the new academic year in August 1980, another *special* short term 'Stage Carriage' licence was issued to the company:-

TGR 4902/Sp/21   **Ridgeway** to **Tenby.** Period of operation 1/9/1980 to 28/2/1981.

Under the new 1980 Road Traffic Act (mentioned above) the full term 'Stage Carriage' licence was applied for on 4th March 1981 with a PG prefix as follows:-

PG 4902/55   **Ridgeway** to **Tenby,** via: B4316 Saundersfoot, Sandy Hill, Twy Cross and Tenby.
Monday-Friday only.   *Granted 29/4/1981.*

Throughout the years management had their share of troubles which included serious accidents and stolen vehicles. On 26th October 1980, a Bristol MW6G saloon registered EMR 304D (17) was stolen by a joy-rider/s from Milford Haven and crashed down a 15ft embankment into a river at Blackbridge on the B4325 road between Milford Haven and Neyland. The bus was damaged beyond repair and consequently towed away to a local breakers yard at Johnston.

By 22nd August 1981 there were 72 licenced vehicles in the Silcox fleet, but this had been reduced to 61 by October 1985, after the loss of some contract work.

BHU 976C (22) above was a Bristol FLF6B 'Lodekka' fitted with a Gardner 6LW engine by its previous owners Bristol Omnibus Company (C7176). The ECW body seated H38/32F and arrived here by April 1976, passing to Stagecoach, Perth in August 1986.

Right: Two Bristol FLF 'Lodekkas' were acquired from Bristol Omnibus Co in April 1978, 538 OHU and BHU 976C. Seen here is one of the pair **538 OHU** (20) a FLF6G with ECW H38/32F body, new to Cheltenham & District Transport (7075) in December 1962. It was re-registered ABX 172A in March 1987 and withdrawn 5 months later in August 1987 passing to a dealer and to Reed School of Motoring, Hyde, Manchester in December 1987. Its cherished registration number **538 OHU** was subsequently used on four other Silcox vehicles. Below is a photograph of the same FLF6G - after its re-registration to **ABX 172A.**

Below: This photograph of bus No 20, formerly **538 OHU** was taken on 18th April 1987, shortly after its re-registration to **ABX 172A.** The roof dome of its ECW body had certainly taken a battering from the low tree branches during its nine years working in Pembrokeshire. To the left of the picture is another former Bristol Omnibus vehicle (C7111), 804 SHW a Bristol FLF6B (retrofitted with a Gardner 6LW engine). *(V. Morgan).*

Above: ETD 949B (19) was an odd-ball vehicle in the fleet – the only Daimler ever owned. This 1964 Daimler CRG6LX nevertheless had a Gardner 6LX power unit, Silcox's preference of engine and carried a Northern Counties H43/31F body. It was acquired from Lancashire United (179) in 1978 and photographed here on 30th July 1978. In May 1980 it was replaced by Bristol FLF6G, RWC 942D which apparently was in a worse state and quickly exchanged for another FLF6G, FLJ 154D. *(V. Morgan)*.

Above: Another vehicle acquired from Lancashire United (208) in 1978 was **LTE 261C** (23) pictured here in June 1979. This was a Marshall B50F bodied Leyland 'Leopard' PSU3/3R with manual transmission, and was withdrawn in January 1982.

Above: Silcox bought six Bristol RESL6G with ECW B42F bodies from Newport Borough Council (101-5/7) in late 1978/9, which were registered JDW 301-5/7F. JDW 305F was not operated and used as a source of spares to keep 101-4/7 (31-4/7) running. 31/4 outlasted the others by running for 24 months. **JDW 301F** (31) is seen here at the depot on 27th September 1980.   *(V. Morgan).*

Above: Two Bristol REs were purchased from Western National O C (2353/62) 839/42 SUO in 1978. Pictured here is **842 SUO** (26) a 1964 Bristol RELH6G with ECW C45F coachwork which arrived in October 1978 to join its sister 839 SUO. This one however, 842 SUO had a very brief stay of just one year when it was withdrawn and sold for scrap.   *(V. Morgan).*

Above: **WBX 871T** (149) was one of an identical pair of Leyland 'Leopard' PSU3E/4Rs (WBX 870/1T) delivered in 1979 with Duple 'Dominant' Express II, C53F coachwork built to full 'grant' specification. This view was taken at Sophia Gardens, Cardiff after a 'dirty' journey eastwards along the M4 Motorway on 19th January 1980. *(V. Morgan).*

Above: This second view of **WBX 871T** (149) was taken at Tenby coach park on 14th December 1996, after the bodywork had been repanelled and all the bright-work removed. It looked somewhat different! *(V. Morgan).*

Above: 538 OHU was a cherished registration mark originally removed from Bristol FLF (20) in March 1987 (see page 110). After a 13 year period fitted to Leyland 'Leopard' AJD 162T (146), **538 OHU** was transferred to this 'Leopard' **WBX 871T** (149) in April 2000. When 149 was withdrawn in March 2004 the cherished mark was transferred to a former MoD Leyland 'Tiger' E673 WWD (204). I took this photograph on 25th May 2004 at Silcox's 'graveyard' behind Waterloo Garage. *(V Morgan).*

Above: This Bristol MW5G, **7793 NG** (25) with ECW C39F body was new to Eastern Counties O C in 1960, and was acquired from Tally Ho, Kingsbridge, Devon in September 1978 along with YNG 784 (24) another Bristol MW5G with ECW C39F body.

Above: This view of **JHK 456C** (27) was taken at 'The Works' on 27th September 1980. It was another Bristol MW6G with ECW DP43F body, new to Eastern National O C (1432) in January 1965, passing to Silcox by January 1979 who re-seated it to DP45F. It was sold to Wacton Trading, Bromyard in August 1986 for scrap. *(V. Morgan).*

Above: A nice shot of **804 SHW** (29) taken on 24th May 1987. This was a 1963 Bristol 'Lodekka' FLF6B (retrofitted with a 6LW engine) which arrived from Bristol Omnibus Co (C7111) in January 1971. Its ECW body seated H38/32F, and during the era of mass re-registering in 1989, its cherished registration number was transferred to Leyland 'Leopard' PSU5C, YBX 608V (150). Alternatively, the Bristol was re-registered ADE 146A, and operated until March 1990 when it passed to a few dealers before seeing further service with 'Top Deck Travel' of Horsell, Surrey in May 1990 who re-registered it KGH 891A and operated it in Europe.

Above: Two ECW bodied Bristol MW6Gs captured with one shot. **Left: HFM 590D** (28) was a 1966 example and right **1231 FM** (39) was new in 1963, both acquired from Crosville in 1979. 1231 FM remained in Crosville livery throughout its three year stay with Silcox working at one of the local oil refinery sites. This view was taken on 27th September 1980. *(V. Morgan).*

Above: I picked up this excellent photograph of **SWY 334L** at a sales event in 2008. It depicts the first Bedford in the fleet for 35 years. **SWY 334L** (49) was a 1972 Bedford YRT with 'Willowbrook 001' B55F body, acquired from Wigmore, Dinnington in September 1979. Sold on in July 1982, it then passed to Grenville Motors at Troon, Cornwall in September 1982 – a company that had a penchant for the Bedford marque.

Above: **YBX 608V** (150) was the one and only 'new' 12 metre Leyland 'Leopard' PSU5C/4R coach to enter the Silcox fleet. Fitted with Duple 'Dominant II' C57F coachwork (not to grant specification) it was delivered in August 1979, and is seen here at Sophia Gardens, Cardiff on an Excursion 24th November 1984. During the era of re-registration in 1989, **YBX 608V** received cherished registration mark **804 SHW** as shown **below** and lost all of its bright-work (chrome trim) after a re-paint. The cherished registration was removed in December 2000 when the coach was sold to Irish Ferries, Pembroke Dock and re-registered CDE 391V. *(VM)*

Above: This particular vehicle had quite a quite a rare combination of chassis/body manufacturer, only 15 of the type were built. **MRU 126F** (41 later 43) had a Bristol RELH6G chassis fitted with Duple 'Commander III' C49F coachwork, and was new to Hants & Dorset (918) in June 1968. Silcox acquired this coach in April 1979 together with MRU 124F (40 later 42), both leaving the fleet a year later when they were sold to a dealer for scrap.

Above: Another Bedford YRT with Duple 'Dominant' C53F body arrived in early 1980 from National Travel (South West) 490. Registered **LAE 890L** it was new to Wessex Coaches, Bristol in April 1973 prior to the sale of Wessex's business to the National Bus Company in August 1974. This was the third of three Bedford YRTs bought as a temporary measure to cover a particular school contract until more Bristol LHs could be located. It left Pembroke Dock in 1982, sold to Arlington Motors (dealer) with no further trace.

Above: New to Southdown Motor Services in December 1963 was this Leyland 'Leopard' PSU3/1RT registered **109 CUF**, fitted with Marshall B51F bodywork. It was one of two Southdown PSU3/1RT type 'Leopards' 109/115 CUF (50/1) acquired in November 1979 via Western National Omnibus Co. Both were withdrawn in 1985 with their cherished registration numbers immediately transferred to two new DAF SB2300 /Plaxton coaches.

Above: In March 1980, two former Black & White Motorways 1967 Leyland 'Leopard' PSU3/3RT's (KDD 283/9E) were acquired. Both were fitted with Plaxton 'Panorama' C47F coachwork and arrived at Pembroke Dock via Blackpool owners. Pictured here is **KDD 283E** (32) which only ran for eight months, after which it was used for spare parts.

Above & Below: BBX 915V (151) was the first of three new PSU3E/4R type Leyland 'Leopards' to arrive in 1980, and was another 'grant aided' coach fitted with Duple 'Dominant II' Express C53F coachwork. It's seen here at Cardiff on 19th March 1988 repainted into the new style coach livery which had been introduced in 1983 to match the new Plaxton 'Paramount' bodied Leyland 'Tigers' delivered that year. After a refurbishment at the company's body-shop later in its working life, all the external bright-work was removed along with the luggage boot, and in July 2000 it received a cherished registration number: **SIL 9611 see below**. It was withdrawn in October 2003 and succumbed to the scrap-man's torch by December 2004. The cherished registration number SIL 9611 was not re-used by the company. *(V. Morgan).*

Above: Delivered in April 1980 to full grant specification was another Leyland 'Leopard' PSU3E/4R registered **BDE 140V** (152) which was fitted with this 'high capacity' Duple 'Dominant' B63F body (3 + 2 seating). This vehicle again was fitted with a heavy duty front bumper bar, similar to NDE 86R (143) shown on page 104. The photograph was taken on 24th May 1987, and shows another experimental style logo – SC denoting Silcox Coaches, and only used for a short while in the mid-1980s. **BDE 140V** was re-registered with a cherished registration number **SIL 9612** in August 2000 as shown below.   *(V. Morgan).*

Above: SIL 9612 (152) was previously registered **BDE 140V** (see top of page) and upon withdrawal in September 2003 reverted to its original registration BDE 140V. The cherished registration number SIL 9612 was not re-used by the company. *(V. Morgan).*

Above: **BDE 143V** (153) was numerically the last new Leyland 'Leopard' delivered to the company in April 1980, and last of the 1980 order, built to full grant specification. It was identical to BBX 915V (15) delivered a month earlier (see page 120) with Duple 'Dominant II' Express C53F body, and served the company for 21 years. This view was taken at Tenby on 26th March 1988 after a repaint into the new style coach livery – adding the blue stripe. It was re-registered SIL 9613 when 20 years old, rather pointless I would have thought as it was withdrawn for scrap a year later! SIL 9613 was then transferred to a M o D 'Tiger' E98 LLP (200).

Above: Another vehicle with a rare combination of chassis/bodywork was **UTD 291H** (91) a 1970 Bristol LH6L with Northern Counties B39D body, which was acquired from Lancashire United (328) in 1980. This view was taken on 4th June 1982.

Above: No less than four former Ribble Motor Services 10 metre Leyland 'Leopard' PSU4A/4Rs with Plaxton 'Panorama' C36F bodies arrived in 1980 via National Travel (South West). They were registered KCK 976/7/87/9H and received Silcox fleet numbers 76/77/86/89 respectively. Pictured here on 3rd May 1987 in the company's 1983 coach livery, is **KCK 987H** (86) which was new to Ribble in April 1970.   *(V. Morgan).*

Above left & right: **KCK 976H** was another 10 metre 'Leopard' identical to KCK 987H (Top) which arrived in July 1980 via: Shamrock & Rambler - National Travel (South West) 416. These short length 'Leopards' were quite nippy – they were fitted with the same running units as the 11 metre chassis; 680 engine etc, but had a remarkably lower un-laden weight due to its short length and only 36 seats. In 1993 however, Silcox rebuilt the front end as shown above right, and fitted a home-made radiator grille derived from the original. Note the windscreen wipers which have also been modified to sweep the screen from above.

123

Above: Amongst the large intake of second-hand vehicles in 1980 were a pair of very tidy Leyland 'Leopard' PSU3C/4Rs (103/4) LPT 903/4P, from Trimdon Motor Service, Trimdon Grange. They were fitted with Willowbrook B55F bodies and were new to Trimdon M S in August 1975. Pictured here is one of the pair, **LPT 903P**. Both were sold to a dealer in August 1987, with LPT 904P ironically returning to Trimdon M S in October 1987.   *(V. Morgan).*

Above: In December 1980, two Bristol LH6Ls arrived from Hants & Dorset (3518/9) NLJ 518/9M. Captured here on 18th July 1987 is **NLJ 518M** (108) with ECW B43F bodywork working one of the numerous school contracts in Pembrokeshire. It was new to Hants & Dorset in October 1973, and taken out of service by Silcox in late 1988 with extensive fire damage and subsequently scrapped in 1992.   *(V. Morgan).*

Above: Second-hand Bristol LHs continued to be purchased in 1981 with SPK 116/9/20M arriving from National Bus Company subsidiary London Country (BL16/9/20). **SPK 116M** (116) seen here at Tenby was the third one to arrive - in August 1981.

Above: SPK 119M (119) was another Bristol LHS6L with ECW B35F body, that was new to London Country (BL19) in October 1973. It is pictured here at Waterloo Garage, Pembroke Dock on 1st April 1991 after a repaint into the smart new style of local bus livery in 1990, re-appearing as seen complete with fleetnames and the local authority bi-lingual branding 'BWS DYFED BUS'. All local authority supported services within the county had to display the branding – failure to comply would result in a fine from the local authority. Incidentally, the registered starting point of service 357 to Monkton was here at Waterloo Garage. *(V. Morgan).*

Above: New to Hebble Motor Services, Halifax in July 1971 was this 11 metre Leyland 'Leopard' PSU3B/4R registered **JHD 377J** with Plaxton 'Panorama Elite II' coachwork. It was acquired in January 1981 from National Travel (East) and given fleet number 127 by Silcox, who re-seated it with 47 bus seats in 1991. It was withdrawn in July 1992 and later broken up. Just visible behind the coach is a grey Morris Minor 1000 which appears in several of my views. It was good reliable transport.   *(V. Morgan).*

Above: Another batch of six Bristol LH6Ls were received in 1981 from West Yorkshire Road Car Co (1177-82) OWT 783-8M. Unfortunately there's insufficient space to reproduce photographs of each individual vehicle owned, so I have chosen **OWT 787M** (f/n 7) to represent this batch of Eastern Coach Works B45F bodied LHs, which all passed to Trimdon Motor Services in August 1987 via Wacton Trading (dealer) Bromyard.   *(V. Morgan).*

SILCOX'S CENTENARY

1982 was the company's centenary and to celebrate the historic occasion two new Leyland 'Tiger' coaches were ordered and delivered in February 1982. Both were fitted with Plaxton 'Supreme VI' Express coachwork seating 57, built to full grant specification and lettered 'SILCOX CENTENARY COACH 1882-1982' as shown on the next page. Within a year there were a total of six new 'Tigers' in the fleet which had all been acquired through the 'grant scheme' before it ended in March 1984. Management however were not impressed with these new 'Tigers' as they were continuously breaking down with overheating problems, and due to their unreliability all six were exchanged for new DAF SB2300s by September 1985. It's not known how the directors managed to exchange these 'Tigers' without refunding the 50% grant received towards their purchase, as conditions applied to the grant scheme requested that *the operator refunds the grant if the vehicle was sold or ceased to be used for stage service within 5 years of its delivery'*.

On 12th May 1982, another 'Stage Carriage' licence was applied for to operate a Sunday's only summertime service, June to August on the following route:-

PG 4902/56   **Pembroke Dock (Car Park)** to **Saundersfoot (Arcade)** via: A4139 to Pembroke and Lamphey, A4139 & B4584 to Freshwater East, B4584 & A4139 to Jameston, A4139 & B4585 to Manorbier, B4585 & A4139 to Lydstep, Penally and Tenby, A478 & B4136 to Saundersfoot.   *Granted 7th July 1982.*

Ten months later the following 'Stage Carriage' licence was asked for:-

PG 4902/57   **Pembroke Dock (Albion Square)** to **Pembroke (Railway Station)**
via: Bush Street, Laws Street, Water Street, London Road, Waterloo Garage, Ferry Lane, Bush Hill, unclassified road to Golden Hill (Devon Drive), unclassified to junction Derry Lane/Bush Hill, Bush Lodge, The Green, Main Street Pembroke and East End Pembroke.   *Monday – Saturday inclusive.*
Granted 25th May 1983.   Surrendered 14th September 1983.

In the meantime a special 'Short Term' licence was issued to operate the above service:-

PG 4902/Sp/22   **Pembroke Dock (Albion Square)** to **Pembroke (Railway Station)**
Period of operation: 4th April 1983 to 3rd October 1983.

February 1983 witnessed delivery of the last three 'Grant Aided' vehicles purchased by Silcox, which incidentally became the last *'new'* Leylands in the fleet. They were Leyland 'Tiger' TRCTL11/2R, NDE 147/748/9Y (157-9) with Plaxton 'Paramount 3200' coachwork, introducing an additional style of livery incorporating the blue line. This particular style of livery was applied to much of the fleet thereafter, some with the blue line and some without - including the double decker fleet, which looked quite impressive. The fleet at this point totalled 62 vehicles.

Simultaneously, the communities of Milford Haven and Pembroke Dock were beginning to feel the effect of Esso Petroleum's refinery closure at Herbrandston in March 1983. This came as a terrific blow to south Pembrokeshire which was already suffering from high unemployment. At the time of Esso's peak, there were three other refineries in the area, Texaco, Gulf and Amoco, and an oil terminal owned by BP. Over production was blamed for its closure. The Esso refinery was demolished during the late 1980s and the site redeveloped into The South Hook LNG terminal.

Above: Silcox were a very early customer for the Leyland 'Tiger' introduced in 1981. **JDE 189X** (156) seen here at Cardiff was the first registered from a batch of three, but last to be delivered in March 1982. Purchased with the government's 'New Bus Grant', this 'Tiger' had a TRCTL11/2R chassis with Duple 'Dominant IV' Express C53F coachwork incorporating a Scottish Bus Group front end. Within 13 months, six grant aided 'Tigers' with varying coachwork had arrived and were the last vehicles purchased under the grant system. All six had left the fleet by September 1985 as the directors were not pleased with them.

Above: Two new Leyland 'Tigers' delivered in February 1982, JDE 972/3X were lettered for Silcox's Centenary 1882 – 1982. Captured here at Sophia Gardens, Cardiff is **JDE 973X** (155) a TRCTL11/3R with Plaxton 'Supreme VI Express' C57F coachwork, which introduced another style of livery incorporating blue lines, identical to its partner JDE 972X (154). This style of livery was used on several repaints in following years.

Above: Pictured here receiving delivery of the two 'Centenary Coaches' **JDE 972/3X** (154/5) in February 1982 are Managing Director Leonard W Silcox (centre), his eldest son Keith Wm Silcox, company secretary (right) and a representative of the coach dealer.

Above: New in February 1983, **NDE 748Y** (158) was another 'grant aided' Leyland 'Tiger' TRCTL11/2R with Plaxton 'Paramount 3200' coachwork seating 49, and is seen here at the Severn Bridge motorway service area in July 1983. This and sister vehicles - NDE 147/749Y (157/9) were the last 'new' Leylands in the fleet and the last vehicles purchased with the aid of the government's grant scheme which eventually ended in March 1984.

<u>Above</u>: This 9.5 metre Plaxton 'Supreme IV' bodied Leyland 'Leopard' PSU4E/4R, **AJD 162T** (146) was new in March 1979 to Glenton Tours, London SE15. Silcox acquired this 43 seat coach from Bicknell, of Godalming, Surrey in November 1983 and immediately painted it into the new style livery matching the Leyland 'Tigers' delivered earlier that year. It's seen here at the Royal Welsh Showground, Llanelwedd (Builth Wells) on 24th July 1986. *(V. Morgan)*.

<u>Above</u>: In March 1987, Leyland 'Leopard' **AJD 162T** (see above) was re-registered with cherished number **538 OHU** removed from a Bristol FLF6G 'Lodekka' originally owned by Bristol Omnibus Co. The new **538 OHU** (146) was captured here at Sophia Gardens, Cardiff accompanied by several other Silcox Coaches on WRU International day 4th April 1987, three weeks after its re-registration. Withdrawn in May 2000, it returned to AJD 162T (not carried) enabling the mark to pass to WBX 871T. *(V. Morgan)*

Above: Captured here at the 'old' Carmarthen Bus Station on 23ʳᵈ May 1984 is **WFH 170S** (131) a 1978 Leyland 'Leopard' PSU3E/4R with Plaxton 'Supreme IV' C53F body. New in February 1978 to National Travel (South West) it was acquired from Hants & Dorset (3030) in November 1983. It later received some refurbishment and a cherished registration mark as seen below.

Above: Leyland 'Leopard' **KSU 409** (131) seen here on 17ᵗʰ April 1995 was actually WFH 170S (see top of page) newly refurbished. It had been re-registered with cherished mark KSU 409 in May 1988 returning to WFH 170S (not carried) after withdrawal in May 2005. KSU 409 was then transferred to a former M o D Leyland 'Tiger' E125 ODE (202).   *(V. Morgan)*.

Above: **AFH 182T** (132) was another Leyland 'Leopard' PSU3E/4R which had been new to National Travel (South West) f/n 182 in September 1978. It arrived at Pembroke Dock in November 1983 from NBC subsidiary, South Wales Transport (151). Its Plaxton 'Supreme IV' coachwork looks quite smart repainted into Silcox's newly adopted livery. This picture was taken on 3rd May 1987, just four months before it was re-registered with cherished registration 817 FKH in September 1987 (see below).   *(V. Morgan).*

Above: Leyland 'Leopard' **817 FKH** (132) was a re-registration of AFH 182T (see top of page), in September 1987. The cherished mark had been removed from Silcox's DAF SB2300/Plaxton coach (163) dating from 1985, which had left the fleet. When this Leyland was withdrawn in February 2003, the registration passed to a Mercedes-Benz Sprinter, f/n 27.   *(V. Morgan).*

Above: Three former National Bus Company Leyland 'Leopards' found a good home at Pembroke Dock in November 1983. This particular one **DAD 258T** (133) was a 12 metre PSU5C/4R chassis, with 680 engine uprated to 175 b h p (fitted Friedmann & Maier fuel pump). Coachwork was the standard Plaxton 'Supreme IV' seating 57 passengers, and was new to National Travel (South West) f/n 258 in April 1979, but was acquired via South Wales Transport, Swansea (153). A sister National Travel (South West) vehicle, DAD 254T was also acquired, arriving in February 1984 from NBC subsidiary Hants & Dorset (3037).

Above: Sophia Gardens, Cardiff is the backdrop for this view of **A53 VGD** (160) working a 'Private Hire' commitment on the occasion of the WRU International, 4th April 1987. Silcox Coaches would always be well represented at Cardiff on these Welsh Rugby Union events, on several occasions service buses (if fitted with tachograph) would be used to transport supporters on the 200 mile round trip to Cardiff. **A53 VGD** (160) was a 1984 Mercedes-Benz L608D with Coachcraft C21F conversion to its otherwise van derived body. It had been acquired from Keenan. Coalhall, Strathclyde in July 1984.   *(V. Morgan).*

Above: In early 1985, the company purchased two more former National Bus Company Leyland 'Leopards' registered KAD 346/8V from Black & White Motorways, Cheltenham (346/8). Both 'Leopards' had PSU5C/4R type chassis fitted with Plaxton 'Supreme IV' C57F coachwork as seen in this view of **KAD 346V** taken at Aberystwyth Railway Station on 3rd August 1985. *(V. Morgan).*

Above: The last three Bristol LHs purchased by Silcox were registered OCA 631/4P and KTT 40P (31/4/40) all arriving from the National Coal Board at Rotherham, South Yorkshire in July 1985. They had latterly been used as non PSVs (un-licenced) conveying personnel to work during the controversial one year long 'Miner's Strike'. Seen here is Bristol LH6L, **OCA 631P** (31) with standard Eastern Coach Works B43F body which was new in March 1976 to Crosville Motor Services, Chester (SLL631). This and OCA 634P left the fleet in August 1990 upon arrival of three new Mercedes-Benz 709Ds, with **OCA 631P** finding a new home at Irwell Valley Coaches. Eccles, Greater Manchester in December 1990.

Above: B538 XDE (164) was the second of seven DAF SB2300/Plaxton coaches purchased by the company in 1985/6 to replace the Leyland 'Tigers'. Six were acquired new, the seventh had been a demonstrator for 5 months. All seven had the SB2300DHS585 rear engine chassis with identical Plaxton 'Paramount' coachwork of varying seating capacities. I took this view of B538 XDE at Tenby on 7th June 1986, shortly before it was given a cherished registration number - as shown below. *(V. Morgan)*.

Above: PVO 624 was the cherished registration number transferred to DAF SB2300DHS585 (*B538 XDE* above) in July 1986. This view was another taken at Sophia Gardens, Cardiff on 4th April 1987, with A53 VGD parked immediately behind (see page 133). This cherished mark had previously been carried on a Leyland 'Tiger Cub' in the fleet since 1964 (f/n 20 later 60). *(V. Morgan)*.

Above: **A9 WLS** was the new cherished/personalised registration mark given to *PVO 624* (originally *B538 XDE* see page 135) after its refurbishment and renumbering **109** in late 1992. Silcox bought thirteen personalised registration numbers (A-WLS) in 1992, applying them initially to the coach fleet. By December 1992, the cherished registration PVO 624 had been transferred to a Leyland 'Leopard' LMA 59P (59), and died with that vehicle in 2005 – no further trace. *(V. Morgan).*

Above: Unfortunately, **A9 WLS** (109) came to a sad end on 18th June 1997, when it skidded on a wet road and collided with an oncoming vehicle. The driver was seriously injured in the accident at Holyland Road (A4075) Pembroke. Salvage of this coach passed to a scrap dealer in October 1997, and the personalised registration was lost with the vehicle.

Above: Silcox purchased this particular Plaxton 'Paramount' bodied DAF SB2300DHS585, **B222 NUT** (165) from the dealer Yeates of Loughborough, where it had served as a demonstration vehicle for five months. It arrived at Pembroke Dock in June 1985, with coachwork identical to the other DAF SBs in the fleet. However, B222 NUT was sold after two years to a dealer, and eventually passed to an operator at Warnham, West Sussex complete with its cherished registration.

Above: Another new DAF SB2300DHS585 acquired in September 1985 with Plaxton 'Paramount' C53F coachwork was **115 CUF** (166). It was registered with this cherished mark from new, removed from withdrawn Southdown Motor Services, Leyland 'Leopard' (51). Sophia Gardens, Cardiff is the backdrop for this picture taken on 1st February 1986. The coach was sold privately to Gwynne Price Coaches, Trimsaran in August 1990 with a proviso that the cherished mark 115 CUF be returned. It was eventually returned in June 1992 - in exchange for a 'personalised' registration mark – A6 GPC, which it carried thereafter.   *(V. Morgan)*.

Above: This DAF SB2300DHS585 was new in April 1986 registered as **C392 CDE** (168). It operated as such for a few weeks before receiving cherished registration mark **109 CUF** in June that year, removed from another former Southdown Leyland 'Leopard'. The 'new' **109 CUF** had identical looking Plaxton 'Paramount' coachwork to the earlier DAF SB2300's in the fleet, but only seated 49. Captured here at Museum Avenue, Cardiff on 7th March 1987 this coach was in pristine condition. Nevertheless, in early 1992 it was refurbished and repainted, receiving a 'personalised' registration mark A7 WLS in March 1992 as shown below.
(V. Morgan).

Above: DAF SB2300, **A7 WLS** (168) was carrying its third registration mark when I photographed it here at an industrial estate off Tyndall Street, Cardiff on 6th March 1993. It was registered C392 CDE when new in 1986, but quickly received cherished mark *109 CUF* eight weeks later (see above). Refurbished to seat 53 and repainted in March 1992 it was then given 'personalised' mark **A7 WLS** which remained on the coach until September 1998 when it was sold to a dealer, reverting to its original C392 CDE.

Above: Captured here on 24th May 1987 at Manor House Wildlife Park, St Florence, Tenby, is **587 NCG** (167) another DAF SB2300DHS585 with Plaxton 'Paramount' C55F coachwork. It was new to Silcox as *C429 ADE* in September 1985 and received the cherished mark **587 NCG** in September 1986. This registration mark left with the coach when it was sold. *(V. Morgan).*

Above: This coach **VAW 527** (169) was the penultimate Plaxton 'Paramount' bodied DAF SB2300DHS585 in the fleet. It was delivered and entered service a month ahead of its stable-mate (168) C392 CDE - *109 CUF* in March 1986. In October 1994, VAW 527 lost its cherished registration in favour of a 'personalised' mark A11 WLS, later receiving fleet number 111. *(V. Morgan).*

Meanwhile, in September 1984 owing to lack of patronage several un-remunerative services were surrendered. The list included: PG 4902/6, 7, 8, 24 and 46, with PG 4902/31 Maidenwells – Pembroke Dock following in March 1985 and PG 4902/23 Tenby – Whitland in November 1985.

Above: Three of these ECW bodied Bristol LH6Ls were acquired from Greater Manchester PTE (1320/23/4) in 1982. New in 1974 and numerically the first to arrive was **BNE 763N** (63) pictured here on 18th April 1987. This and BNE 767N (67) followed other Silcox Bristol LHs to Trimdon Motor Services, Trimdon Grange in December 1987. Trimdon M S bought several surplus Silcox buses. *(V Morgan).*

DEREGULATION

Bus deregulation in Great Britain was brought about by the 1985 Road Traffic Act, introduced by the Conservative government of Margaret Thatcher. The Act scheduled to be implemented on 26th October 1986 was basically the transfer of operation of bus services from public bodies to private companies as legislated by the Act. It abolished Road Service Licencing and allowed the introduction of competition on local bus services for the first time since 1930. To operate a service, all an accredited operator was required to do was to provide 56 days' notice to the Traffic Commissioner of their intention to commence, cease or alter operation on a route.

Having said that, the transition into deregulation actually began on 6th January 1986, with various provisions of the Act coming into force on that day:-

1   The term 'Stage Carriage Service' changed to 'local service'.
2   The term 'Express Carriage' was abolished.
3   Requirement to notify 'Express Services' abolished.
4   Licensing of 'Stage Carriage Services' abolished - changed to 'local service registration',

From 1st March 1986, the layout of 'Local Service Registration' (previously Stage Carriage licensing) changed to a different format. The following registrations are in accordance with paragraph 10 of schedule 6 to the 1985 Transport Act, and lists the *new* 'Local Services' Silcox registered with the Traffic Commissioners *before* 1st March 1986:-

PG/0049/4902   **Nubian Crescent/Wellington Rd/St Anne's Rd** to **Milford Grammar School**
via: Waterloo Road, St Lawrence Hill, Hamilton Terrace, Great North Road and Steynton Road.   *To run on School days only.*   *D/Deck operation.*
Numbered: Route A: Hakin – Milford Schools Service.

PG/0050/4902   **Croft Avenue (Hakin, Milford Haven)** to **Milford Grammar School**
via: Picton Road, Waterloo Square, Hamilton Terrace and Steynton Road.
To run on School days only.   *D/Deck operation.*
Numbered: Route B: Hakin/Hubberston – Milford Haven Schools Service.

PG/0051/4902   **Saundersfoot Arcade** to **Saundersfoot Arcade**
via: Tenby, Castle Ridgeway, Manorbier Castle, Pembroke Castle and Tenby.
Tour operating once a week increasing to 3 times per week at peak season as required, May to September.   *Single deck operation (56 or more).*
Numbered: Three Castles Tour.

PG/0052/4902   **Saundersfoot Arcade** to **Saundersfoot Arcade**
via: Tenby, Pembroke, Castlemartin, Stack Rocks, St Govens, Bosherston, Pembroke and Tenby.
Tour operating once a week at beginning and end of season, increasing to daily in height of season as required April to September.
Numbered: Stack Rocks & Bosherston Tour.   *S/deck operation (56 or more).*

PG/0872/4902   **Waterloo** to **Monkton (Spar Supermarket)**
via: Bush Estate, Laws St, Albion Square, Sunderland Ave, Belle-Vue Terrace, High St, Bush Hill, Main St (Pembroke), Common Road and Monkton.
Route number: 357.   *Local service, Monday – Saturday.*   *D/Deck operation.*

Giving the obligatory notice, the local authority Dyfed County Council implemented the 1985 Road Traffic Act two months early, bringing in deregulation on 31st August 1986. This was to coincide with the new academic year, issuing new school contracts and renewal of tendered 'local services'.

The following registrations of local bus services under section 31 of the Act were made by the company to commence with effect from 31st August 1986 and supported by Dyfed C C in accordance with their planned transition into deregulation of local bus services:-

PG/5051/4902   **Tenby (Upper Park Road)** to **Milford Haven (Robert Street)**
via: Jameston, Manorbier, Pembroke, Pembroke Dock, Neyland and Waterston.
Two hourly service Pembroke to Milford, extending to Tenby in summer. Extra local journeys Pembroke, Pembroke Dock, Jameston and Tenby.
Route number: 359/357. *Mon-Sat excluding public holidays. S/deck operation.*

PG/5052/4902   **Tenby (Upper Park Road)** to **Pembroke Dock (Albion Square)**
via: Manor House Park, St Florence and Sageston.
One journey in to Tenby and two out of Tenby, plus off peak journeys which vary according to time of year.
Route number 360. *Mon-Sat excluding public holidays. S/deck operation.*

PG/5053/4902   **Cosheston (Mount Pleasant)** to **Bush School**   via: Pembroke Dock.
Route number 362. *To run on School days only. S/deck operation (56 or more).*

PG/5054/4902   **Tenby (Upper Park Road)** to **Pembroke Dock (Albion Square)**
via: Saundersfoot, Kilgetty, Cresselly, Sageston and Carew.
Two hourly service Tenby to Carew, three journeys extending to and from Pembroke Dock, with additional journeys on school days.   *Hail & Ride.*
Route number 361. *Mon-Sat excluding public holidays. S/deck operation.*

PG/5055/4902   **Pembroke Dock (Waterloo Garage)** to **Pembroke Dock (Waterloo Garage)**
via: Bush School, Pennar Park and Pembroke Dock.
One shopping journey and School journeys.
Route number 363. *Mon-Sat excluding public holidays. S/deck operation.*

PG/5056/4902   **Pembroke Dock (Water St Car park)** to **Pembroke Dock (Water St Car park)**
via: Stackpole, Bosherston, Castlemartin, Angle, Rhoscrowther and Hundleton.
Friday only – Tues & Fri during school holidays, with 2 journeys each direction.
Route number 365/366.   *Hail & Ride.*   *S/deck operation (56 or more).*

PG/5057/4902   **Green Meadow Estate** to **Grove School**
via: Pembroke and Bishops Park. *To run School days only, morning & afternoon.*
Route number 367.   *S/deck operation (56 or more).*

PG/5058/4902   **Tenby (Upper Park Road)** to **Tenby (South Parade)**
via: Saundersfoot, Kilgetty, Stepaside, Amroth and Wisemans Bridge.
Route number 351/352/353. *Mon-Sat except public holidays. D/deck operation.*

PG/5059/4902   **Tenby (South Parade)** to **Tenby (South Parade)**
via: Serpentine Road and St John's Hill. (Town service).
Route number 350.   *Mon-Sat except public holidays. S/deck operation.*

PG/5060/4902   **Dale** to **Milford Grammar School**   via: Marloes and Herbrandston.
To run on School days only.
Route number 314.   *Hail & Ride.*   *S/deck operation (36 – 55).*

PG/5061/4902   **Neyland** to **Haverfordwest (Bus Station)**   *To run on School days only,*
via: Little Haven, Portfield, Trafalgar Road and Stokes Avenue.
Route number 312.   *Hail & Ride.*   *S/deck operation (36 – 55).*

PG/5062/4902   **Tenby (Upper Park Rd)** to **Haverfordwest (Bus Station)**
via: Saundersfoot and Narberth.
Mon-Fri except public holidays, one journey in each direction. Extra journeys in summer including Saturday.
Route number 319.   *S/deck operation 56 or more.*

The above list of 'new' services, were council supported/tendered services operated on behalf of the local authority, Dyfed County Council.

Bus deregulation inevitably brought about numerous problems for operators nationwide. Silcox faced competition on their more profitable routes almost immediately from two completely new operators. The first competitor to arrive was Teifion Hughes (PG 6346) in August 1987, trading as 'Pennar Taxis' with a 16 seat minibus on the Pembroke Dock to Monkton route. Fortunately the service was short lived – the licence was cancelled on 15th April 1989.

Above: As mentioned earlier, Silcox were a comparatively late starter in the bus industry, so had not experienced competition on local services before deregulation came along in 1986. Deregulation prompted a local taxi operator 'Pennar Taxis' to challenge Silcox on their busy Pembroke Dock to Monkton service with this 16 seat Talbot Express minibus converted to PSV specification by Dormobile. It's seen here at Water Street car park, Pembroke Dock, terminus of his Monkton service on 26th March 1988. *(VM).*

Next on the scene were partners John Moran and John Barrow trading as M & B Coach and Bus Company Ltd, from 2 Nelson Walk, Tenby, who were granted a five year licence PG 6399, for 10 single deck and 2 double deck vehicles on 1st April 1988. The following month they registered five local services commencing 16th May in direct competition with Silcox, operating services beginning from Tenby to Kilgetty, Saundersfoot, Amroth, Lydstep and Kiln Park Caravan Park. When their partnership broke up in July 1989, John Barrow continued operating alone, renaming the business Tenby Bus & Coach Co Ltd, running on the same 'O' licence PG 6399SI, and from the same address. Two months later, the licence changed to PG 6510/SI, which authorised three extra vehicles, and by November that year a further six local services were registered.

In May 1990, Tenby Bus & Coach Company's operating centre moved to the Old RAF Buildings, Carew Airfield, Sageston, and at the start of the academic year September 1990, they increased their vehicle licences by ten, to cover newly acquired school services, gained by tender from the local authority. Their school services, which had previously been operated by Silcox, were all surrendered between February and April 1991 together with all their local bus services. These supported/tendered services including school services immediately returned to Silcox, and a receiver was finally appointed to close down the activities of Tenby Bus & Coach Co on 12th July 1991.

Competitor M&B Coach & Bus Co, later Tenby Bus & Coach Co, operated three of these front wheel drive Talbot Pullman minibuses, challenging Silcox on their busy Tenby to Lydstep and Kiln Park service. **E618 HHP above** was previously a demonstrator for Peugeot-Talbot, Coventry and arrived together with **E134 NDE left** in May 1988. Talbot built the bodywork on both 22 seaters, which are seen here at the bus stand in Upper Park Road, Tenby. *(V. Morgan).*

Above: One of the 'Front Line' coaches owned by competitor Tenby Bus & Coach Company was this DAF SB3000DKV601 with Caetano 'Algarve' C49FT coachwork. Registered **G952 VBC** it was acquired new in September 1989 and is captured here working for a Northern Ireland tour operator 'Consort Travel'. The tour operator's sign attached to the windscreen gives the destination as 'Italian Adriatic (Rimini)'.
(V. Morgan).

Above: In 1990, Tenby Bus & Coach Co, successfully tendered for nine schools services previously operated by Silcox. This former Southdown Motor Services (1825) Leyland 'Leopard'/Plaxton, **UUF 325J** was one of ten vehicles acquired in August 1990 by Tenby Bus & Coach company for their school services. It's seen here at their depot, the 'Old RAF Buildings', Carew Airfield, Sageston already withdrawn on 1st April 1991. UUF 325J was one of the last vehicles acquired by that establishment, and passed to Morgan (Atlas Coaches) Gorseinon via J Sykes the dealer in July 1991.
(V. Morgan).

Silcox suffered considerable competition from Tenby Bus & Coach Co, and in response to the fierce competition minibuses were introduced. Many more were added subsequently to Dyfed C C requirements, featuring DiPTAC (Disabled Persons Transport Advisory Committee) specifications.

After Tenby Bus & Coach Company's demise, Silcox took over the lease of their booking office at 2 Nelson Walk, Tenby, moving their tours booking office from nearby 6 Trafalgar Road, Tenby.

Competition however did not end there. In later years First Group subsidiary 'First Cymru Buses' challenged Silcox in the Pembroke area – more about that later.

In the meantime, other 'new' local services registered by Silcox were:-

PG/1581/4902   **Tenby (Upper Park Rd) to Saundersfoot (Ridgeway)**
via: Haywood Lane, Serpentine Rd, New Hedges (village), and Twy Cross.
Sunday – Saturday (between Spring Bank Holiday and Mid-September 1987).
Route No 351.   *Starting 24/5/1987.*   *D/decker operation.*

PG/1759/4902   **Pembroke Dock (Laws St) to Pembroke (East End)**
via: Bush Street, Meyrick Street, Laws Street, Albion Square, Pembroke Street, Melville Street, Sunderland Avenue, Victoria Road, Bellvue Terrace, High Street, Bush Street, Dark Lane and Main Street (Pembroke).
Thursday & Friday only, every 30 min, 10 15 – 15 15. Normal stopping.
           Starting 4/2/1988.   *D/decker operation.*

PG/1813/4902   **Tenby Esplanade (South Beach) to Tenby Esplanade (South Beach)**
via: Tudor Square, The Norton, The Glebe, Lady Park and Upper Hill Park Est.
Monday – Saturday.   *Hail & Ride service.*
           Starting 5/4/1988.   *S/deck operation (17-35).*

PG/1922/4902   **Tenby (Upper Park Rd) to Tenby (Upper Park Rd)**
via: Lady Park Estate, Upper Hill Park, Heywood Lane and Knowling Mead.
Monday – Saturday.   *Hail & Ride service.*
           Starting 22/7/1988.   *S/deck operation (36-55).*

PG/1925/4902   **Tenby (The Salterns Car Park) to Tenby (The Salterns Car Park)**
via: South Parade (Circular).   *Park & Ride service.*
Daily service every 15 min (10 00 – 18 00) until 4/9/1988. Limited stopping.
Numbered: Park & Ride.   *Starting 25/7/1988.*   *D/decker operation.*

PG/1938/4902   **Milford Haven (Hamilton Terrace) to Carew (Market)**
via: Neyland, Honeyborough, Pembroke Dock and Pembroke.
Sundays only.   *One journey in each direction.*   *Limited stopping.*
Numbered: Milford Haven to Carew Market.
           Starting 7/8/1988.   *D/decker operation.*

PG/0049/4902   Both routes were extended due to the merger of Milford Grammar School and
PG/0050/4902   Milford Central School.   *Starting 7/9/1988.*

Additionally, in 1988 there were numerous timetable changes after M & B Coach and Bus Company (Tenby Bus & Coach Co) began operating their registered services around the Tenby area.

Above: This former United Automobile Services 1969 Bristol VRTSL6G, **WHN 411G** arrived at Silcox via South Wales Transport (902) in April 1986. For a short while it operated in SWT livery, but eventually received this pleasing new style livery to its ECW H39/31F bodywork. After sale to a Carlton breaker in 1997, it was rescued for preservation, and remains in preservation today.

(V. Morgan).

Above: OCD 770G (70 later 77) was one of three Bristol VRTSL6Gs with ECW H39/31F bodies acquired for the new academic year in August 1986. This particular bus was ordered by Bristol Omnibus Co, but diverted to Southdown (100) in 1969. It came to Silcox from National Bus Group subsidiary, Brighton & Hove Bus & Coach Co (2100) and was finally scrapped by 1996. *(VM)*

Above: This 1971 Bristol VRTSL6G with ECW H39/31F body, **UUF 111J** (111) is seen here at Silcox's Tenby depot on 24th May 1987. It was new in April 1971 to Southdown M S (511) from whom it was acquired in August 1986. *(V. Morgan).*

Above: Captured here pulling away from the bus stop at Laws Street, Pembroke Dock on 26th March 1988 is **WCD 524K** (24) another Bristol VRTSL6G with ECW H39/31F body acquired from Southdown M S (524) in August 1986. This was new to Southdown in November 1971. These Bristol VRTs were acquired to work the new school services gained from Dyfed C C tendering during the transition into deregulation. *(V. Morgan).*

Above: Throughout the period of time Silcox tried a varied assortment of coachwork and coachbuilder, but Belgian coachbuilder Jonckheere was not favoured. Only one example of that manufacturers products was ever acquired, a 1982 Jonckheere 'Bermuda' bodied DAF MB200DKTL600, seen here at the depot on 24th May 1987. **WRK 3X** (154) was new to a London operator, but arrived via Roman City, Bath in September 1986. It left two years later - joining the fleet of Islwyn Borough Transport, where it was re-registered IIB 1825 and given fleet number 59. *(V. Morgan).*

Above: This Leyland 'Leopard' PSU3A/4R, **HPT 320H** (129 later 9) was one of four 'Leopards' acquired from Creamline Services, Tonmawr, West Glamorgan upon their demise in 1987. Also acquired from Creamline in March 1987 were HPT321H, YTG138H and for spares, LJD 926K. HPT 320H, seen here on 26th March 1988 had a Plaxton 'Derwent' B55F body. *(V. Morgan).*

Above: This Bristol VRTSL6G, **JOV 713P** (71 later 4) with Metro-Cammell-Weymann H43/33F body had been new to West Midlands PTE (4713) in November 1975. Silcox purchased this from Crosville Motor Services (HVG967) in May 1987, and a year later bought one of its sisters, a Bristol VRT registered JOV 700P (70) originating from West Midlands PTE via Eastern National Omnibus Co, JOV713P was captured here on 24th May 1987 just a few days after its entry into service.   *(V. Morgan).*

Above: Pictured here at Cardiff on 19th March 1988 is **D901 HBX**, later A3 WLS (171) an integrally built Duple 425, which seated 59 and delivered in July 1987. Built by Hestair-Duple it was fully integral, fitted with Cummins L10 engine and manual transmission. Only 130 of these Duple 425s were built, and was one of a pair purchased new by the company. They were a remarkably durable vehicle as this particular vehicle is still operating for Mounts Bay Coaches, Penzance at 30 years old.   *(V. Morgan).*

Above: The second Duple 425 acquired by Silcox was originally registered *E522 MDE* (172) and delivered in March 1988 fitted with 55 seats and a toilet. In October 1992 it received this 'personalised' registration mark **A2 WLS** and was renumbered (102), whilst its twin D901 HBX pictured opposite was re-registered A3 WLS. **A2 WLS** was later re-seated to C57F and reverted to its original registration *E522 MDE* in February 2003 when it was sold. *(V. Morgan).*

Above: Another example of Silcox's rebuilding work is seen here on **AAW 411K** (41) a 1972 Leyland 'Leopard' PSU3B/4R, with Plaxton 'Panorama Elite Express II' bodywork. Also noticeable in this view taken on 21st April 1992 is that it's been re-seated to C53F using an assortment of unmatched seats. This coach came from Brown, Trench in August 1987 and was sold to a dealer in September 1996, who sold it for further use to an owner at Stratford upon Avon in 1997. *(V. Morgan).*

Above: Two more Bristol VRT/ECW were acquired in August 1987 from Stevenson, Spath (Uttoxeter) registered AJA 418/21L. New in 1973 to the large fleet of **S**outh **E**ast **L**ancashire **N**orth **E**ast **C**heshire PTE, they had been ordered by North Western Road Car Co, which had been absorbed by SELNEC in January 1972. This one, **AJA 421L** (21) is pictured outside the company's paint shop at Waterloo Garage on 3rd April 1988. Both of these Bristol VRTs gave the company 10 years' service. *(V. Morgan)*.

Above: MHX 530P (30) was another Leyland 'Leopard' PSU3C/4R with Duple 'Dominant' C53F coachwork, and was acquired in August 1987 from dealer/operator J Alwyn Evans, of Tregaron, Cardigan. It was captured here on 3rd April 1988, painted in another new style of livery, introduced in late 1987. This 'Leopard' had been new in June 1976 to the Royal Arsenal Cooperative Society, London SE18 as f/n K128. *(V. Morgan)*.

Above: **VCW 1L** (1 later 61) was another Leyland PSU3B/4R 'Leopard' with Duple 'Dominant' C49F coachwork, which had been new to Burnley, Colne & Nelson (1) in June 1973, built to the 'New Bus Grant' specification. It was taken into stock in July 1987 ex Worthington. Collingham, Notts and was re-registered KDE 161L by March 1991 when its cherished registration was sold. Two years later Silcox rebuilt the front end as shown below. Ironically in June 1988, its sister VCW 2L was operated on loan from the dealer - Wacton Trading of Bromyard. *(V. Morgan).*

Above: This was the rebuilt front end of **KDE 161L** f/n 61 (originally *VCW 1L*) picture and information at top of this page.

Above: Silcox acquired this Leyland 'Leopard' PSU3D/4R, **OKY 54R** as a <u>running chassis</u> in June 1988. The chassis was overhauled and retrofitted it with a DAF engine, and later dispatched to Willowbrook Coachbuilders where it received this new Willowbrook 'Crusader' C51F body, entering service as No 54 in April 1989. Sold to a dealer in December 1992 it was re-acquired in April 1993, and received cherished registration mark VAW 527 two years later (see below). It was photographed here at Stradey School car park, Llanelli on the occasion of Llanelli RFC playing New Zealand 28ᵗʰ October 1989. *(V. Morgan)*.

Above: In March 1995, **OKY 54R** (54) emerged from the body shop after a front end 'face lift' fitted with a Duple 'Dominant' two piece windscreen. This meant reconstructing the fiberglass aperture – a neat job too! At the same time it was given a cherished registration mark **VAW 527** which it carried until withdrawn in September 2002. It was finally scrapped in 2004. *(V. Morgan)*.

Above: By comparison, Silcox were quite late introducing mini-buses into their local service fleet. Their first arrived in October 1988 when they took delivery of **F77/8 TDE** (7/8), an identical pair of Mercedes Benz 609Ds bodied by PMT as 24 seaters. They were purchased in response to the fierce competition from M & B Coach and Bus Co, (later Tenby Bus & Coach Co) in the Tenby area. In subsequent years, several more were added to the fleet, all built to the DiPTAC specification (Disabled Persons Transport Advisory Committee) to operate the Dyfed C C tendered operations. I took this picture on 8th April 1989. *(V Morgan)*

Above: MHS 19P (19) was one of just five Alexander bodied Leyland 'Leopards' operated by the company. It had chassis type PSU3/3R and was acquired from Central SMT (T241) via Perry, Bromyard, and is seen here at Tenby on 30th June 1990. *(VM)*

In July 1989, the company registered another 'seasonal' local service:-

PG/2405/4902   **Tenby (The Salterns Car Park)** to **Tenby (The Salterns Car Park)**
                       via: South Parade (Circular).   *Park & Ride Service.*
                       Daily service every 15 min (10.00 – 18.15) incl Sun & B/H until 1/9/1989.
                       Numbered Park & Ride.   *Starting 24/7/1989.*   *D/Decker operation.*

The service operated on behalf of the local authority, permitted closure of Tenby High Street to traffic during the peak holiday period, thereafter becoming an annual event.
Licence PG/5062/4902 was cancelled from 6/1/1990, followed by cancellation of PG/5053/4902, PG/5054/4902, PG/5057-9/4902 from 2/9/1990.

On 7th February 1990, renewal of the company's 'O' Licence PG 4902/SI (International) was applied for. A five year licence was granted to operate 2 minibuses, 55 single deck and 9 double decker vehicles expiring 28th February 1995. Transport managers given as: K W & L W Silcox.

Other local services registered in 1990 were listed as follows:-

PG/2769/4902   **Haverfordwest (Bus Station)** to **Pembroke (Gateway Store)**
                       via: Merlins Bridge, Freystrop Cross, Hook, Llangwm (Garen), Houghton, Burton, Pembroke Dock and Bethany.   *Mon – Sat except public holidays.*
                       Route No 358.   *Normal stopping.*   *Starting 2/9/1990.*   *D/decker operation.*

PG/2770/4902   **Burton** to **Haverfordwest (Bus Station)**
                       via: Houghton, Freystrop Cross and Tasker Milward Voluntry Control Sch.
                       Schooldays only, 1 outward and 2 inward journeys.
                       Route No 358.   *Starting 3/9/1990.*   *D/decker operation.*

PG/2881/4902   **Tenby (Upper Park Road)** to **Tenby (South Parade)**
                       via: Moreton, Saundersfoot, Kilgetty, St Davids, Summerhill and Amroth.
                       Route No 351/352.   *Hail & Ride.*   *Starting 3/9/1990.*   *D/decker operation.*

PG/2883/4902   **Pembroke Dock (Albion Square)** to **Tenby (South Parade)**
                       via: Cresselly, Begelly Church and Wooden. (Schools).
                       Mon – Fri during school term.   *Starting 3/9/1990.*   *S/deck operation (36-55).*

PG/2921/4902   **Haverfordwest (The Patch, RAF Estate)** to **H'west (Barn Street Voluntry Sch)**
                       via: Mount Airry Infants School.
                       Two daily journeys Mon – Fri during school term.
                                     Starting 10/9/1990.   *D/decker operation.*

Furthermore, due to the surrender of school contracts by Tenby Bus & Coach Co in February 1991, Silcox were asked by Dyfed C C to make additional school journeys to six of their registered local services. The additional journeys were registered to commence from 22nd February on services under: PG1581/4902, PG1922/4902, PG2881/4902, PG2883/4902, PG5051/4902, PG5056/4902.

Permission was sought after from the Traffic Commissioners on 17th April 1991, for an additional operating centre at The Milford Docks, Milford Haven, to replace the operating centre at Brunel Quay, Neyland SA73 1PY, which had been used since the closure of Neyland Ferry in 1975. Permission was was granted, but vehicles were kept in a yard at Victoria Road /Hakin Bridge.

Above: This Bristol VRTSL6G registered **GNJ 567N** (67), was fitted with Gardner 6LXB engine and ECW H43/31F body. It was acquired in August 1990 from Williams of Cambourne, Cornwall, and was new to Southdown Motor Services, Brighton (567) in December 1974. GNJ 567N marked the end of an era at Waterloo Garage – after a long association with the Bristol marque it was the last Bristol purchased and came to a sad end in October 1993 when it crashed into a disused hotel at The Norton, Tenby.

Above: Pictured here at Westgate Hill, Pembroke outside Pembroke Castle is **H736 EDE** (6) one of the Mercedes-Benz 709Ds with Dormobile bodies acquired new in August 1990 to fullfil the requirements of Dyfed C C supported services. By the time I took this view on 12th April 2003 it had received this all over advertisement livery for a catering equipment company at Kilgetty.

Above: Silcox had a strange method of selecting registration numbers for new vehicles, they were picked at random from a block of marks issued to their associate motor dealership business, W L Silcox & Son. The registration marks used on three new Mercedes Benz delivered in August 1990 were H736/743/754 EDE. Seen here at Tenby on 14th July 1991 is **H743 EDE** f/n 3, one of the three Mercedes Benz 709Ds with Dormobile B29F bodies, built to DiPTAC specification, later re-seated to B27F. *(V Morgan).*

Above: This Dormobile B33F bodied Mercedes Benz 811D, **H227 GDE** (f/n 2) was new to Silcox in January 1991, and is seen here on 27th May 1991 loading up at Park Road, Tenby for service 352 to Kilgetty (Rylands Lane) via Heywood Lane (Tenby), New Hedges, Saundersfoot, Ridgeway, Valley Road and Fountain Head. The service, which was *partly* funded by the local authority was shared with The South Wales Transport Co, who operated the service with full funding and interavailability of tickets. *(V. Morgan).*

Local services registered by the company during 1991 were:-

PG/3108/4902   **Tenby (Upper Park Road)**   to   **Tenby (South Parade)**
via: Saundersfoot, Kilgetty, Narberth, Robeston Wathen, Canaston Bridge, Haverfordwest and Withybush Hospital. *One daily return journey, Mon – Sat.*
Route No 381.   *Starting 22/4/1991.*   *S/deck operation (17 – 35).*

PG/3153/4902   **Pembroke Dock (Waterloo Garage)** to **Pembroke Dock (Waterloo Garage)**
via: Water St, Laws St, Albion Square, Bethany, Bush Lodge and Ferry Lane.
Park & Ride service.   *12ᵗʰ -14ᵗʰ July 1991 only.*   *D/decker operation.*

PG/3220/4902   **Tenby (Salterns Car Park)**   to   **Tenby (Town Centre)**
Daily service Monday – Sunday, every 15 min 10.00 - 18.15 until 1/9/1991.
Park & Ride service.   *Starting 20/7/1991.*   *D/decker operation.*

PG/3297/4902   **Pembroke (The Green)**   to   **Pembroke (The Green)**
via: Pembroke, St Daniels Hill and Grove Estate.   *Daily, Monday to Saturday.*
Route No 357.   *Starting 17/9/1991.*   *S/deck operation (17-35).*

PG/3297/4902   was cancelled from 1/10/1991, and PG/0050/4902 surrendered from 28/10/1991.

Brothers -   Keith and David Silcox were both made company directors in August 1991.

Above: Silcox Motor Coach Co bought four of these integrally built 'LAG Panoramic' coaches of Belgian manufacture between 1991-3. All four were acquired second-hand and fitted with 11.6 litre DAF engines, the company's preference at this point. Pictured here at Tyndall Street, Cardiff on 1ˢᵗ February 1992 is **D218 XPK** which was acquired from Berryhurst Coaches, Kennington London SE11, in August 1991. In November 1992 it received a personalised registration mark **A6 WLS** which was carried until its sad end in June 1993 - it was destroyed by fire. Two months later the registration mark A6 WLS was transferred to its successor, a second-hand Auwaerter-Neoplan N122/3 coach previously registered B170 BFE.   *(V. Morgan).*

Above: The second 'LAG Panoramic' integral coach purchased by the company in August 1991 is seen here on 21ˢᵗ April 1992 displaying the cherished registration mark **GSK 676** which it received in October 1991. Previously registered *D753 APK*, it was new in January 1987, and latterly operated with Hogg of Boston, Lincolnshire. After carrying the cherished registration GSK 676 for thirteen months it received the personalised registration mark A4 WLS, (see below) which remained with the vehicle until its sale to Moseley the dealer at Taunton fourteen months later. Moseley re-registered it D980 NCV and returned the plates to Silcox for further use on a Van-Hool bodied Volvo B10M. *(V Morgan).*

Above: This is a different view of the same 'LAG Panoramic' pictured at top of this page. I took this picture on 6ᵗʰ March 1993, just four months after it received the 'personalised registration' mark **A4 WLS**. *(V. Morgan).*

Above: Bus no 84 was a very tidy 1975 Leyland 'Leopard' PSU3C/4R registered **GNL 840N**, fitted with the lightweight Alexander 'Y type' 11 metre aluminium body seating 62, (3+2 seating). New to Tyne & Wear PTE in July 1975, it had several owners before arriving at Pembroke Dock, together with GNL 839N in April 1991. Sold to a dealer in 1997, it later passed to Goodwin Farms Ltd for staff transport in January 1998. *(V. Morgan)*.

Above: This Duple 'Dominant' coach bodied Leyland 'Leopard' PSU3E/4R, re-registered **BUR 712S** (f/n 12) arrived in January 1992 from Stephenson, Rochford, Essex. New in June 1978 to Woburn Garage, London WC1, as *XWX 169S* it had been re-registered *FIL 6784* with a subsequent owner. Silcox fitted it with 53 bus seats before it entered service in February 1992, and is seen here at Haverfordwest bus station working a Haverfordwest town service on 9th April 1993. *(V. Morgan)*.

Above: Also acquired from Stephenson, Rochford, Essex in January 1992 was this Leyland 'Leopard' PSU3C/4R with Plaxton 'Panorama Elite III' C53F coachwork. It was new to Yeates of Runcorn in July 1975 as *LMA 59P*, running as *LMA 59P* (59) with Silcox until December 1992, when it underwent removal of its bright-work, a re-paint and received cherished registration mark **PVO 624**, as seen here on 28th March 1993. *(V. Morgan).*

Above: This view of **PVO 624** (previously *LMA 59P* - see above) was taken on 11th April 2004 after it had received a tremendous amount of bodywork including re-panelling and a 'home made' front grille. It was finally laid to rest after 30 years in May 2005 and scrapped on site at Waterloo Garage. The cherished registration mark presumably died with the vehicle as it was not re-used by the company. *(V. Morgan).*

Above: As mentioned earlier, the directors of Silcox had a penchant for the DAF marques in the 1990s. **9195 PU** (112) pictured here was a second-hand DAF SB2300 with Plaxton 'Paramount' C53F coachwork dating from May 1984, which arrived in January 1992 from Travelfar, Henfield, West Sussex with its original registration *A263 BTY*. It was re-registered **9195 PU** before entering service in January 1992 and is seen here at Sophia Gardens, Cardiff on 21st March 1992. In August 1992 it was again re-registered with a personalised registration mark A12 WLS, as shown below. *(V. Morgan).*

Above: This is a different view of the same DAF SB2300 pictured above. Previously registered **9195 PU**, *originally A263 BTY*, it received personalised mark **A12 WLS** in August 1992 and was re-registered A81 VDE upon sale in June 1997. *(V. Morgan).*

163

Above: New to National Travel South West as *WFH 166S* (166) in 1977, this 12 metre Leyland 'Leopard' PSU5C/4R with Duple 'Dominant' C53F coachwork came from Stephenson, Rochford, Essex in January 1992 as *WFH 166S*. It ran as WFH 166S until June 1992 when it received cherished registration 115 CUF, and in August 1992 received **9195 PU** as shown here on 9th April 1993. Later re-seated to C57F, it was re-registered (allocated) TDE 708S upon withdrawal in December 2000. *(V. Morgan)*.

Above: The first Volvo in the fleet was this 1985 B10M-61 with Caetano 'Algarve' C49FT body registered *B722 MBC*. New to Parks of Hamilton, it arrived from Ageneralink, Dundee in January 1992. In April 1992 it was re-registered **A14 WLS** as seen here outside Felinfoel RFC on 27th February 1993. It received a new registration B89 ADE upon sale in January 1998. *(V. Morgan)*.

Above: J387 ODE (5) was another Mercedes-Benz 811D delivered in April 1992 with Crystals B31F bodywork finished by Whittaker to full DiPTAC specification. This was withdrawn in December 2007 and subsequently scrapped. *(V. Morgan).*

Above: GSK 676 (72) was one of three Willowbrook 'Warrier' re-bodied Leyland 'Leopards' acquired from Glyn Williams, Cross Keys, Gwent in August 1992. Originally registered *HWY 720N* it was chassis type PSU3B/4R and seated 55. The other two were registered HWY 719N/NGV 288M (79/28) with chassis type PSU3B/4R/PSU5/4R respectively. All three rebodied in 1988, entered service with Silcox in Augst 1992 carrying original registrations, this one, GSK 676 *(HWY720N)* received its cherished mark in January 1993, with NGV 288M receiving its cherished mark 109 CUF at the same time. *(V. Morgan).*

Above: Seen here at Bute Street, Cardiff on 6th February 1993 is **A15 WLS** (115) a 1988 Volvo B10M-61 with Plaxton 'Paramount 3200' C57F coachwork acquired from Frames-Rickards. Brentford, Essex *(E167 OMD)* in December 1992. It received the personalised registration before entering service, and returned to its original mark E167 OMD upon sale in April 1999, to an Irish operator – Hogan, Thurles, County Tipperary. *(V. Morgan).*

Above: This Leyland 'Tiger' TRCL10/3ARZM with Plaxton 321 coachwork, and personalised registration **A11 WLS**, was new to Bebb, Llantwit Vardre, Mid-Glam registered *J47 SNY* in August 1991. The coachwork built after Duple's merger with Plaxton, was based on the Duple 320 shell with a clear Plaxton flavour to the interior. Acquired in December 1992, it was fitted with the economical Cummins L10 engine and a manual transmission. Re-registered J328 PDE *and* operated as such for a few days, it passed to a dealer in September 1994, and was exported to Malta in January 1995, where it was re-registered: Y-0934 with Canco Supreme. Zetjun, Malta. This photograph was taken on 7th November 1993. *(V. Morgan).*

Above: This splendid view of **A8 WLS** (108) was taken at Tyndall Street, Cardiff on 6th March 1993. Silcox acquired this, their fourth and last 'LAG Panoramic' from Berryhurst Coaches, Kennington London SE11 in January 1993, registered as F628 SRP. Again fitted with the DAF 11.6 litre engine, it was re-registered **A8 WLS** before entering service in January 1993, and reverted to its original mark F628 SRP upon sale to a dealer in February 2000. *(V. Morgan).*

Above: K651 TDE (9) a Mercedes-Benz 814D with Crystals B31F bodywork was captured here on Silcox's yard - as delivered on Saturday 26th June 1993. I was in the right place at the right time to photograph this vehicle. On that particular day, I was working a 'Rail Replacement Service' - serving all stations from Whitland to Pembroke Dock with the Davies Bros, Plaxton bodied Leyland 'Leopard' OUT 11W, which is just visible parked in the background. *(V. Morgan).*

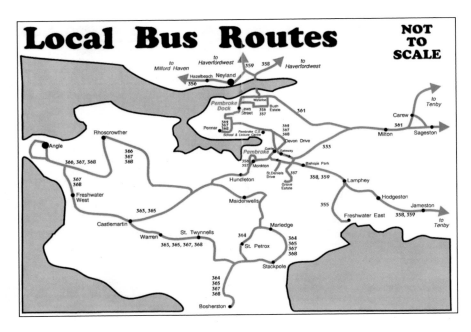

Dyfed County Council bus route maps showing services operating in south west Dyfed, dated June 1993.

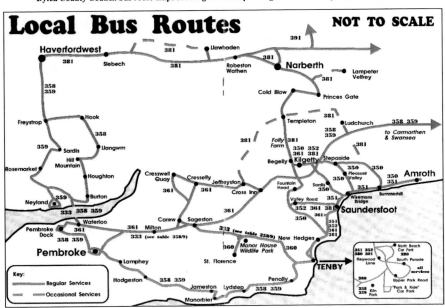

New local services registered by the company from July 1992 – July 1994 are listed below:-

PG 3629/4902   **Tenby (Salterns Car Park)** to **Tenby (Salterns Car Park)** via: Town Centre.
Daily service Monday – Sunday, every 15 min 10.00 – 18.15, until 5/9/1992.
Park & Ride service.   *Starting 20/7/1992.*   *D/decker operation.*

PG 3997/4902   **Pembroke Dock (Waterloo Garage)** to **Pembroke Dock (St Daniels Drive)**
via: Bush St, Laws St, Bethany, Pennar, Devon Drive and St Daniels Drive.
Daily service, Monday to Friday only.
Route No 362/367/368.   *Starting 7/6/1993.*   *S/decker operation (36-55).*

PG 3998/4902   **Pembroke Dock (Laws Street)** to **Jameston**
via: Bethany, Pembroke town, Bishops Park, Lamphey and Freshwater East.
Route No 355/362. Mon – Sat. Starting 7/6/1993. S/decker operation (36-55).

PG 3999/4902   **Tenby (Upper Park Road)** to **Manorbier**
via: Penally and Lydstep.   *Daily service, Monday – Friday only.*
Route No 358/359.   *Starting 7/6/1993.*   *S/decker operation (17-35).*

PG 4016/4902   **Tenby (Salterns Car Park)** to **Tenby (Salterns Car Park)** via: Town Centre.
Daily service, Monday – Sunday, every 15 min 10.00 – 18.00, until 4/9/1993.
Park & Ride service.   *Starting 26/7/1993.*   *Single/Double-decker operation.*

PG 4084/4902   **Pembroke (Gateway Store)** to **Angle (circular)**.
via: St Daniels Drive, Hundleton, Maidenwells, Angle and Castlemartin.
Schools service, to operate on school days only Mon – Fri.   *Normal stops.*
Route No 366.   *Starting 2/9/1993.*   *S/decker (17-35 & 36-55).*

PG 5056/4902   To transfer **Angle** journeys on to PG 4084/4902 above, and amend timetable.
Starting 2/9/1993.

PG 4171/4902   **Tenby (Salterns Car Park)** to **Tenby (Salterns Car Park)** via: Town Centre.
Daily service, Monday – Sunday, every 15 min 10.00 – 18.15, until 2/9/1994.
Park & Ride service.   *Starting 25/7/1994.*   *S/decker (36-55) & D/decker.*

PG 4172/4902   **Tenby (Upper Park Road)** to **Tenby (South Parade)**
via: Amroth, Saundersfoot, Tenby, Jameston, Pembroke, Bosherston,
Castlemartin, Angle and Hundleton.   *Service operating Monday – Sunday.*
One circular journey per day from 29/5/94 to 2/9/94.   *Normal stopping.*
                                               S/decker operation (17 – 35).

Local service registrations cancelled in 1993:-

PG 1938/4902   Milford Haven to Carew Market.   Cancelled from 24/3/1993.

PG 5060/4902   Dale to Milford Haven Comp. School. Cancelled from 2/9/1993.

PG 2921/4902   Haverfordwest (Furzey Park) to Barn Street School.
                                    Cancelled from 2/9/1993.

Above: Only three Leyland 'Atlanteans' were ever operated by Silcox, all arriving in August 1993 from Camm of Nottingham. New to South Yorks PTE (1707/12/59) CWG 707/712/759V in 1979-80, they had chassis type AN68A/1R. **CWG 759V** (75) seen here at Tenby on 7th November 1993 had Roe bodywork to H45/29D layout, the others had Alexander bodies. *(V. Morgan)*.

Above: The only Auwaerter 'Neoplan' to operate with Silcox came from Amberline, Liverpool (*B170 BFE*) in 1993. It entered service in August 1993 re-registered **A6 WLS**, receiving a 'new' registration mark B48 ADE upon sale in 1996. The seating layout of its 'Neoplan' coachwork was CH57/20CT, and is seen here at Cardiff on 26th November 1994. *(V. Morgan)*.

Above: Museum Avenue, Cardiff is the backdrop for this particular shot of **A16 WLS** (116) a 1991 Toyota Coaster HDB30R with elegant Caetano 'Optimo I' C21F coachwork. Previously owned by Harry Shaw Coaches, Coventry (*H75 HAW*) it received the personalised registration mark **A16 WLS** upon entering service with Silcox in October 1993. The Toyota Coaster midi-coach was quite a popular choice with south Wales coach operators, as they were ideally suited for rural communities. This view was taken on 18th February 1995, but the next time I photographed it the personalised registration A16 WLS had been removed and exchanged for a 'new' registration mark H59 JDE in preparation for its disposal to a dealer (See below).   *(V. Morgan)*.

Above: Previously registered *A16 WLS* (*originally H75 HAW*), H59 JDE awaits collection by the dealer in April 1996.   *(VM)*.

Above: Van-Hool coachwork was not a preferred choice at Silcox, only three of that make were ever operated. Seen here at King Edward VII Avenue, Cardiff on the occasion of the Welsh Rugby Union cup final 7th May 1994 is **A4 WLS** (104) a 1989 Volvo B10M-60 with Van-Hool 'Alizee' C49FT body acquired from Berkeley Coaches, Paulton, Avon in January 1994 registered *F866 XJX.* It received its personalised registration mark in March 1994 and its identity returned to F866 XJX upon sale in January 2002.
(V. Morgan).

As a consequence of the 1994 round of re-tendering for the network of local authority supported services branded 'Bws Dyfed' (Dyfed Bus), Silcox significantly increased their network of services. They successfully tendered for new contracts together with contracts previously operated by The South Wales Transport Co. The list of services registered by Silcox to operate on behalf of Dyfed County Council, and commencing on 5th September 1994 were as follows:-

PG 4204/4902   **Kingsbridge & Cosherston   to   Pembroke C S School**
via: Waterloo and Pembroke Dock (all stops). *School days only. Hail & Ride.*
Route No 369/371.   School service.   Starting 5/9/1994.   S/decker (36-55).

PG 4205/4902   **Pennar Park   to   Pembroke C S School**
via: Pennar and Bethany. *School days only. Normal stops.*
Route No 362. School service. Starting 5/9/1994. S/decker operation (36-55).

PG 4206/4902   **Haverfordwest (Bus Station) to Carmarthen (Bus Station)**
via: Withybush Hospital, Robeston Wathen, Narberth, Whitland and St Clears.
Previously operated by South Wales Transport.
To operate 3 journeys per day Mon-Sat.   Normal stops and Hail & Ride.
Route No 322.   Starting 5/9/1994.   S/decker operation (36-55).

PG 4207/4902   **Bush St / Ferry Lane Junction   to Pembroke C S School**
via: Laws Street, Albion Square and Bethany.
Route No 357. School service. Starting 5/9/1994. S/decker operation (36-55).

PG 4208/4902   **Haverfordwest (Bus Station)** to **Pembroke Dock (Laws Street)**
via: Milford Haven, Waterston, Neyland, Cleddau Bridge and Waterloo.
To operate 1 journey per day Mon - Sat.   *Normal stops and Hail & Ride.*
Route No 333.   *Starting 5/9/1994.*   *S/decker operation (36-55).*
This registered service was a <u>non-starter</u> - it was cancelled from 4/9/1994.

PG 4209/4902   **Pembroke Dock (Laws Street)** to **Carmarthen (Bus Station)**
via: Pembroke (Gateway Store), Pembroke (Station), Bishops Park, Lamphey,
Milton, Sageston, Redberth, Kilgetty, Llanddowror, St Clears and Carmarthen.
Route No 332.   *School days only.*   *Starting 5/9/1994.*   *S/decker (36-55).*

PG 4210/4902   **Tenby (Upper Park Road)** to **Pendine (Shops)**
via: Saundersfoot, Kilgetty, Wisemans Bridge, Stepaside, Summerhill, Amroth
and Pendine.   <u>Previously shared with The South Wales Transport Co.</u>
Route No 351.   *Daily Mon-Sat.*   *Starting 5/9/1994.*   *S/decker (17-35).*

PG 4211/4902   **Tenby (Upper Park Road)** to **Haverfordwest (Bus Station)**
via: Saundersfoot, Kilgetty, Templeton, Narberth and Withybush Hospital.
<u>Previously shared with The South Wales Transport Co.</u>
Route No 381.   *Daily Mon-Sat.*   *Starting 5/9/1994.*   *S/decker (36-55).*

PG 4212/4902   **Pembroke Dock (Waterloo/Llanion Pk)** to **Trewent Beach, Jameston** or **Tenby**
via: Pembroke and Lamphey.
Route No 355/362.   *Daily Mon-Sat.*   *Starting 5/9/1994.*   *S/decker (17-35).*

PG 4213/4902   **Haverfordwest (Bus Station)** to **Little Haven (Haven Fort)**
via: Broad Haven.   *To operate on Saturdays & school holidays only.*
Route No 311.   *Starting 5/9/1994.*   *S/decker (17-35).*

PG 4214/4902   **Pembroke Dock (Llanion Pk or Laws St)** to **Merchants Park or Hundleton**
via: Pennar Park, Devon Drive, Pembroke and St Daniels Drive.
Route No 362.   *Mon-Fri only.*   *Starting 5/9/1994.*   *S/decker (17-35).*

PG 4215/4902   **Pembroke and Pembroke Dock areas** to **Pembroke C S School**
Route No 375/376.   *School service.*   *Starting 5/9/1994.*   *S/decker (36-55).*

PG 4216/4902   **Tenby (Upper Park Road)**   to   **Kilgetty (Post Office)**
via: Saundersfoot, Amroth, Summerhill and Stepaside.
Route No 350.   *Daily Mon-Sat.*   *Starting 5/9/1994.*   *S/decker (36-55).*

PG 4217/4902   **Tenby (Upper Park Road)**   to   **Carmarthen (Bus Station)**
via: Saundersfoot, Kilgetty, Llanddowror and St Clears.
<u>Previously operated by The South Wales Transport Co.</u>
Modified from 24/11/1997 to include Bro-Myrddin School, Carmarthen
Route No 333.   *Daily Mon-Sat.*   *Starting 5/9/1994.*   *S/decker (36-55).*

A total of seven new buses were ordered to operate the above services, but simultaneously five established local services were withdrawn as from 5th September 1994. These were:-

PG 2769/4902, PG 2881/4902, PG3108/4902, PG 3997/4902 and PG 3998/4902.

Above: **M174 BDE** (17) was one of seven new vehicles purchased by Silcox in August 1994 to fulfil the newly acquired local authority tendered contracts on the 'BWS DYFED' network of services. **M174 BDE** was a 9.8m Dennis Dart with East Lancs B40F bodywork and was purchased direct from East Lancs as a cancelled order for Derby City Transport. I captured **M174 BDE** here outside the bus station at Blue Street Carmarthen on its arrival from Tenby on 17th September 1994. His bus stand No 4 was already occupied by the bus I was driving, HCS 793N a Leyland Leopard in the backdrop. This was just 10 days after Silcox had commenced operating the new local service to Carmarthen - a service previously operated by South Wales Transport. The Bws Dyfed sign displayed in the window was a stipulation for the contract – otherwise a fine of £60 was imposed by the local authority. *(V Morgan).*

Above: This Wadham Stringer B29F bodied Mercedes Benz 709D registered **M361 CDE** (f/n 1) was also purchased in August 1994 for the new 'BWS DYFED' contracts and is seen here at Carmarthen bus station on 24th September 1994. *(V. Morgan).*

174

Above: Another Mercedes Benz 709D acquired for the 'Bws Dyfed' work arrived in November 1994 fitted with a Mellor B27F body. This one was registered **M368 CDE** (8) and is seen here when it was 11 years old exiting the 'rebuilt' Carmarthen bus station working a Carmarthen 'Town Service' 208 to Brynmeurig. Silcox received much tendered work from the reformed Carmarthenshire County Council in 2005, service 208 latterly operated by Taf Valley Coaches was part of it. M368 CDE is seen here on 23rd September 2005 with all over advertisement for PRP Training Ltd, Pembroke Dock, and 'Pembrokeshire Bus' windscreen sticker.

Above: This Mellor B27F bodied Mercedes Benz 709D, registered **M674 CDE** (7) was also new in November 1994 and together with M368 CDE (upper view) were the only two Mercedes Benz in the fleet to be fitted with side facing destination boxes. It's seen here at Waterloo Garage on 7th April 1996, and for a minibus had a long working life of 19 years. *(V. Morgan).*

Above: Seen here at the depot on 17th April 1995, minus all its bright-work (chrome trim) is **EHW 294W** a 1981 Volvo B58-61 with Duple 'Dominant II' C55F coachwork. It was acquired from a Gwent operator, Kerricabs of Newport in September 1994 to cover the extra school transport work designated by the local authority in 1994. *(V. Morgan).*

Above: Three 9 metre Dennis Darts were ordered in August 1994 as previously mentioned for the 'Bws Dyfed' network of services. **M17 SMC** (17) seen here at Carmarthen bus station on 28th January 1995 was one of the trio registered with personalised registrations M16-8 SMC (16-8), delivered in November that year fitted with Marshall SPV, DP31F bodies. *(V. Morgan).*

176

Above: By 1995 the necessity of a double decker on schools had changed to high capacity single decker buses fitted with 3 + 2 seating. As a direct result of this the company purchased their last double decker **GNF 13V** f/n 31, seen here on 17th April 1995 (note they would not use fleet No 13). This was a 1980 Leyland 'Titan' TNTL11/1RF with Park Royal H47/26F body acquired from Capital Citybus, London (100) in March 1995, passing to Gemini, Swansea in August 1998 where it was destroyed by fire in November 1998. GNF 13V and Leyland Atlantean CWG 707V were the last two double decker's operated by Silcox. *(V. Morgan).*

Above: Pictured here outside the companys registered office at Waterloo Garage on 7th April 1996 is **K507 RDE** a 1993 Leyland-Daf 400 (LDV) with a body conversion to PSV standards by Pearl, seating 16 passengers. It was acquired from Kennings Hire in 1996 and used mainly for a school contract. *(V. Morgan).*

On 7th February 1995, renewal of the company's 'Operator Licence' PG 4902/SI was applied for. The maximum five year licence was granted to operate 62 single deck and 9 double decker vehicles expiring 28th February 2000. Operating Centres were given as Waterloo Garage, Milford Dock Co, Milford Haven and North Beach Car Park, Tenby, although a few vehicles 'slept out overnight' at other locations.

Only two local service registrations were made during 1995, which were:-

PG 4399/4902   **Haverfordwest (Bus Station)** to **Tenby (South Parade)**
via: Freystrop Cross, Rosemarket, Neyland, Pembroke Dock, Pembroke, Lamphey, Jameston and Penally. *Sunday only, spring B/H to first Sunday in Sept. Route No 359.*   *Starting 28/5/1995.*   *S/decker operation (36-55).*
Note: This service was cancelled from 25/5/1997.

PG 4463/4902   **Tenby (Salterns Car Park)** to **Tenby (Salterns Car Park)** via: Town Centre. *Daily service, Monday - Sunday every 15 min, 10.00 – 18.15 until 1/9/1995. Park & Ride service.*   *Starting 24/7/1995.*   *S/deck & D/deck operation.*

In April 1996, the three original counties that had formed 'Dyfed' were reinstated. The new Pembrokeshire County Council was reinstated and able to make their own transport arrangements. However, the first local service registered by Silcox in conjunction with Pembrokeshire C C was the annual Tenby Park & Ride service:-

PG 4672/4902   **Tenby (Salterns Car Park)** to **Tenby (Salterns Car Park)** via: Town Centre. *Daily service, Monday – Sunday every 15 min, 10.00 – 18.15 until 31/8/1996. Park & Ride service.*   *Starting 23/7/1996.*

PG 1581/4902 & PG 5052/4902 were both cancelled from 25/5/1996 & 26/5/1996 respectively.

Above: F585 OOU was one of four Iveco Daily 49.10 purchased in April 1996, for use on the 'Bws Dyfed' network of services. This one from Bristol City Line (7585) and its sister F580 OOU (7580) had Dormobile B23F bodies.   *(V. Morgan).*

Above: Seen here at Carmarthen on Sat 8th March 1997 is **A6 WLS** (106) a 1990 Volvo B10M-60 with Caetano 'Algarve' C49FT coachwork, which arrived from Thompson, Uxbridge London in April 1996 registered G903 WAY. Silcox re-registered this with personalised registration mark **A6 WLS** before it entered service in April 1996, returning it to the original registration upon sale to a dealer in January 2001. *(V. Morgan).*

Above: The next major change to the fleet came in early 1997 when the company started buying surplus Ministry of Defence left-hand drive Leyland 'Tigers' with Plaxton 'Derwent II' bodies. This picture taken at the rear of Waterloo Garage on 18th May 1997 shows one of the first 26 purchased between 1997/8, before its conversion to right-hand drive. Apparantly they were easily converted to RHD as the components were interchangable from one side to the other. They also converted LHD M o D buses for other operators, and interestingly some of these M o D 'Tigers' gave the company up to 20 years use. The very last one A3 WLS (222) was still operational when the company ceased trading on 5th June 2016. *(V. Morgan).*

Above: Originally registered 82 KF 37 with the Ministry of Defence, this 1987 Leyland 'Tiger' TRCTL11/3LZ with Plaxton 'Derwent II' DP54F was first to arrive in December 1996, already registered D578 DPM for civilian use. After conversion to RHD and an emergency door fitted to the off side rear, it entered service in June 1997 as f/n 96 but was later renumbered 207 as shown here at King Edward VIII Avenue, Cardiff on 20th May 2000, seen working a private hire to the W R U cup final. It was re-registered **A11 WLS** in March 2002, together with other M o D 'Tigers' in due course. *(V. Morgan).*

Above: In due course Silcox fitted destination boxes to most of the former M o D 'Tigers' as displayed here by **D577 DPM** (220) at Haverfordwest bus station on 21st June 2000. Seen here working the 311 service to Broad Haven it had been re-seated to B71F before entering service in April 1998 with 3 + 2 seating, and re-registered A8 WLS in March 2002. The personalised registration mark appears to have been lost when the bus was withdrawn in November 2014 - as there was no further trace of it. *(V. Morgan).*

Above: Originally registered 87 KF 46 and new to the M o D in October 1987, this Leyland 'Tiger' became E141 ODE (212) when licenced by Silcox in September 1997. It retained the DP54FA seating layout throughout its working life, but was fitted with a destination box and later repainted into school bus livery, as seen here on 27th September 2010. The personalised registration mark **A4 WLS** was added in June 2010 - and removed in September 2011 when the bus was withdrawn. *(V. Morgan).*

Above: Another of the Plaxton 'Derwent II' bodied 'Tigers' to receive a destination box was **NSV 324** (221) seen here 13th April 2003. Previously registered 82 KF 41 by the M o D, this cherished registration mark was given to the bus when it was first licenced by the company in September 1998. I took this picture on 13th April 2003. *(V. Morgan).*

Above: One of the second batch of M o D 'Tigers' bought in May 1998 is seen here on 8th October 2001. This was new in September 1987 as 87 KF 26, and was first licenced by Silcox in March 1999, using cherished registration mark **109 CUF** (225). This particular M o D 'Tiger' also received a destination box, but was not 'upseated' it retained its 54 dual purpose seats. However, in September 2009 the cherished registration mark **109 CUF** was sold, and replaced by a personalised registration mark – SIL 6637 as seen in the picture below. *(V. Morgan).*

Above: SIL 6637 (225) seen here on 30th May 2010 was actually a re-registration of 109 CUF (225) the Plaxton 'Derwent' bodied Leyland 'Tiger' TRCTL11/3LZ, seen in the upper view. It was re-painted into the yellow school bus livery during the summer term school holidays 2009 - the time of its re-registration. There was no further record of its personalised registration mark - **SIL6637** after withdrawal from service in 2014 – when it succumbed the scrapmans torch. *(V. Morgan).*

Above: This former M o D Leyland 'Tiger' TRCTL11/3LZ was new to the M o D in September 1987 as 87 KF 44. Silcox registered this with a personalised registration mark **A7 WLS** (224) in January 1999, and equipped it for one-person operation complete with a destination box. The yellow school bus livery was applied in early 2009, and the photograph was taken on 22nd March 2009.

Above: What an odd looking body this former M o D vehicle had! Registered with cherished registration **GSK 676** (229) it was a Leyland 'Leopard' PSU5D/5L with Wadham Stringer 'Vanguard' B54F body, new to M o D in Dec 1983 as 51 AC 03. Converted by Silcox from L H D, it entered service in August 1999, and was withdrawn with a broken chassis in 2004. *(V. Morgan).*

183

Above: **P779 WDE** (179) was a 12 metre Dennis Javelin with Caetano 'Algarve II' C51FT coachwork new to Silcox in May 1997. It was delivered in the livery of 'Grand UK Holidays' as seen here, for contracted use on the Norwich based UK Holiday Group's coach holidays. This photograph was taken at Llanelli on 10th February 1998. *(V. Morgan).*

Above: It was always worthwhile to 'hang around' Carmarthen bus station to see what vehicle would operate the Pembrokeshire Council supported 322 service from Haverfordwest at 10.03. The tightly scheduled 3 times daily service, advertised as 'normally operated by a low floor easy access bus' was on the morning of 25th November 2013 operated by Dennis 'Javelin' **9195 PU**, which had been re-registered from *(P779 WDE above)* six months earlier. This sold for £10 at the official recievers auction. *(V. Morgan).*

Above: Another 12 metre Dennis Javelin arrived in March 1998 registered **R531 HDE** (182). Fitted with attractive Marcopolo 'Explorer II' C53F coachwork, it was built at the Portuguese plant of the Brazilian coachbuilding company, Marcopolo. This coach received severe roof damage in 2007 when it struck a low bridge with 9ft 9ins clearance at Golden Hill Road, Pembroke. Silcox's coachbuilders did an excellent repair to its roof which had been peeled open - to the second window pane like a 'sardine tin'. After its repair it was repainted in overall white livery, which it retained until its sale by the official receiver in June 2016.

Above: Formerly a Ministry of Defence (Army) Dennis 'Javelin' and new in April 1993 as 15 KL 44, this 10 metre Wadham Stringer C48F bodied coach arrived in December 1998. It was registered **K721 UDE** (230) and was identical to its partner K722 UDE (231) which arrived together via Stones of Leigh, Gtr Manchester. This was sold in April 2006 to Chicago Bridge & Ironworks, a construction company located at South Hook, Milford Haven, but was still maintained at Waterloo Garage.

The local services registered from 1998 - 2000 were as follows:-

PG 6015/4902   **North Beach Car Park** to **North Beach Car Park**
via: Salterns Car Park, South Parade and Upper Park Road, Tenby.
Daily service, Monday – Sunday every 20 min. 10.00 – 18.00
Park & Ride service. Starting 22/7/1998 until 5/9/1998.

PG 6072/4902   **Pembroke (Gateway Store)** to **Haverfordwest (Bus Station)**
via: Pembroke Dock, Neyland and Johnston.   *Mon – Sat (except B/H).*
Route No 382.   *Starting 2/11/1998.*   ***Cancelled from 31/5/1999.***

PG 6073/4902   **Haverfordwest (Bus Station)** to **Carmarthen (Bus Station)**
via: Narberth and St Clears. (Re-routing service registered under PG 4206/4902).
Route No 322.   *Starting 5/10/1998.*   *Mon – Sat (except B/H).*

PG 6100/4902   **Pembroke Dock (Waterloo Garage)** circular service via: Pembroke, Maidenwells, St Petrox, Bosherston, Stackpole, Freshwater East and Lamphey.
Route No 387.   *Starting 3/11/1998.*   *Tuesday & Thursday only.*

PG 6101/4902   **Pembroke Dock (Waterloo Garage)** circular via: Pembroke, Hundleton,
Angle, Castlemartin, Merrion, St Twynnels, Maidenwells and Pembroke.
Route No 388.   *Starting 4/11/1998.*   *Wed & Fri only, 2 journeys per day.*

PG 6134/4902   **Tenby (Upper Park Road)** to **Cardigan (Finch Square)**
via: Kilgetty, Narberth and Crymmych.
Route No 390.   *Starting 24/11/1998.*   *Tuesday & Saturday only.*

Left: Two of these former London Buses Optare 'Metroriders' found a home at Pembroke Dock for a brief period. **H689 YGO** (14) seen here and its partner H681 YGO arrived via Richmond, Epsom in February 1999 but left after less than two years use. They were re-numbered 89/81 respectively before leaving to a dealer in December 2001, passing to Nu-Venture, Aylesford, Kent soon after.

Above: Another strange looking body was this Marshall 'Campaigner' B54FA body fitted to a former M o D Leyland 'Tiger' TRCTL11/3R. It arrived from the M o D as 20 KB 58 in April 2002, and received civilian registration number **A153 VDE** upon entry to service a month later carrying f/n 232. This view was taken on 14th April 2002 at 'The Works'. *(V. Morgan).*

Above: Captured here at Haverfordwest bus station on 17th August 1999, before redevelopment of the site is **D603 MKH** another Fiat-Iveco 'Daily' 49.10 with Robin Hood 'City Nippy' B25F body acquired in March 1999. In the background a Richards Bros DAF SB220, P901 PWW is seen working a shuttle bus service to the Pembrokeshire County Show at Withybush. *(V. Morgan).*

Above: In June 1999 another chassis manufacturer made an appearance at the Silcox establishment. The choice this time was a German built MAN 18.310 fitted with Marcopolo 'Continental 340' C49FT coachwork and registered T143 RDE (187). Silcox were not very impressed with it, as a return to Dennis 'Javelin' chassis was made the following season. T143 RDE was just 2 months old when I photographed it here on 17th August 1999, and it left the fleet in January 2005. *(V. Morgan).*

Above: This former Ministry of Defence 1983 Leyland 'Tiger' TRCTL11/3R with Marshall 'Campaigner' B57F bodywork arrived at Pembroke Dock in October 2003, from First Somerset & Avon (2217). Originally registered 20 KB 47 with the M o D it was registered **A649 YOX** when purchased by Southern National, predecessors of First Somerset & Avon where it carried a yellow livery. The destination equipment was fitted by Silcox who gave it f/n 235. This passed to a construction company in 2006. *(V. Morgan).*

Above: Seen here at Pensarn, Carmarthen on layover before its 15.00 return journey to Pembroke Dock on 12th May 2010 is **T142 RDE** (186), a Dennis Javelin with Salvador Caetano 'Cutlass' C53F body. It was in a livery promoting 'Great Days Out by Bus', sponsored by Pembrokeshire C C, and carried an advertisement for the Manor House Wildlife Park near Tenby. The 333 service had been revived by Silcox in January 2010, commercially operated with one return journey daily on Wednesdays and Fridays only.

(V. Morgan).

Above: This is another photograph of **T142 RDE** (top of page) the Caetano bodied Dennis Javelin, taken on 16th July 2014 after a repaint and re-registration to **M18 SMC**. It certainly looks like a different vehicle. *(V. Morgan).*

Above: After taking delivery of their MAN coach a year earlier, Silcox returned to the Dennis marque for their millennium year purchases, receiving a pair of 12 metre 'Javelins'. This Javelin, **W108 NDE** (188) arrived in March 2000 fitted with Berkhof 'Axial 50' C51FT coachwork, and carried the livery of 'David Urquhart Travel' for contracted use on that particular travel agents coach holidays. It later received the livery of 'Grand UK Holidays' and eventually passed to Edwards Coaches, Llantwit Fardre with Silcox's school contracts in June 2016. *(V. Morgan).*

Above: The second 12 metre Dennis 'Javelin' to arrive in the millenium year is seen here on 7th July 2001, leaving Magor Service area of the M4 Motorway, near the Severn Bridge. This Javelin, **W109 NDE** (189) arrived in May 2000 fitted with a Marcopolo 'Continental 340' C53F body and was sometime later repainted in all over white livery for 'Grand UK Holidays' which was carried until November 2013. **W109 NDE** also passed to Edwards Coaches, Llantwit Fardre with Silcox's school contracts in June 2016. *(V. Morgan).*

Above: N356 MDE was another former Ministry of Defence Dennis 'Javelin' previously registered D-GF-25. This one had bodywork built by U.V.G (Bus & Coach) Ltd to B54FA layout, it was a model named 'Unistar'. It was acquired in November 1999, but underwent conversion from LHD to RHD, removal of the Ambulance type door at the rear end and re-seated to DP55F. Finally registered **N356 MDE** it entered service in May 2000, and is pictured here on 14th April 2002. *(V. Morgan)*.

The only local service registered by the company during 2000 was the usual Tenby Park & Ride:-

PG7344/4902 **Tenby (Salterns Car Park)** to **Tenby (Salterns Car Park)** via: Town Centre.
Daily service, Monday – Sunday, every 15 min, 10.00 to 18.15.
Park & Ride service. Starting 24/7/2000. Finishing 1/9/2000.

Silcox also registered their withdrawal of Sunday services on PG 1759/4902, Pembroke Dock (Laws Street) to Pembroke (Tesco Store) to take effect from 23/12/1999.

This however prompted a local coach proprietor Richard Lewis (T/A Barneys Coaches), Pembroke to register an alternative Sunday service running hourly (PG 7203/6915), commencing on 23rd January 2000 from Pembroke Dock (Leo's Car Park) to Monkton via Bush Estate, Laws St, Pembroke (Main St), Grove Estate and Monkton.

Richard Lewis later registered another local service:-

PG 7341/6915 Pembroke Dock (Irish Ferries) to Pembroke via: Pembroke Dock, to operate
Monday – Sunday for daytime sailing at approx 13.00. *Starting on 28/6/2000.*

On 12th April 2001, Silcox applied to the Department of Transport to change the location of their Milford Haven outstation from 'The Milford Docks' SA73 3AF to D.A.D Munro (South Wales) Ltd, Waterston Industrial Estate, Waterston, Milford Haven SA73 1DF.

The new outstation at Waterston previously occupied by a construction company, was authorised in May 2001, and by May 2008 had moved to Lloyd & Pawlett, Victoria Depository, Waterston Industrial Estate. Three years later it moved once more to Plot 8A Waterston Industrial Estate.

Above: In December 2000, two second-hand Mercedes Benz 709Ds were purchased from Dublin Bus. Pictured here is former Dublin Bus 93 D 10006, (f/n ME6) a 1993 Mercedes Benz 709D with Eurocoach B23F bodywork which received registration number **L632 XBX** and fleet number 20 when licenced in June 2001. *(V. Morgan).*

Above: The second Mercedes Benz 709D acquired in December 2000 from Dublin Bus (ME1) was identically fitted with Eurocoach B23F bodywork. Previously registered 93 D 10001, it received registration **L784 SEJ** (19) with Silcox, and was licenced in March 2001. This also had a long working life – it was 'retired' in June 2013 and sold for scrap in July 2014. *(V. Morgan).*

Above: A nice shot of a beautiful coach seen leaving Waterloo Garage on 14th April 2002. **Y199 JDE** was yet another 12 metre Dennis Javelin with Berkhof 'Axial 50' C51FT coachwork, acquired new in March 2001. *(V. Morgan).*

Above: Also new in March 2001 was **Y201 JDE** (21) the company's first 'low floor' Dennis Dart SLF, with impressive looking Salvador Caetano 'Compass' B38F bodywork. This bus operated with the company through to their demise in June 2016, and was sold at the official receivers auction for £1,500 to Cainey. Thornbury, Gloucester. I photographed this vehicle at the Tenby outstation on 14th April 2002 about to depart on the 381 service to Haverfordwest, a service supported by Pembrokeshire C C and at one time shared with South Wales Transport. *(V. Morgan).*

Above: **V675 FPO** (22) was another Dennis Dart SLF with an earlier Caetano 'Compass' body which seated 40. This was new to Wilkinson, Staines in December 1999, and acquired from White Rose, Thorpe, Surrey, through the dealership of S C C, Waterlooville in September 2001. It's seen here on 13th April 2003, and left the fleet in February 2005. *(V. Morgan).*

Above: Admittedly not the best photograph, but considering that this rare vehicle only operated for 10 months before its sad end, I had to include it. **Y733 OBE** (194) was a Mercedes Benz 'Atego' 1223L (lorry chassis, 6.37 litre engine) with rare Ferqui C35FT (Spanish built) coachwork, which was new in April 2001 as a demonstrator. Silcox acquired this coach in September 2001 from the dealers Optare of Crossgates, Leeds but unfortunately it burnt out on the M4 Motorway in July 2002. *(V. Morgan).*

The only local service registrations recorded in 2001/2 were:-

PG 7667/4902   **Tenby (Salterns Car Park)** to **Tenby (Salterns Car Park)** via: South Parade.
Daily service, Monday – Sunday, every 15 min. 10.00 – 18.15 until 31/8/2001.
Tenby Park & Ride service.   Starting 23/7/2001.

PG 7808/4902   **Hubberston (Haven Drive)** to **Hubberston (Haven Drive)**
Daily service Monday – Saturday except Bank Holidays.
Route No 300.   Starting 7/1/2002.
Note: *This service was issued with a <u>new format </u>registration number;*
<u>PG0004902/30</u>   *PG0004902/30 six weeks later in 2/2002. All local service registrations*
thereafter had the new format.

PG0004902/31   **Hubberston** to **Haverfordwest** (Withybush Showground) via: Milford Haven
Route No 302.   Starting 30/6/2002.

On 2nd December 2002, company secretary and director of Silcox Motor Coach Co Ltd, David William Silcox (Leonard Silcox's son) relinquished his position, with Mrs Rosalind Margaret Silcox director (Leonard Silcox second wife) taking his place as company secretary and director.

The new board of directors were then given as: Leonard William Silcox; Rosalind Margaret Silcox; Keith W Silcox; Doreen Ellen Miller and Thomas Egan Miller.

Above: After a break of four years, the company invested in another Plaxton bodied coach for the 2002 coaching season. Pictured here at Waterloo Garage on 14th April 2002, just 10 weeks after delivery, is **CU51 HVS** (195) a Dennis R410 with Plaxton 'Paragon' C49FT coachwork. It was sold to Moseley (dealer) in April 2008 and quickly passed to Taylor's of Yeovil where it operated in full Silcox livery minus Silcox lettering – which was replaced with Taylor's name.   *(V. Morgan).*

Above: Another coach holiday company Silcox contracted to was Alfa Coach Holidays of Chorley, Lancs. The Alfa livery was applied to this 12 metre Dennis 'Javelin' **CV02 HBN** (196) which was acquired new in March 2002 fitted with Caetano 'Enigma' C53F coachwork. It was withdrawn in July 2011 and sold for scrap a year later. A very short life! *(V. Morgan).*

Above: Fleet number 24 was carried by **CV02 HBO** a Dennis Dart SLF with Caetano 'Compass' B33F body delivered in April 2002. I captured this one on the bus stand at Upper Park Road, Tenby on Sunday 30th August 2009, complete with advertisements for the legendary Llanelli RFC 'Scarlets' – well supported across west Wales. **CV02 HBO** was about to commence service 349 to Haverfordwest, terminating at Withybush Hospital (Haverfordwest). This service was operated by First Cymru Buses Monday - Saturday, but the local authority tendered Sunday service had successfully been won by Silcox. *(V. Morgan).*

Above: The second Caetano 'Compass' bodied Dennis Dart SLF delivered in April 2002 was consecutively registered **CV02 HBP** (23) and is seen here at Eastern Avenue, Pembroke Dock working the company's frequent 357 service to Monkton via Pembroke town on 7th August 2007. This bus worked continuously until its M O T (C o F) expired in May 2016, and was sold at the official receivers auction in July 2016 for scrap, regarded as un-roadworthy without a Certificate of Fitness. *(V. Morgan).*

Above: This Mercedes Benz 413CDi 'Sprinter' **FY02 YHF** (197) with 16 seat coachwork by Optare was new to Silcox in August 2002 and normally carried coach livery. Nevertheless, it's seen here at North Beach car park Tenby on 13th July 2004 working the newly registered annual Tenby Park & Ride service, supported by the local authority. All of the Silcox lettering had been covered by vinyl stickers promoting the free service from the car park to the walled town and harbour. The service which operated annually during the peak summer holiday period, allowed closure of the walled town streets to normal traffic. *(V. Morgan).*

Above: This very unusual coach **FY02 WHD** (194) was another Mercedes Benz 'Atego' 1223L which came as a replacement for the 'Atego' lost in a fire a month earlier. Delivered in August 2002, **FY02 WHD** had the same type lorry chassis, and carried the same fleet number as its predecessor Y733 OBE (194) but was built by a different coachbuilder. Having very pleasing lines, this coachwork was built by Optare with a C39F body named 'Solera'. This was photographed on 13th April 2003, and to promote its lines even further a rear view is included below.   *(V. Morgan).*

Above: This photograph shows the very neat lines of the Optare 'Solera' C39F coach, **FY02 WHD** (194) built on the Mercedes Benz 'Atego' lorry chassis – see also the picture above.   *(V. Morgan).*

TURBULENT TIMES

After David Silcox's sudden departure from the company in December 2002 there were major issues concerning the car dealership business operated by the associated company, W L Silcox & Son Ltd, of which David Silcox had been manager. Their Rover and LDV dealership had ended in January 2003 followed by complete closure of the remaining car dealership (Renault, Kia and Jeep) along with the motor car repair business and petrol station on 8th April 2003.

A rift had emerged between the brothers David and Keith Silcox, directors of the business four months earlier, and in a statement to the local newspaper, a member of Silcox's staff said 'pressures from new competition such as internet car sales had had a significant impact on the business. Even though the Welsh Development Agency had tried to help, it was difficult to compete with the internet when people could buy a car for a few thousand pounds cheaper than a local dealer'.

David Silcox in the meantime independently started a car and van hire business some 400 metres away from Waterloo Garage at Paterchurch, London Road, Pembroke Dock, and later expanded to include a Self-Storage business.

Above: W L Silcox & Son Ltd, Waterloo Garage, Pembroke Dock. This is a view of their Texaco petrol station, garage forecourt, car showroom and motor car workshops circa 2002. In the foreground is Eastern Avenue, with London Road and the famous pub named 'The First and Last' (painted white) on the left hand side. Part of the bus garage (with vents on the roof) can be seen on the right, behind the car showroom and car workshops.   *(The Omnibus Society collection).*

The company's troubles however did not end there as notification was issued from the Department of Transport (VOSA) in May 2003 of a public enquiry (No 26898) to be held on 16th June 2003, where consideration of disciplinary action against the transport manager's repute would be taken with regard to their maintenance facilities. The end result of this public enquiry was: 'That the operator be given a final warning with regard to their maintenance facilities'.

Simultaneously, the management of Swansea based '2 Travel Ltd' and 'First Cymru Buses Ltd' were eagerly watching the precarious situation and offered assistance.

Despite all these difficulties, Silcox Motor Coach Company continued as normal with additional work constantly arriving.

Above: This was Silcox's Tenby depot/outstation at the North Beach car park on 13th April 2003, where a total of 15 vehicles were parked. Cleaning, fuelling and daily vehicle check facilities were provided here from a company owned shed at the car park entrance.

The following local service registration was granted under short notice on 19/6/2003:-

PG0004902/35 **Maidenwells** to **Maidenwells** via: Pembroke, Lamphey and Freshwater East.
Service to run Monday – Sunday including b/holiday 19/7/2003 – 28/9/2003.
Route No 387. (Summer timetable). Starting 19/7/2003. Four journeys daily.

Service 387 was soon amended and re-registered for winter operation on Tue/Thu/Sat only:-

PG0004902/36 **Maidenwells** to **Maidenwells** via: Pembroke and Lamphey.
Route No 387. (Winter timetable). Starting 30/9/2003. Tue/Thu/Sat, only.

PG0004902/37 **Carmarthen** to **Amroth** via: Johnstown, Laugharne and Pendine.
To run every Sunday - except bank holidays.
Route No 222.   Starting 25/1/2004.

The 222 Sunday service above was the first of many services gained from <u>Carmarthenshire C C</u>, through successful tendering. This extended the company's operating area into Carmarthen.

Local services cancelled from 29/7/2003 were PG0004902/14 & 15 (previously PG 6101/4902 & PG 6100/4902 respectively) with route Nos 388 & 387. These route numbers were re-used later.

As from 2nd September 2003, PG0004902/24 (previously PG 4217/4902) service 333 Tenby to Carmarthen was extended to start from Pembroke Dock (Laws Street), with continued funding from Pembrokeshire C C until November 2008 when it became commercially operated (see page 218/29).

Successful tendering of a local service to Carmarthenshire County Council in January 2004 brought-

Above: **RIL 1476** (25) previously registered *G445 LEP* was acquired as **RIL 1476** from a Birmingham operator in June 2003. New in 1990, this Mercedes Benz 811D had bodywork built by L.H.E. to C24FL layout, converted to DP16FL by Silcox in 2006 for the newly acquired tendered service 387/388, operating from Pembroke to Angle via Bosherston and Stackpole which was branded 'Coastal Cruiser'. It received this special livery to promote the daily service, and by March 2008 received a completely new redesigned all over branding for the same 'Coastal Cruiser' service.

Above: Captured here at Tenby outstation carrying an all over branding for the free bus service to the 'Asda' store at Pembroke Dock is **VAW 527**, (previously *D372 UVL*) a 1986 Leyland 'Tiger' TRCTL11/3R with Duple 'Caribbean II' C53F coachwork. It was acquired in June 2003 from James Bros, Llangeitho, Cardiganshire, and was given this cherished registration in September 2003 when it was first licenced. Finally withdrawn in February 2009, it was cut up at Waterloo Garage in November 2010.

-Silcox their first tendered work for that authority, which inevitably soon led to further awards within the county. The Carmarthenshire C C tendered services registered in February 2004 were:-

PG0004902/38 **Carmarthen (Bus Station)** to **Middleton Hall** via: Capel Dewi.
Monday – Saturday, except Christmas day, Boxing day and New Year's day.
Route No 166.   Starting 5/4/2004.   Normal stops/hail & ride.

PG0004902/39 **Carmarthen (Bus Station)** to **Abergwili (Church)** via: Abbey Mead.
Monday – Saturday, except Christmas day, Boxing day and New Year's day.
Route No 281.   Starting 5/4/2004.   Normal stops/hail & ride.

PG0004902/40 **Carmarthen (Bus Station)** to **Brynmeurig Estate**.
Monday – Saturday, except Christmas day, Boxing day and New Year's day.
Service to replace a similar service withdrawn by Bysiau Cwm-Taf.
Route No 208 (later 207/208). Starting 5/4/2004. Normal stops/hail & ride.

PG0004902/41 **Carmarthen (Bus Station)** to **Russell Terrace** via: St Catherine Street.
Monday – Saturday, except Christmas day, Boxing day and New Year's day.
Route No 205.   Starting 5/4/2004.   Normal stops/hail & ride.

PG0004902/42 **Carmarthen (Bus Station)** to **Johnstown**.
Monday – Saturday, except Christmas day, Boxing day and New Year's day.
Route No B11.   Starting 5/4/2004.   Normal stops/hail & ride.

PG0004902/43 **Carmarthen (Bus Station)** to **Abbey Mead.**
Monday – Saturday, except Christmas day, Boxing day and New Year's day.
Route No B12.   Starting 5/4/2004.   Normal stops/hail & ride.

PG0004902/44 **Carmarthen (Bus Station)** to **Heol Bolahaul** (Cwmffrwd).
Monday – Saturday, except Christmas day, Boxing day and New Year's day.
Route No B13.   Starting 5/4/2004.   Normal stops/hail & ride.

PG0004902/45 **Carmarthen (Bus Station)** to **Richmond Terrace**.
Monday – Saturday, except Christmas day, Boxing day and New year's day.
Route No B14.   Starting 5/4/2004.   Normal stops/hail & ride.

Pembrokeshire supported services registered February and April 2004 were:-

PG0004902/46 **Tenby (Upper Park Road)** to **Pendine** via: Saundersfoot and Kilgetty.
Mon – Sat, incl B/H, except Christmas day, Boxing day and New Year's day.
Route No 351.   Starting 5/4/2004.   Normal stops/hail & ride.

PG0004902/17 **Tenby – Amroth,** (previously PG4216/4902) was *cancelled from 5/4/2004, and was re-registered as* PG0004902/47 *below.*

PG0004902/47 **Tenby (Upper Park Road)** to **Amroth,** via Saundersfoot.
To operate every Sunday, summer only - as timetabled.
Route No 350.   Starting 2/5/2004.   Normal stops/hail & ride.

On 11th September 2004, Leonard W Silcox, entrepreneur and driving force behind the Silcox Motor Coach Company sadly passed away at the age of 81. Leonard, with an engineering degree had designed and assisted with the construction of his own bus and coach bodies in the immediate post war period 1949-54, photographs and details of these vehicles can be seen on pages 25-32.

The funeral was held at St Andrews Presbyterian Church, Pembroke Dock, with the coffin being carried into the church the evening before by six long serving employees. Family and friends were joined by a very large number of present and retired Silcox employees. As the cortege passed the Silcox premises on the way to Parc Gwyn Crematorium at Narberth, a number of Silcox Coaches and their drivers were lined up in front of the premises to allow more of the staff to pay their respects.

After Leonard passed away, his son Keith and grandson Jason took full control of the family concern, Keith becoming the new Managing Director.

Further local services awarded to Silcox by Carmarthenshire C C arrived in November 2004:-

PG0004902/48   **Carmarthen (Bus Station)** to **Johnstown (Davies' Estate)**.
                   via: St Davids Hospital, Johnstown and Maridunum School.   Mon – Sat.
                   This service replaced a similar service withdrawn by Bysiau Cwm-Taf.
                   Route No 226/228.   Starting 9/11/2004.
                                   Service cancelled from 4/9/2005 - passed to Morris Travel.

PG0004902/49   **Carmarthen (Bus Station)** to **Bancyfelin (Fox & Hounds)**,
                   via: Johnstown and Parc-y-ffordd.   Monday - Saturday
                   This service replaced a similar service withdrawn by Bysiau Cwm-Taf.
                   Route No 241.   Starting 9/11/2004.
                        Service later incorporated into 222/224 operated by Bysiau Cwm-Taf.

Above: L865 LFS (10) was one of two Mercedes Benz 711Ds acquired from Coakley Bus, Motherwell, Scotland in October 2004. L865 LFS is seen here exiting Carmarthen bus station on tendered service 208 to Brynmeurig Estate on 27th July 2005, again not displaying a destination blind. This and its partner L867 LFS (11) had Plaxton 'Beaver' B25F bodies. *(V. Morgan).*

Above: This Mercedes Benz 'Sprinter' 410D with a Mellor B14FL conversion and tail lift was new in March 1998 to Wrexham C B C, registered as **R414 VCC**. It passed to Silcox in April 2004 where it was given f/n 27, and re-registered with cherished registration 817 FKH in May 2004, as seen below. It was seen here on 25th May 2004, before its re-registration. *(V. Morgan)*

Above: This is the same Mercedes Benz 'Sprinter' as seen above - registered R414 VCC, which had been re-registered **817 FKH** in May 2004. I captured **817 FKH** (27) here on Crackwell Street, Tenby working the annual 'Tenby Park & Ride' service from North Beach car park to picturesque Tenby harbour on 30th August 2009. It was a free service operated at 15 minute intervals on behalf of Pembrokeshire C C, enabling closure of all streets within the walled town between 10.00 – 18.15 each day during the peak holiday period July/August. *(V. Morgan)*

Above: This Optare 'Alero' **YN04 LXJ** (26) was purchased in April 2004 to operate Carmarthenshire County Council's newly introduced Carmarthen Town Dial-a-Ride services. Silcox gained this contract together with seven other services in Carmarthen after successful tendering to the Carmarthenshire authority. The 'Alero' however was not a good choice of vehicle and was replaced by an Optare 'Solo' in less than 2 years. **YN04 LXJ** is seen here leaving Carmarthen Bus Station on the service's first day of operation 5/4/2004 - minus a destination blind. That would normally be regarded as an offence committed by the operator, resulting in a fine from the local authority, but on this occasion the blind was not delivered on time!   *(V. Morgan).*

Above: Pictured at the same location as the 'Alero' above, some 2 years later, is this 8.5 metre Transbus 'Dart' **CU04 AUW** (28) with Transbus 'Mini-Pointer' B29F bodywork. It was purchased in May 2004 for the new services at Carmarthen, but is captured here working a <u>Pembrokeshire</u> supported service 322 to Narberth on 12th August 2006.   *(V. Morgan).*

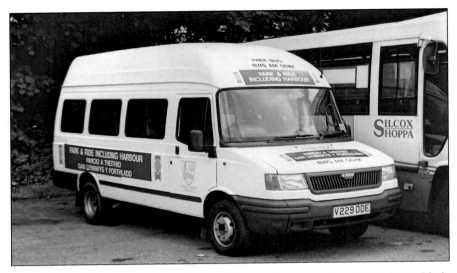

Above: **V229 DDE** (29) was one of the four LDV 'Convoy' 16 seat mini-buses acquired from Netherwood House School, Saundersfoot in May 2004. It was seen here at North Beach car park Tenby on 7th August 2005 still displaying the Netherwood House School's logo on the front doors, but also carrying branding for the Tenby 'Park & Ride' service, which it was operating that day to the harbour. *(V. Morgan).*

Above: As we have already seen, Silcox had several styles of liveries but this attractive looking coach must have the best livery of all. New to the company in February 2005, ready for the new 'Silcox Coach Holiday' season, carrying personalised registration **CU54 KWS** (Keith Wm Silcox) and f/n 198, was this Volvo B12B with Caetano 'Enigma' C53FT coachwork. It was downseated to C49FT for extra passenger comfort – more leg room on the companys own holiday programme. This coach was sold at auction by the administrators in July 2016 with no further trace! This picture was taken on 15th April 2007. *(V. Morgan).*

Above: Delivery of this MAN 14.200 with MCV 'Evolution' B40F bodywork in March 2005 was quite a change from the usual purchases. Nevertheless, the management were quite pleased with **CU05 DME** (30) as it went on to stay in their possession until the company's demise in June 2016, sold at the auction to Autocar of Five Oaks Green, Kent. It was seen here at Tenby about to leave on the company's lengthy route to Haverfordwest, service 381 via Saundersfoot and Narberth. *(V. Morgan).*

Right: This was the badly faded sign placed outside Town Wall Arcade, Tenby (Nelsons Walk), pointing towards Silcox's coach tour booking office; No 2 Nelson Walk. It will be noticed that Silcox were also booking agents for the 'National Express' services.

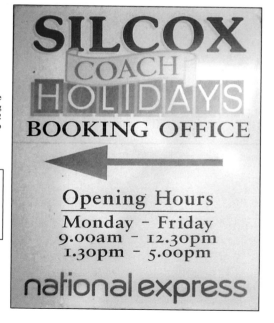

Local service registrations made by the company during 2005/6 were as follows:-

PG0004902/50 **Tenby (Salterns Car Park)** to **Tenby (Salterns Car Park)** via South Parade.
Monday – Sunday including bank holiday, 10.00 – 18.13, until 4/9/2005.
Park & Ride circular service. *Limited stops.* *Starting 2/7/2005.*

PG0004902/51 **Tenby (North Beach C P)** to **Tenby (North Beach C P)** via Tenby Harbour.
Monday – Sunday including bank holiday, 10.00 – 18.13, until 4/9/2005.
Park & Ride (Walled Town scheme). *Limited stops.* *Starting 2/7/2005.*

PG0004902/52 **Haverfordwest (Bus Station)** to **Haverfordwest (Bus Stn)** Town circular.
Monday – Saturday except bank holidays.
Route No 301. *Starting 9/1/2006.*

PG0004902/53 **Haverfordwest (Bus Station)** to **Haverfordwest (Bus Station)**
via: Little Haven and Walton West. *To run on schooldays only.*
Route No 310. *Starting 9/1/2006.*

The services numbered 301/310 above had previously been operated by First Cymru Buses Ltd, and were awarded to Silcox by Pembrokeshire C C, through successful tendering.

Service No 390, Tenby to Cardigan was cancelled from 29/5/2006 (PG0004902/19). Additionally, the school service Pembroke Dock (Ferry Lane) to Pembroke Secondary School was cancelled from 5/1/2006 (PG0004902/1).

Above: Captured here at Glangwili Hospital Carmarthen, working a new extension to the 222 Sunday service on 1st May 2006 is **CV55 AXW** (16) a 33 seater Optare 'Solo' M920. It's on lay-over here before the 16.05 return journey to Amroth, via Carmarthen Bus Station, Laugharne and Pendine, operated by Silcox on Sundays only, contracted to Carmarthenshire C.C.   *(V. Morgan).*

Above: It was mentioned on page 204 that Silcox purchased an Optare 'Solo' to replace the unreliable 22 month old Optare 'Alero' - well this was the replacement vehicle, **CV55 BAU** which even took the Alero fleet number **26. CV55 BAU** was a 22 seat Optare 'Solo' M780SL new in February 2006, and is seen here at Carmarthen on 7th April 2006, working the local authority tendered Carmarthen Town 'Dial-a-Ride' service, which included this B11 timetabled service to Llanllwch.   *(V. Morgan).*

Above: This Caetano 'Enigma' C49FT bodied Volvo B12B registered **CV55 AZN** (199) was delivered February 2006 in full 'Grand UK Holidays' livery for that particular coach holiday company's contracted work. However, it was repainted into Silcox Coach Holidays livery by July 2009 after the 'Grand UK Holidays' contract had ended. CV55 AZN is seen here at Waterloo Garage on 4th November 2006. *(V. Morgan).*

Above: Alfa Coach Holidays, Chorley, Lancs was another coach holiday company which Silcox contracted to on a regular basis, hence the Alfa livery on this Volvo B12B, **CU06 ANP** (184) with Caetano 'Enigma' C49FT coachwork. This was new in April 2006, and I captured it here outside the Boar's Head Hotel, Lammas Street, Carmarthen on 16th August 2006, unloading a coach load of holidaymakers on a day excursion from Tenby. This particular part of Lammas Street was the towns original bus terminus before the bus station was built in 1975, but is still the official pick up and drop off point for touring coaches. *(V. Morgan).*

Above: Seen here at Bridge Street, Tenby, overlooking Tenby Harbour, is another Mercedes Benz 'Sprinter' 410D, **S862 BHR** (12) working the towns 'Free Park & Ride' service from North Beach car park to the Harbour on 30th August 2009. S862 BHR is pictured carrying the livery of the 'Coastal Cruiser' service beneath the vinyl stickers applied for the P & R service. *(V Morgan)*

Above: This Volvo B10M-56, **D113 GHY** with Alexander 'P type' B54F body was new to Badgerline in 1987, and was acquired from First Somerset & Avon in February 2007. It remained in 'First' livery throughout its stay here, on contract work for Shaw's at the South Hook LNG Terminal. It returned to PSV use with a later owner, C A Rees of Llanelli in January 2009. *(V Morgan)*

Above: **H613 UWR** was a Volvo B10M-60 with Plaxton 'Paramount 3500' bodywork to C46FT layout on arrival in October 2006. It was new in April 1991 to coach operator Wallace Arnold Tours, and acquired by Silcox from First Western National (2258) via Munden (dealer) Bristol. H613 UWR is pictured here ready to leave the depot for Blackpool on 15th April 2007 for a full refurbishment. Incidentally it broke down on that journey - in mid Wales, and had to be recovered. *(V. Morgan).*

Above: This was **H613 UWR** (178) after Silcox spent around £20,000 on a full refurbishment, complete with a new look front end and P60 wing mirrors (drop mirrors) simular to the Irizar. The conversion by John Walker Styling/Blackpool Coach Services (Burton Rd) FY4 4NW was probably the last Plaxton 'Paramount' conversion carried out by them before their demise in 2007, and was one of just 2 dozen Plaxton 'Paramount' front end rebuilds carried out by Blackpool Coach Services. It finally entered service in July 2007 as a 50 seater, but was it worth spending all that money to renovate a sixteen year old coach in addition to its purchase cost. This photograph was taken on 4th May 2008, but see next page. *(V Morgan).*

Above: In September 2014, the Volvo B10M-60 seen opposite, H613 UWR (178) was re-registered with cherished registration mark **NSV 324**. That registration mark had previously been used on a former M o D Leyland 'Tiger' (221), which by now had been withdrawn. In its new guise, **NSV 324** (*H613 UWR*) is seen here at Trostre Park, Llanelli on 24th September 2014, on a lay-over between school journeys. It was working one of the longest school journeys in Wales, starting from Milford Haven, it picked up children along its 60 mile route via Haverfordwest to St Michaels Independent School at Llanelli. *(V. Morgan).*

Above: **N952 NAP** (11) was a Mercedes Benz 709D with Alexander 'Sprint' B23F bodywork, which had been new to Stagecoach 'East Kent' in 1996. It arrived at Silcox in May 2007 via Munden, Bristol and is seen here alongside the ancient 'Town Wall' at South Parade, Tenby on 24th March 2008, accompanied by Optare 'Solo' YC51 HAO. Visible on the right hand side of this view is the entrance to 'Nelson Walk' (Town Wall Arcade), where the company had an enquiry office/tours booking office, previously occupied by competitor Tenby Bus & Coach Co, and acquired after their demise in 1991. *(V. Morgan).*

Above: This Mercedes Benz 'Atego' 1324L with Ferqui 'Solera II' (Optare 'Solera') C37FT coachwork arrived at Pembroke Dock in March 2007 registered **YX07 AWV** (197). This was Silcox's third coach built on the 'Atego' chassis, and had been displayed at the 2006 Eurobus-Expo exhibition prior to delivery, carrying registration number YX56 AFV. That registration mark nevertheless was voided due to its first licensing not being until March 2007, after the change of 'age identifier' numbers. It was exchanged for registration mark **YX07 AWV** before delivery. This coach was in great demand here due to its size, and remained with the company until their demise – sold to a local operator at Narberth through the administrator's online auction. This photograph was taken on 15th April 2007.   *(V. Morgan).*

Above: Silcox acquired this Optare 'Solo' M850, **MX04 VLT** (10) in June 2007 as a 29 seater, but reduced it to 27 seats to allow extra wheelchair space. It was previously operated by Hutt of Finstock, Oxford but new to Stagecoach (47155) in April 2004. Silcox withdrew it from service in 2015 with engine failure, and was sold as a non runner at the administrator's auction July 2016 to Go-Goodwins, Eccles, Gtr Manchester. I photographed it here at Tenby outstation on 30th September 2007.   *(V. Morgan).*

Above: Another former Ministry of Defence 12 metre Dennis 'Javelin' to arrive at the stable was **P384 YHT** (177) in August 2007. New in July 1997 to the Royal Navy, it had previously been registered *17 RN 09, P539 SUS, 17 RN 09*, and received its Bristol registration P384 YHT whilst with the dealer. The coachwork was built by UVG to C70F layout, but increased to 71 seats by Silcox. This coach was sold by the administrator's at the auction for £4,050.   *(V. Morgan).*

Above: This particular Optare 'Solo' M950, **MX07 BAO** (22) was one of a pair - MX07 BAO/BCE delivered in March 2007. MX07 BAO was fitted with 30 seats at the time this photograph was taken on 30th August 2009, but was later upseated to 33. It's seen here at Upper Park Road, Tenby on a short working of the 352 service - terminating at Saundersfoot. This vehicle passed to Pickford, Chippenham after the administrator's auction.   *(V. Morgan).*

In the meantime a wide variety of issues arose from the company's operations at Carmarthen. Firstly, there were operational problems on services 207/226/228 which included lack of destination blinds as seen in the photographs on page 203/5 and secondly, problems recruiting 'quality' drivers, which resulted in drivers travelling daily from Pembroke Dock to operate three buses based at their unregistered Carmarthen outstation, located at 'Smiths Mechanical Services Ltd' (Tachograph Centre), Allt-y-cnap Road, Johnstown, Carmarthen. Their plan to extend into Carmarthen failed, as Carmarthenshire C C terminated the contract for the 'Dial-a-ride' services B11-B14 owing to poor performance. In turn Silcox cancelled their remaining four tendered Carmarthenshire services and retreated back to Pembroke Dock after only four years. The services cancelled were:-

PG0004902/38	Service No 166	Cancelled from 30/12/2007.
PG0004902/39	Service No 281	Cancelled from 1/1/2008.
PG0004902/40	Service No 207/208	Cancelled from 30/12/2007.
PG0004902/41	Service No 205	Cancelled from 30/12/2007.
PG0004902/42-45	Service No B11-B14	Cancelled from 30/12/2007.

All of the above services passed to First Cymru Buses, registered to start from 31/12/2007.

In September 2008, two more family members were appointed directors of the company, Mrs Maria E Silcox; wife of Keith W Silcox (MD) and his son Jason Ian Silcox.

Above: Seen here at Blue Street, Carmarthen on 27th February 2010, having exited Carmarthen bus station through the tunnel beneath 'Greyfriars Shopping Centre' is dealer registered **SN08 AAJ** (34) an Alexander-Dennis 'Enviro 300'. This was new to the company in March 2008 as a 55 seater, but was later converted to 47 to accommodate wheelchairs. Delivered in this all-over yellow livery, **SN08 AAJ** was working the 10.30 am Pembrokeshire C C supported, three times daily 322 service from Carmarthen to Haverfordwest bus station via Narberth and Withybush Hospital. *(V. Morgan)*.

Above: The company's first VDL Bova 'Futura' was delivered in April 2008. Dealer registered **WA08 JVX**, it received f/n 100, and was built in the Netherlands by the Dutch manufacturer VDL Bova, having model number FHD127.365 it was fitted with 53 seats and a toilet. It was seen here when just two months old, on 22nd June 2008, carrying the livery of Silcox Coach Holidays – a livery it retained until the company's demise. *(V. Morgan).*

Above: Another dealer registered coach arrived at the establishment in May 2008. **YN08 NKJ** (101) was a 12 metre Alexander-Dennis 'Javelin' with Plaxton 'Profile' C53F coachwork, and is seen here on 28th June 2009 lettered in the livery of 'Silcox Coaches'. The company however, must have received an excellent payment in August 2012 to repaint this coach into an all-over advertisement for 'Samsung Electronics Co Ltd', for use during the 2012 Olympic Games. It returned to normal fleet livery immediately afterwards. *(V. Morgan).*

After serious consideration in October 2008, Pembrokeshire C C decided to withdraw support on the unremunerative daily 333 service operated by Silcox between Pembroke Dock, Tenby and Carmarthen (PG0004902/24). The registration was cancelled from 10/11/2008, but Silcox unwisely decided to register the service on a commercially operated basis as shown below:-

PG0004902/54   **Pembroke Dock** to **Carmarthen (Bus Station)** via Tenby.
To operate one journey in each direction on <u>Wednesdays & Fridays</u> only.
Route No 333.   *Starting 12/11/2008. (See also page 229).*

In April 2009, the following council funded services were registered:-

PG0004902/55   **Haverfordwest (Withybush Hospital)** to **Tenby (Upper Park Road)**.
To operate on Sundays only (on behalf of Pembrokeshire C C)
Route No 349.   *Starting 6/4/2009.*   *(Operated by First Cymru Mon-Sat).*

PG0004902/56   **Haverfordwest (Bus Station)** to **Wiston.**
To operate Monday-Saturday (Operated on behalf of Pembrokeshire C C).
Route No 313.   *Starting 6/4/2009.*

PG0004902/57   **Hubberston** to **Milford Haven Comprehensive School.**
To operate on schooldays only.
Route No 319.   *Starting 20/4/2009.*

PG0004902/58   **Haverfordwest (Bus Station)** to **Cashfields Estate**   *(Monday-Saturday).*
Route No 303.   *Starting 6/4/2009.*   *(Operated on behalf of Pembs C C).*

Above: In June 2009, five Ford Transit mini-buses were leased from Day's Rental Company for use as 'Crew Mini-buses' at the South Hook LNG Terminal. Pictured here at Waterloo on 28th June 2009 is 'Crew Mini-bus No 4' **CV57 HMU** a Ford Transit 16 seater dating from 2007. The other four Transits operated are listed in the fleet-list on page 280.   *(V. Morgan).*

Above: WA04 EWT (102) was a pre-used Volvo B12M with Van-Hool 'Alizee' C49FT coachwork which arrived in March 2010 from a Gloucestershire operator, Astra Coaches, Andoversford. This coach was new to Astra Coaches in March 2004 as a 49 seater with toilet, but the toilet was removed by Silcox, increasing the seating capacity to 53. This photograph was taken on18th March 2011. *(V. Morgan)*.

Above: This Optare 'Solo' M710SE, registered **YJ10 EXU** was one of a pair purchased by Pembrokeshire C C in April 2010 for their 'Coastal Bus Service'. The pair of 23 seaters – YJ10 EXU/EXV were operated and maintained by Silcox staff on behalf of the local authority, and received fleet numbers 36/7 in the Silcox series. **YJ10 EXU** is seen here with this very colourful branding at South Parade, Tenby, on lay-over whilst the driver took his well earned lunch break on 18th June 2014. *(V. Morgan)*.

Above: In addition to the Optare 'Solos' mentioned on the previous page as owned by Pembrokeshire County Council, they also owned a couple of coaches which operated school services in the county. Pictured here at Tenby on 27th September 2010 is **DX10 DXR**, one of a pair of Autosan A10-12T coaches owned and operated by the local authority, but maintained at Silcox's workshops.
(V. Morgan).

Above: Acquired from Trent-Barton (901) in May 2010 was this 1996 Dennis 'Dart' SLF, **P901 CTO** (38) with Plaxton 'Pointer' B40F bodywork. It was captured here at South Parade, Tenby on 25th July 2010 still in the Trent-Barton livery, working the annual Tenby Park & Ride service between South Parade and Salterns car park via Upper Park Road and Park Road at 15 minute intervals on behalf of Pembrokeshire C C. This bus eventually received fleet livery in 2013, and was re-registered **SIL 9613** in April 2015, but was withdrawn a month later due to engine failure. It appeared on the administrator's auction list in June 2016 minus its cherished registration mark, selling for £10 - as scrap.
(V. Morgan).

Above: Bus number 39, **T430 KAG** was another Dennis 'Dart' SLF with Plaxton 'Pointer' B34D body acquired in June 2010. New in February 1999, this one came from London United (DP30) and was later converted to B35F layout by Silcox upon removal of its centre doorway. This also came out of service in 2015, and sold for £10 at the administrator's auction.   *(V. Morgan).*

Above: This 2001 Bova 'Futura' FHD12-370 registered **RLZ 1670** received fleet number 236. It had previously carried cherished registration *Y14 DLC* with Dealtop Coaches, Clyst St Mary, Devon and was acquired by Silcox in September 2010 as a 49 seater with toilet. It's toilet was removed before conversion into a 70 seat coach (3+2 seating) for the carriage of school children, and sold to Llew Jones, Llanrwst, North Wales in the final auction. This view was taken on 27 september 2010.   *(V. Morgan).*

Above: **P771 BJF** (237) was a 1997 Dennis 'Javelin' with Caetano 'Algarve' C70F coachwork (3+2 seating) acquired from Tilley, Wainhouse Corner, near Bude, Cornwall in October 2010. P771 BJF was new to Tilley in January 1997 but had carried a personalised registration mark *TIL 1260* for a period of time during Tilley's ownership, reverting to P771 BJF again before disposal. In May 2012 however, Silcox re-registered it with a much used cherished registration, as seen below. *(V. Morgan).*

Above: **804 SHW** (237) pictured here at Tenby on 6th October 2013 is the same vehicle as shown in the upper view – P771 BJF. The registration mark **804 SHW**, originally salvaged off a Bristol 'Lodekka' had been used by the company for several re-registrations, but was removed by the administrators in June 2016, and sold at a separate auction from the coach. *(V. Morgan).*

Above: Another Dennis 'Javelin' purchased in October 2010 for school contract work was **S488 UAK** (238) seen here with Plaxton 'Premiere 320' coachwork seating 57. It arrived at the Silcox stable from Jones, Burley Gate (Hereford & Worcester) and was new in January 1999. This coach regularly worked a school contract from Milford Haven and Haverfordwest to St Michaels Independent School, Llanelli.

(V. Morgan).

Right: In June 2010, a pair of preserved Bristol MW6Gs arrived at Waterloo Garage, a mark which had left the fleet almost 30 years earlier in 1982. The two ECW coach bodied 39 seater MWs, registered **617 DDV** and 573 UVX respectively were owned by the Bluestone Leisure Park, but were maintained and operated by Silcox staff, and ran on Silcox's operator discs. They were used to perform local tours for the holidaymakers and guests of Bluestone, but only operated for one season before they were sold. **617 DDV** seen here on 18th March 2011 had been restored to its former glory, in the livery of Royal Blue its original operator.

(V. Morgan).

Left: In December 2010, two more Optare 'Solo' M710SEs arrived at Waterloo Garage registered YJ60 LRL/N respectively. These again were again owned by Pembrokeshire C C and given fleet numbers 41/2 in the Silcox series for identification purposes during maintenance. Operated on behalf of the local authority, both were painted in the livery of 'The Little Green Bus', with bi-lingual branding for the council tendered 'Little Green Bus' services, numbered 301/303/304/305. **YJ60 LRL** (41) is seen here on 26th June 2011.

Below: The second Optare 'Solo' 26 seater supplied to Silcox by the local authority in December 2010, for use on 'The Little Green Bus' network of services at Haverfordwest was also seen on 26th June 2011. This was registered **YJ60 LRN** with a Silcox fleet no 42.

Local services registered in 2010 on behalf of Pembs CC, branded 'The Little Green Bus' were:-

PG0004902/59   **Haverfordwest (Withybush Hosp)** circular via: Bus Station, Tesco, Furzey Park, Trafalgar Rd, Portfield. Route No 304. Mon – Sat. Starting 11/11/2010.

PG0004902/60   **Haverfordwest (Bus Station)** Town circular via: Pembrokeshire College and Leisure Centre.   Route No 305. Mon – Sat. Starting 11/11/2010.

Above: Two former London General, Dennis 'Dart' SLF's (LDP 103/7) were purchased in November 2011 and were pressed into service without receiving fleet livery. Seen here at Tenby during the drivers lunch break on 3rd December 2011 is **S103 EGK** (43) a Plaxton 'Pointer' B29D bodied SLF, which soon lost its centre doorway. See picture below. *(V. Morgan).*

Below: Silcox did a neat job of converting **S103 EGK** (above) into single entrance layout as shown here when it emerged from the 'Works' as **B29F**. It retained the same seating capacity by re-arranging the seats to allow a larger wheelchair space on the nearside. Simultaneously, in May 2012 it was re-registered with the much used personalised registration mark **A4 WLS**, and later received branding for the Tenby to Haverfordwest (Withybush Hospital) 381 service. It sold at the administrator's on-line auction in July 2016 for £400 without the personalised registration number. *(V. Morgan).*

Above: Former London General (LDP 107) **S107 EGK** (44) was another 1998 Dennis 'Dart' SLF with Plaxton 'Pointer' B29D body, and numerically the second SLF acquired from that source. It was captured here at the 'Works' on 6th May 2012 before conversion to single entrance B29F layout, and its sprucing up – note the tape holding the destination display together. *(V Morgan)*.

Below: **A5 WLS** was the end result of a splendid refurbishment to **S107 EGK** (44) pictured above. It was another very tidy refurbishment to a former London General Dennis 'Dart' SLF carried out in-house at Pembroke Dock in July 2012. **A5 WLS** *(S107 EGK)* is seen here on 23rd April 2013 loading up at Tenby (Upper Park Road), departure point of 352 service to Kilgetty (Rylands Lane) via New Hedges, Saundersfoot and Valley Road. This 'SLF' also received route branding before the company's sad end in June 2016, and with its personalised registration mark removed by the administrator for a separate sale, it sold at auction for £100. *(V. Morgan)*.

Above: In March 2012 two more former London General Dennis 'Dart' SLF's (LDP 90/113) were purchased via Metrobus London (388/7). One of the pair **S113 EGK** (45) is seen here at Tenby on 11th October 2012, converted to single door layout by Silcox, re-seated to B31F layout, repainted and branded for the busy Tenby to Haverfordwest 381 service, via Saundersfoot. See also the photograph below.

(V. Morgan).

Below: **A15 WLS** was the personalised registration mark given to S113 EGK (45) above in August 2015. This picture has a sad tale to it – as it was taken on Sunday 5th June 2016, Silcox's last day of operation. After trading ceased on 5th June all vehicles returned to the base at Pembroke Dock to await their fate – sold off by the administrator through an on-line auction. All the company's personalised and cherished registrations were removed before sale, creating a separate auction for registration marks. **A15 WLS** returned to its original registration S113 EGK and sold for £850.

(V. Morgan).

Above: Pictured here at Waterloo Garage on 6th May 2012 is **S638 JGP** (46) another 1998 Dennis 'Dart' SLF Plaxton 'Pointer' with B29D bodywork. New to London General (LDP 90) with cherished registration mark *WLT 990* in December 1998, it was later re-registered S638 JGP and eventually passed to Metrobus London (388) from whom it was acquired in March 2012.

(V. Morgan).

Above: This view of the former London General (LDP 90) Dennis 'Dart' SLF, **S638 JGP** (46) was taken at Tenby outstation on St Davids day 1st March 2013. It had been converted to single door by then, and re-painted into fleet livery complete with branding for the Tenby – Haverfordwest 381 service. In October 2014 it received cherished registration mark KSU 409, running as such until May 2015 when it was finally withdrawn with mechanical failure. Its cherished plate was removed by the administrator in June 2016, reverting to S638 JGP. It was sold at the administrators auction for £25.

(V. Morgan).

Above: This Optare 'Solo' M710SE with Optare B23F bodywork, **YJ60 KFP** was a dealer loan operating with Silcox in April 2011. I captured this at Upper Park Road, Tenby on 7th April 2011 working the Pembrokeshire C C supported service 351, Tenby to Pendine. The following month it was replaced with another dealer loan – Optare 'Solo' MX58 AAN. *(V. Morgan).*

On 8th December 2011, the company asked for authorisation of a new outstation located at Plot 8A Waterston Industrial Estate, Main Road, Waterston SA73 1DP, to replace Victoria Depository, at Waterston Industrial Estate. Authorisation was granted for nine vehicles at that location, and simultaneously an increase of three licence discs was made totalling 74. Directors were given as KW & RM Silcox and TE & DE Miller.

Four months later the 'Bus Service Operator Grant' (Fuel Duty Rebate) was cut by 25% and a 27% reduction made in 'Local Transport Service Grants' to the local authorities. This had a detrimental effect on rural bus services and bus operators, and as a direct result of this, there were several service cuts and curtailments. Cancelled services were:-

PG0004902/31	Service 302. **Hubberston** to **Haverfordwest.**	Cancelled from 30/9/2012.
PG0004902/47	Service 350. **Tenby** to **Amroth.**	Cancelled from 30/9/2012.
PG0004902/55	Service 349. **Haverfordwest** to **Tenby** (Sun only).	Cancelled from 30/9/2012.
PG0004902/57	Service 319. **Hubberston** to **M/Haven Comp Sch.**	Cancelled from 1/10/2012.
PG0004902/54	Service 333. **Pembroke Dock** to **Carmarthen.**	Cancelled from 21/11/2012.

Operation of service 333 above had been taken over by Silcox as a commercially operated service Wed/Sat only in November 2008, after Pembrokeshire C C withdrew the funding of a *daily* 333 service. Silcox allegedly withdrew this service because the bus was full – full of concessionary pass holders, and as the reimbursement rate was low, coupled with the aforementioned reduction in fuel duty rebate, the service was un-remunerative and cancelled.

In December 2012, Silcox were notified of a forthcoming public inquiry regarding adverse maintenance issues, to be held at Cardiff in April 2013. Transport Manager Keith W Silcox was also summoned to attend the meeting where consideration of his repute as manager would take place. The company and Keith were issued with final warnings, and licences were reduced to 65 vehicles.

Above: WA08 GPO (103) was a VDL Bova 'Futura' with C48FT (to C50FT) coachwork acquired in February 2012 from Rover European, Horsley, Glos. Registered as *WA08 GPO* when new, it carried registration *TO08 DRH* for a while at Rover European.

Above: XUD 367 (241) previously *P883 FMO, 1760 VC, P883 FMO* was one of three coaches acquired from Bodman, Worton, Wilts in June 2012. It had a Dennis 'Javelin' 12m chassis and Berkhof 'Axial' C53F bodywork new in April 1997. *(V Morgan)*

Above: Seen here outside Llanelli Police Station on 5th July 2012, on layover between school journeys – Milford Haven to Llanelli is **R708 NJH** (239) another 1997 12m Dennis 'Javelin' with Berkhof 'Axial' C53F coachwork, which was also acquired from Bodman, Worton, near Devizes, Wiltshire in June 2012. It received cherished registration mark – RIL 1476 as shown below in October 2012, returning to R708 NJH in the hands of the administrators in June 2016, and sold for £2700. *(V. Morgan).*

Above: Pictured almost on the same patch at Town Hall Square, Llanelli is the same vehicle as above, R708 NJH after it received cherished registration mark **RIL 1476** in October 2012. This photograph was taken on 22nd October 2012. *(V. Morgan).*

Above: The third vehicle acquired from Bodmin, of Worton, in June 2012 was this Volvo B10M-62 with Plaxton 'Premiere 320' C57F coachwork, registered **R50 TGM** (240). The registration indicates it was new to Tellings Golden Miller in May 1998. Again, I captured this coach on layover outside the Police Station, Town Hall Square, Llanelli, whilst working the school contract from Milford Haven to St Michaels Independent School, Llanelli on 3rd July 2012. This coach later received a re-paint in all-over white and was the last Silcox vehicle to receive cherished registration 538 OHU – see below. *(V. Morgan).*

Above: Volvo B10M-62/Plaxton, **538 OHU** was a re-registration of R50 TGM above in June 2013.

Above: The Dennis 'Javelin' chassis was a popular choice with the company in their final years, with no less than 30 passing through their ownership. **M17 SMC** (242), previously *M308 SHN, HIL 7540, M308 SHN* was another 12m 'Javelin' with Plaxton 'Premiere 350' C70F coachwork (3+2 seating), acquired from Mc Leans Coaches, Witney, Oxford in August 2012, and is pictured here on 4th May 2013. This coach was one that slipped through the administrators net – sold with its personalised registration mark to Llew Jones, Llanrwst for £3450. It was new to Walton, Stockton on Tees, Cleveland, in February 1995. *(V. Morgan).*

Above: South Parade, Tenby is the backdrop for this view of former Warrington B T (19) **Y619 GFM**, a Marshall 'Capital' B41F bodied Dennis 'Dart' SLF dating from 2001. Acquired in April 2013, it received fleet number 47 with Silcox, and is seen here about to leave Tenby on service 361 to Pembroke Dock via Saundersfoot, Kilgetty, Sageston, Cresswell Quay and Waterloo. This vehicle was sold at auction to Taf Valley Coaches, Whitland for £800, and regularly operates former Silcox services.

Above: **Y252 XHH** (245) previously registered *Y158 RLC*, was a Dennis 'Javelin' with Plaxton 'Premiere 320' coachwork acquired from the Ministry of Defence in September 2013 as a 57 seater. It was converted to C70F in February 2014 (3+2 seating) and was one of five 'Javelins' acquired from the M o D in 2013/4. **Y252 XHH** and six other Silcox vehicles passed to Edwards Coaches of Llantwit Fardre, along with the school contracts on 6ᵗʰ June 2016. *(V. Morgan)*.

Above: Acquired in January 2014 as *Y183 SRK* was another former Ministry of Defence Dennis 'Javelin' with Plaxton 'Premiere 320' C57F coachwork. This received fleet number 249 and was re-registered **Y154 EBY** in July 2014, when it was converted to C70F (3+2 seating). It was another coach which passed to Edwards, Llantwit Fardre with the school contracts. This view was taken on 16ᵗʰ July 2014. *(V. Morgan)*.

Above: I took this view of **SX02 WDS**, another former Ministry of Defence Dennis 'Javelin' on 6th October 2013. It entered service later that month re-registered **CT02 NAE** carrying fleet number 246. The picture below shows it 13 months later, still in all-over white livery as received.   *(V. Morgan).*

Above: **CT02 NAE** (246) was a re-registration of *SX02 WDS* above, a former M o D Dennis 'Javelin' with Plaxton 'Premiere 320' C57F coachwork. This picture was taken on 9th November 2014, and unlike its sisters, it was not upseated to 70, it remained at 57 and passed to Edwards Coaches, Llantwit Fardre with the school contracts on 6th June 2016.   *(V. Morgan).*

Registration of new local services had stopped in the previous three years, but the registration of PG0004902/61   **Carew Airfield** to **Tenby (Salterns Car Park)**, a Park & Ride service was introduced for the 'Ironman Wales' event and was registered for that one day only – 8ᵗʰ September 2013, and annually thereafter.

In the meantime, the company were experiencing serious financial problems and substantial changes were made to the board of directors. Family members Mrs R M Silcox, Mrs D E Miller and Mr T E Miller left the board on 24ᵗʰ June 2013 and were replaced by new directors and shareholders: Bakerbus Ltd, and Bakers Bus & Coach Ltd, of The Coach Travel Centre, Prospect Way, Biddulph, Stoke on Trent, ST8 7PL, together with a new chairman and financial director, Mr Mark Raymond Ready of Henderson Travel Ltd, These three new director shareholders were all linked to a Barbados based company calling themselves 'Island Fortitude Ltd'.

A summary of Silcox's accounts published on 31ˢᵗ August 2013 stated that the company was worth £647,045 with assets of £337,247 and liabilities amounting to £880,233; cash available £540.

By October 2013, King-Long Direct Ltd, Coventry (owned by the aforementioned Island Fortitude Ltd) had a major shareholding in the Silcox business, and placed a brand new Chinese built King-Long, 57 seat tri-axle coach into the fleet.

Above: The company's first Chinese built King-Long coach was put into the fleet by the new investors King-Long Direct Ltd, in October 2013. Dealer registered **BN63 NYD** (104) was a 13 metre tri-axle King-Long XMQ6130Y coach, fitted with a Cummins 8.9 litre engine coupled to a ZF 6 speed automatic transmission and C57FT coachwork. The investors also placed some pre-owned vehicles into the fleet, most of which had a rather short stay.   *(V. Morgan).*

The association with King-Long (Island Fortitude Ltd) however was short lived. At the time of merger, the Silcox directors thought that securing the outside investment was 'too good an opportunity to miss', but after allegations of 'broken promises' the family decided to take back their ownership, and completed the re-purchase of Silcox Motor Coach Co Ltd from King-Long UK Ltd, (the renamed King-Long Direct Ltd) owned by Island Fortitude Ltd on 6th March 2015. Simultaneously, six second hand vehicles from the Silcox fleet were returned to the former investors King-Long UK Ltd.

On 7th April 2015, Bakerbus Ltd, Bakers Bus & Coach Ltd, and Mr M R Ready, all resigned from the Silcox board. Two weeks later Bakerbus Ltd, and Bakers Bus & Coach Ltd, ceased trading. Henderson Travel Ltd, had been wound up five months earlier, and several other Island Fortitude linked UK companies also fell by the wayside, namely Barnards Coaches, Brijan Tours, Eddie Brown Tours, Guideissue Ltd, and After-Sales Service, Knypersley, Staffs (dealer). It was then revealed by 'Route One Trader' magazine that both directors of the 'Brass Plated' offshore company Island Fortitude Ltd had a criminal past. Island Fortitude however, decided to end their investment in the UK on 11th May 2015.

Silcox's finances nevertheless were still critical, which resulted in the directors looking for alternative investors. This ultimately led to another shareholder joining the board on 28th May 2015, and at the same time Mrs M E Silcox left the board.

The new shareholder, 'New Inn Travel Group Ltd' of 54 Beacon Buildings, Leighswood Rd, Aldridge, Walsall WS9 8AA joined the board with 10k of ordinary shares @ £1, together with Silcox's Transport Manager Hubert John Dix. H J Dix however, quickly resigned from the board in February 2016.

Amidst all these difficulties, Silcox began to face direct competition from competitors First Cymru Buses Ltd, on their Monkton to Milford Haven route. First Cymru Buses registered a 'new' service numbered 355 to run Monday to Saturdays between Monkton and Milford Haven via Pembroke Dock and Neyland, commencing from 13th April 2015. Having very little defence, Silcox quickly amended the timetable on their equivalent 356 service, Monkton to Milford Haven as from 18th May 2015. Fortunately the travelling public remained loyal to 'the old firm' and First Cymru withdrew their competing service from Sunday 3rd January 2016.

In retaliation, Silcox had registered a service to compete against First Cymru's 302 service:-

PG0004902/62   **Haverfordwest (Withybush Hospital)** to **Hubberston (Milford Haven)**.
via: Johnston and Milford Haven.   *Monday – Saturday.*
Route No 306.   Starting 11/5/2015. It appears that a compromise was made here, as Silcox's 306 service was cancelled from Mon 4/1/2016 and First Cymru's 355 service was cancelled a day earlier, Sun 3/1/2016.

Silcox's local service 358, (PG0004902/18) **Tenby** (Upper Park Road) to **Pembroke Dock** (Laws Street) was cancelled from 28/4/2014, and the *final* local service registered by them was:-

PG0004902/63   **Narberth (Moorfield Rd)** to **Carmarthen (Glangwili Hospital)**
via: Carmarthen Bus Station.   *Monday - Saturday.*
Route No 322.   Starting 5/5/2015.

The above Pembrokeshire C C supported 322 service was extended beyond Carmarthen bus station to reach Glangwili Hospital, to assist the travelling public after Withybush Hospital (Haverfordwest) transferred certain medical services to Glangwili Hospital. Furthermore, Pembrokeshire County Council provided Silcox with a suitable VDL SB200 low floor vehicle to operate the re-scheduled service.

Above: This Mercedes-Benz 'Vario' 0814, **V723 GGE** (48) with Plaxton 'Beaver 2' B33F body arrived in November 2013 from another Island Fortitude linked company, Guideissue, Knypersley Staffs (183). It's seen here at the temporary bus stop outside Sainsbury's Store in Upper Park Road, Tenby working the 352 service from Tenby to Kilgetty on 23rd January 2014. This bus was withdrawn in May 2016 with a mechanical fault, and sold as a non-runner at the auction to Richards Bros, Cardigan.
(V. Morgan).

Above: The company's first and only Scania was this 2006 tri-axle example. **YN06 CFZ** (247) a Scania K114EB6 with Irizar coachwork to C65FL layout, arrived in December 2013 from Excalibur Coaches, Peckham, London. Seen here on 9th November 2014 minus front panel - broken down, it was returned to the investors with major issues in early 2015. *(V. Morgan).*

Above: Yet another 12 metre Dennis Javelin in the fleet was **RUI 6748** (250) with Berkhof 'Excellence' C53F coachwork, previously registered *N865 XMO, EUI656, N865 XMO*. It was acquired locally from Edwards Bros of Tiers Cross, Pembrokeshire in February 2014, and was sold by the administrators at the final auction for scrap at £800. *(V. Morgan).*

Above: The second King-Long in the Silcox stable was 'pre-used' but only three months old. **BK63 ZTB** (105) was a King-Long XMQ 6127 with C49FT coachwork, new in November 2013 to Guideissue, Knypersley, another 'linked' member of the Island Fortitude company. It arrived at Pembroke Dock in February 2014, and is seen here expertly driven by D C Bevan, a former coach proprietor at Carmarthen. BK63 ZTB was another coach that passed to Edwards, Llantwit Fardre with the business in June 2016.

Above: This rather untidy looking 1998 Dennis 'Javelin' **R114 SBD** (251) fitted with UVG bodywork to C69F layout (3+2 seating) came from West, South Woodford, London, in May 2014, and previously carried registration *R20 BUS*. This view was taken at Haverfordwest on 16th July 2014 before Silcox's staff spruced it up with a re-paint and re-registration to A11 WLS in November 2014. This also went to Llew Jones, Llanrwst through the final auction July 2016 re-registered R114 SBD. *(V M)*.

Above: Four of these Egyptian built MCV 'Evolution' B27F bodied buses, with MAN 14.240 chassis were placed in service June/July 2014. They came to Pembroke Dock through the company's 'link' with Island Fortitude Ltd. All four, AE08 KTK, AE09 DJO/DJU/DJV (49/52/50/51) had been new to Airparks Ltd, Crawley, West Sussex, two having briefly been operated by Silcox's associated company Guideissue, Knypersley. **AE09 DJO** (52) is seen here at the depot on 16th July 2014. All four had returned to the associated dealer King-Long UK Ltd in October 2014. *(V. Morgan)*.

240

Above: AE09 DJU (50) pictured here was another one of the four MAN 14.240s acquired in July 2014 through their 'associate' company Guideissue Ltd of Knypersley, Staffs. Fitted with MCV (**M**anufacturing **C**ommercial **V**ehicles) 'Evolution' B27F body, **AE 09 DJU** was seen here at Tenby on 13th August 2014 working the 381 service to Haverfordwest via Saundersfoot. Immediately behind is Optare 'Solo' YJ10 EXU (36) branded 'Coastal Bus Service' but working the Tenby Town Service 380. *(V. Morgan).*

Above: MX54 KYJ (99) was another second-hand Optare 'Solo' M920 acquired in May 2015 from Jackett, Gunnislake, Cornwall. It never received fleet livery and was withdrawn by March 2016 – replaced by a new A D Enviro 200. *(V. Morgan).*

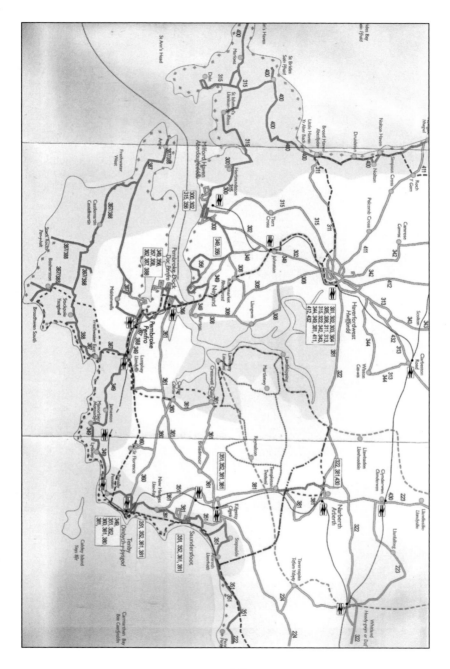

Above: This pair of Dennis 'Dart' SLFs **W794/3 VMV** (56/5) arrived from Leven Valley, Stockton-on-Tees in April 2015 together with Dennis 'Dart' SLF, Y178 CFS (54) seen below. They entered service May 2015 in the liveries they carried upon arrival, but later received fleet livery. All three returned to the finance company in June 2016. *(V. Morgan)*.

Above: **Y178 CFS** (54) was the third Dennis 'Dart' SLF / Plaxton 'Pointer' acquired from Leven Valley, Stockton-on-Tees in April 2015, but was withdrawn in April 2016 following an inspection by a DVSA examiner. *(V. Morgan)*.

Opposite page: An official South Pembrokeshire Route Map dated 2014/5 which was still current at the time of Silcox's demise in June 2016. Local bus routes are coloured – Blue, and the Pembrokeshire 'Coastal Bus Services' coloured – Red. Railway lines are indicated with a thin black line, whilst bus route numbers are given alongside each roadway.

Above: Captured here on layover at Haverfordwest bus station 7th October 2015 is **MX12 DYN** (57) a 28 seat Alexander-Dennis E20D 'Enviro 200'. It was one of a pair (MX12 DYN/DZK) leased from a dealer in July 2015, and had been new to T L C Travel, Bradford in May 2012. They both remained with Silcox until the company's demise in June 2016, when they returned to their lessor. MX12 DYN then passed to another Welsh operator, Phil Anslow & Son Pontypool, Gwent.   *(V. Morgan)*.

Above: This VDL SB200 with Plaxton 'Centro' B45F bodywork, **YJ58 FFN** (59) was purchased by Pembrokeshire County Council in November 2015 for the re-vamped local authority supported service 322 operated by Silcox. The re-scheduled and extended 322 service commenced in May 2015, to provide transport between Withybush Hospital (Haverfordwest) and Glangwili Hospital (Carmarthen) after certain medical services were transferred to Glangwili. When Silcox ceased operations in June 2016, the local authority transferred YJ58 FFN to Taf Valley Coaches of Whitland, with the supported 322 service.

Above: At the point when the Silcox family were desperately trying to find a buyer for the business, three more Alexander-Dennis E20D 'Enviro 200s arrived to replace several un-roadworthy vehicles in the fleet. Numerically the first to arrive in April 2016 was 39 seater **SN16 OGV** (60) which is seen here at the Tenby outstation on the last day of operation 5th June 2016, about to return to Waterloo Garage, Pembroke Dock for disposal. *(V. Morgan).*

Above: 33 seater Alexander - Dennis E20D 'Enviro 200' **SN16 ORS** was also received in April 2016 when the company were short of serviceable vehicles after a fleet inspection by DVSA . This view also was taken at the Tenby outstation as the driver was about to leave for Upper Park Road and commence service 352 to Saundersfoot – on the last day of Silcox operation, 5th June 2016. *(V. Morgan).*

Above: The third Alexander – Dennis E20D 'Enviro 200' delivered in April 2016 to cover vehicle shortages, also seated 33 passengers. All three were dealer registered, with this particular one receiving registration **SN16 ORU**. It was a coincidence to find all three 2016 Enviros parked together at Tenby outstation on the morning of 5th June 2016. *(V. Morgan).*

Above: During the last few weeks of the company's existance, three of these Volvo B11RTs with Spanish built 'Sunsundegui SC7' coachwork appeared in the yard, acquired from three different sources but closely registered - BL14 LSO/U/V. All three were new in August 2014 to Excaliber Coaches, Peckham, London to work National Express contracts. This one, **BL14 LSO** had briefly operated with Barnard, Kirton in Lindsey, Lincolnshire, prior to arrival at Pembroke Dock on loan in April 2016. The view was taken on 30th April 2016. *(V. Morgan).*

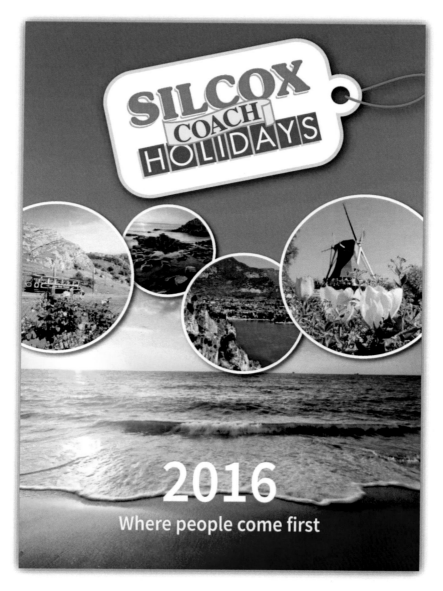

This was Silcox's final Coach Holiday Brochure for 2016, containing 28 pages of British and Continental Holidays that were second to none. Many of their clientel were regulars, frequently enjoying the delights of Scotland, Ireland, North Wales, Devon, Cornwall, Bournemouth, Sussex, Norfolk Broads, Lake District, Blackpool, Yorkshire, London, Isle of Wight, Isle of Man and Jersey. For the more adventurous, there was Lake Garda, Austria, Dutch Bulbfields and Disneyland Paris etc.

As the company's financial situation worsened in 2015, Waterloo Garage together with the frontal area of the yard formerly the petrol station was sold off for development – purchased by the large supermarket chain 'Aldi Stores Ltd' who quickly set about clearing the site to build a new superstore.

All the land situated to the rear of Waterloo Garage was retained as a parking area for the fleet, whilst the garage workshops moved to a far smaller unit at the town's dockyard. The company's registered office moved virtually across the road from Waterloo Garage into temporary accommodation at Unit G, Eastern Avenue, Pembroke Dock, on 14th December 2015.

In April 2016, a DVSA vehicle examiner inspected 42 vehicles from the fleet and issued six immediate and eight delayed prohibition orders together with 18 inspection notices. Two of the prohibitions were 'S' marked and only 14 vehicles were clear of any defects. There were also reports of no pre-planning for the downloading of vehicle data from drivers defect cards, nor any records after June 2015 to show that driver's hours had been checked. Having so many prohibition notices led to vehicle shortages, resulting in the hire and loan of new buses and pre-owned coaches. Five second-hand coaches hired were owned by A P Travel Ltd, of Cowbridge, Vale of Glamorgan, a company whose licence had been revoked two months earlier. A P Travel were at that particular time applying for a new 'O' licence from a new address given as Saundersfoot!

In the meantime, the Silcox family were desperately trying to source a buyer for the business which had liabilities of £1.1m. Furthermore, payment had not been received for the land sold to Aldi.

Ultimately, a local newspaper dated 1st June 2016 stated that interest from Edwards Coaches a principal buyer had fallen through on Friday 20th May, and added that the company protected itself from creditors by filing a notice of intention to appoint administrators at court, and said the notice had given the company breathing space of 10 business days to explore all options and seek a buyer.

Business recovery specialist Wilson Field Ltd, who were initially charged with finding a buyer for the Silcox undertaking, expressed their belief that there was a strong prospect that a buyer could be found, but failed to do so. As a result operations ceased at midnight on Sunday 5th June 2016. Wilson Field were then appointed as administrators.

Concessionary ticket issued on bus No 47
2/6/2016.

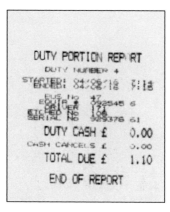

A ticket machine 'Duty Portion Report' (final waybill) for bus
No 47, Y619 GFM dated Saturday 4/6/2016.

248

Local Services operational as at 5th June 2016 were:-

300	Milford Haven Town Service.
301	Haverfordwest Town Circular (Leisure Centre & Top of Town).
303	Haverfordwest Town Circular (Cashfields Estate).
304	Haverfordwest Town Circular (Trafalgar Rd, & Portfield).
305	Haverfordwest Town Circular (College & Leisure Centre).
311	Haverfordwest to Broadhaven.
313	Wiston to Haverfordwest (via: Crundale & Clarbeston Road).
318	Hakin – Milford Haven Comprehensive School.
322	Haverfordwest to Carmarthen (via: Narberth).
351	Tenby to Pendine (via: Saundersfoot, Wisemans Bridge & Amroth).
352	Tenby to Kilgetty (via: Saundersfoot)
356	Milford Haven to Pembroke (via: Neyland & Pembroke Dock).
357	Monkton to Pembroke Dock (via: Pembroke).
360	Tenby to St Florence (Circular).
361	Pembroke Dock to Tenby (via: Cresselly & Kilgetty).
362	Pennar to Pembroke Dock (via: Pembroke Comprehensive School).
371	Kingsbridge to Pembroke Comprehensive School
375	Pembroke to Golden Grove School.
380	Tenby Town Service.
381	Tenby to Haverfordwest (via: Saundersfoot, Kilgetty and Narberth).
387/8	Coastal Cruiser (Winter). Pembroke Dock, Angle & Stackpole (Circular).
387/8	Coastal Cruiser (Summer). Pembroke Dock, Angle & Stackpole (Circular).

There was also a Tesco (Free Bus service) at Haverfordwest, and a total of 31 Pembrokeshire C C contracted Education Transport Services together with two College bus services contracted from Carmarthenshire C C, and a privately operated school contract to an Independent School at Llanelli.

Above: This picture is *my* sad farewell to a much loved and well respected company. It was the last photograph I would capture of a Silcox vehicle, taken at the gateway entrance to Waterloo depot on Sunday 5th June 2016. Nearest the camera is CU54 KWS, (198) with WA04 EWT (102) and YN08 NKJ (101) next in line. WA08 GPO (103) is on the right. *(V. Morgan).*

Consequently, on 24th August 2016 the Deputy Traffic Commissioner revoked the 74 vehicle international licence PG0004902/SI held by Silcox Motor Coach Company Ltd, on financial grounds, and took no action against directors Keith and Jason Silcox regarding the maintenance issues mentioned on page 248. On 31st August 2016, the DTC decided not to take action in regard to Keith Silcox's repute or professional competence as Transport Manager, as he had stated 'it was not his intention to seek employment as a TM in the future'.

Above: Aldi's supermarket - London Road, Pembroke Dock. This store was built during 2016 on the former premises of Silcox Motor Coach Company Ltd. The car parking area to the front of the supermarket was the location of Silcox's Petrol Station, car sales showroom and car repair workshops (see view on page 199). The supermarket was built on the site previously occupied by 'Waterloo Garage' – the bus garage/workshops, which were also known as 'The Works'. *(V. Morgan).*

EPILOGUE

Edwards Coaches of Llantwit Fardre, Pontypridd had examined the possibility of acquiring Silcox Motor Coach Co Ltd as a going concern, but found that the business was not salvageable owing to the level of debt it carried.

However, after Silcox Motor Coach Co Ltd had been put into administration, the management of Edwards Coaches felt obliged to help out by rescuing the majority of staff and customers in a combined effort with Pembrokeshire County Council. Edwards Coaches absorbed a large amount of Silcox's work including the holidays, and by Sunday 5th June 2016 everything was in place ready for their first day of operation the following day, having acquired extra licence authorisation and some extra vehicles from their predecessor's fleet. Edwards' vehicles became out-stationed at the former Silcox yard, Waterloo Garage (by then owned by New Inn Travel, Silcox's parent company) and at North Beach Coach Park, Tenby, owned by Pembrokeshire C C, previously Silcox's outstation. The former Silcox coach tours booking office at No 2 Nelson's Walk, Tenby was also leased for a few months to operate the former Silcox Tours and to promote Edwards' Holidays, but was soon closed due to lack of business, Edwards' holidays were a lot more expensive.

With assistance from the administrators, the local authority *initially* distributed the Local Service routes and Education Transport routes as follows:-

Edwards Coaches	301/303/304/305/356/360/361/208R/210R/220R/222R/223/530/533/535 538/539/540/542/543/586/587/589/591X/601/602/602R/689/690/710 714; 4010X; Pride 1 (Federation); Pride 2A (Federation). St Michaels Independent School, Llanelli.
Edwards Brothers	300/311/313/318
First Cymru Buses	357/362/371/375/381/532
Taf Valley Coaches	322/351/352/536
A Phillips. Trecwn	387/388
Coracle Coaches	Col 17 (Tenby & Carmarthen to Gelli Aur campus, Golden Grove). *On behalf of Carmarthenshire C C.*
M Hayward & Daughter	PC1 (Carmarthen to Pembrokeshire College). *On behalf of Carmarthenshire C C.*

After a very short period, some of the tendered services listed above had a change of operator following the local authority's decision to submit them for re-tendering. The commercially operated Tenby town service, 380 was not taken up at all, that was subsequently cancelled.

The majority of Silcox's 92 staff were re-employed under the Transfer of Undertakings (Protection of Employment) regulations, by the three main operators taking over the relevant Silcox work.

In the meantime, the appointed administrators, Wilson Field, set about disposal of the company's assets and organised several auctions. Vehicles were split into two categories, the expensive and cheaper ranges. The expensive vehicles were allocated to GWA Auctioneers, Clitheroe, Lancs, for an online auction closing 30/6/2016. The others remained at Pembroke Dock, and were auctioned online by Charterfields Ltd, Manchester, with a closing date of 1/7/2016. The cherished registration numbers were also sold off by Charterfields at a separate online auction, as were other assets.

Above: Taf Valley Coaches of Whitland, Carmarthenshire acquired service 322 together with the Pembrokeshire C C owned VDL SB200 with Plaxton 'Centro' B45F bodywork, **YJ58 FFN**. It's captured here exiting Carmarthen bus station for the final part of its journey to Glangwili Hospital, on its first day in service with Taf Valley Coaches, 6th June 2016. *(V Morgan)*.

Above: **Y619 GFM** seen here at Upper Park Road, Tenby on 24th January 2017, is another former Silcox vehicle working the erstwhile Silcox route to Kilgetty. Taf Valley Coaches purchased this Dennis 'Dart' SLF, at the Silcox auction for £800.

Above: South Parade, Tenby is the backdrop for this picture of **YK04 KWD** a 2004 Optare 'Solo' M1020 with B37F body owned by Taf Valley Coaches, Whitland. It was purchased in June 2016 for the 351 Tenby – Saundersfoot - Pendine service inherited from Silcox, and was captured here on 2nd November 2016 working service 351, with a bi-lingual destination display: Pentywyn trwy Saundersfoot (Pendine via Saundersfoot), still carrying the livery of its previous owner, P & O Lloyd. It has since received Taf Valley Coaches' new 'local bus livery' of red and black. *(V. Morgan).*

Above: Captured at the same place - South Parade, Tenby at the same time as the Optare 'Solo' above, was First Cymru Buses' (42684) **CU53 AUP**, a 2003 Transbus 'Dart' SLF working the Haverfordwest – Tenby 381 service, inherited through Silcox's demise. **CU53 AUP** is painted in the livery of 'United Welsh Services' a livery it received in 2014 to celebrate the centenary of 'The South Wales Transport Company' - forerunners of First Cymru Buses. The 381 service has since passed to Taf Valley Coaches, who operate the service with four red and black liveried 2014 Alexander-Dennis 'Enviro 200'. *(V. Morgan).*

Above: Taf Valley Coaches, Whitland were operating **YX14 RZE**, on the Tenby –Saundersfoot – Kilgetty 352 service when I photographed it here at Tenby on 7th July 2016. This Alexander-Dennis 'Enviro 200' was acquired in June 2016 to operate the former Silcox route. *(V. Morgan).*

Above: Pembrokeshire County Council owned Optare 'Solo' **YJ60 LRL** was photographed here at the entrance to Haverfordwest bus station on 2nd November 2016, having arrived in from Broad Haven with accident damage to the front off side corner. **YJ60 LRL** passed to Edwards Brothers, Tiers Cross with the erstwhile Silcox 311 service, Haverfordwest to Broad Haven *(VMorgan)*

Above: The largest portion of Silcox's work passed to Edwards Coaches of Llantwit Fardre near Pontypridd – which is situated some 90 miles away from Pembroke Dock. Edwards Coaches, also retained Silcox's parking facilities and offices at Pembroke Dock and Tenby, and acquired six of their coaches. One of the coaches Edwards acquired from Silcox was this 57 seat Dennis 'Javelin' **CT02 NAE** *(SX02 WDS)* with Plaxton 'Premiere 320' coachwork, which is seen here on lay-over at Llanelli after working the inward journey of a former Silcox school contract to St Michaels Independent School. *(V. Morgan).*

Above: One of the smallest portions of Silcox work was taken over by Coracle Coaches of Carmarthen, who operate this much travelled Volvo B10M-62, Plaxton 'Premiere 350' **(R965 RCH)** on a Carmarthenshire County Council supported College service (numbered Col 17) from Tenby and Carmarthen to Gelli Aur, Llandeilo. *(V. Morgan).*

VEHICLE DETAILS

F/N	Reg No	Chassis make & type	Chassis number	Body make & type	Seating	Date New	Remarks / Additional Information Previous owner	Date acquired	Date W/drawn
5	DE 7244	Thornycroft A2 (long)	14724	Hall Lewis	B20F	9/1927	Ex J. R. Ford. Pembroke.	9/1933	2/1942
1	DE 7985	Guy BB	BB23230	Guy	B31D	11/1930	Ex J. R. Ford. Pembroke.	9/1933	1936
6	DE 8384	Thornycroft A12	20896	Brush	B20F	8/1931	Ex J. R. Ford. Pembroke.	9/1933	2/1942
2	DE 8595	Guy (type unknown)		Guy	B20F	1/1932	Ex J. R. Ford. Pembroke.	9/1933	2/1942
8	GT 9498	Dennis (30cwt)	56115	Short	B18F	10/1931	Ex J. R. Ford. Pembroke.	9/1933	12/1942
3	DM 7678	Guy FBB	FBB23279	Guy	B32R	1929	Ex J. R. Ford. Pembroke.	9/1933	9/1938
7	DE 9151	Thornycroft A6	18310	Thomas & Thomas	B24F	7/1929	Ex J. R. Ford. Pembroke.	9/1933	by 1937
4	DE 9301	Guy Conquest	FC23812	Guy	B32R	5/1933	Ex J. R. Ford. Pembroke.	9/1933	1946
1	HS 5800	Guy ONDF	9445	Guy	B20F	1/1930	Ex Paton. Renfrew, Scotland.	c1936	1938
9	BDE 96	Thornycroft Dainty DF	25720	Grose	C24F	1/1936		lic 3/1936	12/1947
10	BDE 238	Leyland Tiger TS7 (oil)	9272	Leyland	B32F	4/1936	New (Body rebuilt by Silcox 1950)	4/1936	by 11/59
11	CDE 259	Leyland Tiger TS7 (oil)	12917	Leyland	B36R	6/1937	New (Body rebuilt by Silcox to DP35F)	6/1937	6/1956
12	CDE 732	Bedford WTB	111818	Thomas & Thomas	C25F	1/1938	New	1/1938	by 6/48
7	DDE 222	Bedford WTB	112832	Duple	C26F	6/1938	New	6/1938	3/1950
1	DDE 963	Bedford WTB	11432	Thomas & Thomas	C25F	5/1939	New	5/1939	6/1949
3	EDE 16	Bedford WTB	17645	Duple	C26F	6/1939	New	6/1939	5/1950
14	EDE 734	Leyland Cub KP24	202269	Thomas & Thomas	C26F	7/1940	New	7/1940	1951
15	EDE 735	Leyland Cub KP24	202270	Thomas & Thomas	C26F	7/1940	New	7/1940	1951
16	EDE 773	Leyland Cub KP24	202271	Thomas & Thomas	C26F	9/1940	New	lic 10/40	1951
17	AET 456	Dennis Arrow Minor	255029	Fielding & Bottomley	C25F	5/1937	Ex Greaves. Rotherham. Yorks.	1/1941	1952
18	DYN 291	Bedford WTB	111499	Duple	C25F	6/1937	Ex Clarkes Luxury Coaches, London E16.	1/1941	1948
19	FXT 824	Bedford WTB	18919	Duple	C26F	6/1939	Ex Clarkes Luxury Coaches, London E16.	1/1941	by 8/50
	GJ 2086	AEC Regent	661648	Tilling	H27/25RO	10/1930	Hired from London Transport (ST 910)	12/1941	2/1943
	GJ 2097	AEC Regent	661653	Tilling	H27/25RO	11/1930	Hired from London Transport (ST 921)	12/1941	2/1943
	GK 1009	AEC Regent	661665	Tilling	H27/25RO	11/1930	Hired from London Transport (ST 933)	12/1941	2/1943
20	FDE 215	Bristol K5G	57.036	Duple	L30/26R	4/1942	New	4/1942	9/1961
2	FDE 404	Bedford OWB	8956	Duple	B32F	8/1942	New	8/1942	1/1950
5	FDE 410	Bedford OWB	9040	Duple	B32F	8/1942	New	8/1942	9/1949
21	FDE 447	Bedford OWB	8930	Duple	B32F	8/1942	New	8/1942	8/1949
6	FDE 448	Bedford OWB	9246	Duple	B32F	8/1942	New	8/1942	8/1949
28	FDE 517	Guy Arab I 5LW	FD25698	Strachan	L27/28R	1/1943	New (Rebuilt by Silcox FL32/28R 1954)	1/1943	1958
22	FDE 530	Bedford OWB	11489	Duple	B32F	2/1943	New	2/1943	8/1949
23	FDE 531	Bedford OWB	11478	Duple	B32F	2/1943	New	2/1943	2/1949
24	FDE 534	Bedford OWB	11481	Duple	B32F	2/1943	New	2/1943	2/1949
25	FDE 535	Bedford OWB	11562	Duple	B32F	2/1943	New	2/1943	1947
26	FDE 536	Bedford OWB	11601	Duple	B32F	2/1943	New	2/1943	6/1949
27	FDE 537	Bedford OWB	11494	Duple	B32F	2/1943	New	2/1943	4/1950

Fleet No.	Reg.	Chassis	Chassis No.	Body	Seating	Date	Notes	Date in	Withdrawn
29	FDE 609	Guy Arab I 6LW	FD25860	Strachan	L27/28R	6/1943	New	6/1943	1955
30	FDE 733	Guy Arab II 6LW	FD26186	Strachan	L27/28R	3/1944	New	3/1944	by10/1955
31	GDE 124	Guy Arab II 5LW	FD27561	Strachan	L27/28R	5/1945	New	5/1945	1956
32	GDE 235	Guy Arab II 5LW	FD27674	Strachan	L27/28R	9/1945	New (body rebuilt by Silcox in 1954)	9/1945	12/1959
39	JDE 43	Leyland Titan PD1	471702	Leyland	L27/26R	9/1947	New	9/1947	11/1953
33	JDE 426	Bristol L5G	65.056	Strachan	DP35F	12/1947	New	12/1947	1960
34	JDE 427	Bristol L5G	65.057	Strachan	DP35F	12/1947	New	12/1947	11/1958
35	JDE 428	Bristol L5G	65.058	Strachan	DP35F	3/1948	New	29/4/1948	by 4/1959
36	JDE 429	Bristol L5G	65.067	Strachan	DP35F	3/1948	New	29/4/1948	4/1963
37	JDE 430	Bristol L5G	65.068	Strachan	DP35F	3/1948	New	29/4/1948	1/1959
38	JDE 431	Bristol L5G	65.069	Strachan	DP35F	3/1948	New	29/4/1948	by 3/1961
-	ADE 903	Bedford WTL	878163	Duple	B20F	11/1935	Ex E C James, Pembroke Dock.	4/1948	12/48
4	FDE 964	Bedford OWB	20026	Duple	UB32F	6/1944	Ex E C James, Pembroke Dock.	4/1948	11/1950
8	LDE 340	Crossley SD42/7	97985	Silcox	DP35F	5/1949	New	5/1949	4/1953
9	LDE 630	Leyland Tiger PS1/1	493074	Silcox	DP35F	6/1949	New (lic to L W Silcox, Pioneer Bus Service)	7/1949	12/1953
21	LDE 850	Bristol K6G	76.110	Barnard	L27/26R	11/1949	New	11/1949	11/1969
22	LDE 949	Bristol K6G	76.108	D J Davies to Willowbrook (1948)	H30/26R to L31/28R	10/1949	New (Re-bodied in 5/1961 with the s/hand 1948 Willowbrook body off RC 4627 f/n 41)	10/1949	8/1969
23	LDE 950	Bristol K6G	76.109	D J Davies to Willowbrook (1948)	H30/26R to L31/28R	10/1949	New (Re-bodied in 6/1961 with the s/hand 1948 Willowbrook body off RC 4633 f/n 47)	licenced 1/2/1950	by 9/1971
1	MDE 530	Leyland Comet CPO1	493556	Silcox	DP32F	6/1950	New	6/1950	by 7/1953
2	MDE 531	Leyland Comet CPO1	493650	Silcox	DP33F	6/1950	New (lic to L W Silcox, Pioneer Bus Service)	6/1950	1952
7	MDE 532	Leyland Tiger PS1/1	495815	Silcox	DP35F	6/1950	New	6/1950	3/1954
3	NDE 330	Bristol L5G	81.013	Silcox	DP39F	3/1951	New	3/1951	by 5/1967
4	NDE 331	Bristol L5G	81.012	Silcox	DP39F	3/1951	New	3/1951	1967
5	NDE 332	Bristol L5G	81.014	Silcox (re-bodied 6/1961 by Marshall of Cambridge)	FDP39F FDP39F	6/1951	New	6/1951	1972/3
6	NDE 616	Bristol LL5G	81.197	Silcox	DP41F	6/1951	New	6/1951	1964
42	FOP 349	Guy Arab II 5LW	FD26308	Weymann	H30/26R	10/1943	Ex Birmingham Corporation (1349) 11/1951	lic 5/1952	1959
40	FOP 353	Guy Arab II 5LW	FD26397	Weymann	H30/26R	1/1944	Ex Birmingham Corporation (1353) 11/1951	lic 5/1952	1959
41	FOP 366	Guy Arab II 5LW	FD26676	Weymann	H30/26R	5/1944	Ex Birmingham Corporation (1366) 11/1951	lic 5/1952	4/1959
26	FOP 380	Guy Arab II 5LW	FD26897	Weymann	H30/26R	8/1944	Ex Birmingham Corporation (1380) 8/1951	8/1951	11/1958
27	FOP 403	Guy Arab II 5LW	FD27111	Weymann	H30/26R	11/1944	Ex Birmingham Corporation (1403) 8/1951	8/1951	1960
24	ODE 401	Bristol K6G	80.052	MCCW (1940) to Willowbrook (1948) - L31/28R	FH30/24R to FH32/28R	1950	Chassis new (1st body ex Birmingham Corp. trolleybus FOK 90. 2nd body fitted in 9/1961 was also second hand off RC 4630 f/n 42)	5/1952	1971
25	ODE 402	Bristol K6G	80.053	MCCW (1940)	FH30/24R to 32/28	1950	Chassis new (Fitted with second hand body from Birmingham Corp Trolleybus FOK 83)	6/1952	1967
12	ODE 600	Bristol LL5G	81.196	Silcox (converted to half-cab 1959)	FDP41F to DP41F	7/1952	New	7/1952	1/1965

Fleet	Reg	Chassis	Chassis No	Body	Body Code	New	Notes	Acquired	Withdrawn
18	LYL 725	Leyland Royal Tiger PSU1/15	504683	Beccols	C35F	6/1951	Ex Shaw. Oldham, Lancs.	c10/1952	7/1959
19	KAB 338	Leyland Royal Tiger PSU1/15	510745	Burlingham 'Seagull'	C37C	6/1951	Ex W. D. Smith, Fernhill Heath, Worcester.	12/1952	1972
2	LYL 722	Leyland Royal Tiger PSU1/15	504537	Beccols	C35F	4/1951	Ex Spencer's Tours, Oldham, Lancs. Possibly acquired 10/1952.	lic 6/1953	4/1958
9	SDE 400	Leyland Tiger Cub PSUC1/2	542595	Burlingham 'Seagull'	C33C to 41 (4/64)	4/1954	New	4/1954	by 5/1974
39	SDE 450	Bristol K6G	80.051	Silcox	FL32/28F to FL32/27R	chassis 1950	New Stored 1951-4. Body built by Silcox in 1953 and rebuilt to rear entrance layout by 1959.	lic 6/1954	1969
21 to 7	KWW 541	Leyland Royal Tiger PSU1/15	510574	Plaxton 'Venturer' Rebuilt by Silcox	C41C to DP45F	6/1951	Ex J W Kitchin & Sons. Pudsey, Yorks. Body completely rebuilt by Silcox by 4/1963.	3/1954	5/1967
1 to 41	MRH 226	Leyland Royal Tiger PSU1/15	511340	Burlingham 'Seagull'	C37C	2/1952	Ex Bluebird Garages. Hull.	1/1954	1967
-	NJW 300	Guy Arab LUF 6HLW	LUF72332	Burlingham 'Seagull'	C41C	9/1954	Operated on hire from Guy Motors Wolverhampton.	-/1955	-/1955
46	WDE 343	Guy Arab LUF 6HLW	LUF73061	Burlingham 'Seagull'	C41C	5/1956	New	5/1956	2/1969
44	ACK 871	Guy Arab II 5LW	FD27401	Roe	L27/26R	2/1945	Ex Ribble M S, Preston, Lancs (2444)	11/1955	12/1960
45	ACK 875	Guy Arab II 5LW	FD27498	Roe	L27/26R	3/1945	Ex Ribble M S, Preston, Lancs (2448)	6/1956	12/1959
30	MDE 333	AEC Regal III	9621A1033	Burlingham	B35F	4/1950	Ex D J Morrison, Tenby, Pembrokeshire (30)	12/1958	by 5/1959
35	ODE 1	AEC Regal IV	9821E529	Roe	B44F	2/1952	Ex D J Morrison, Tenby, Pembrokeshire (36)	12/1958	1965
29	UDE 111	AEC Reliance	MU3RV175	Plaxton 'Venturer III'	C39C	5/1955	Ex D J Morrison, Tenby, Pembrokeshire (42)	12/1958	1970
43	YDE 444	AEC Reliance	MU3RA1051	Burlingham	B45F	7/1957	Ex D J Morrison, Tenby, Pembrokeshire (43)	12/1958	1969-70
34	OHA 298	AEC Regal III	9612A1220	Harrington	C37F	5/1950	Ex Grey Garages. Tenby (34) (subsidiary company of D J Morrison, Tenby)	12/1958	1967
15	DDB 268	Bristol L5G	71.053	Windover	C32F	4/1949	Ex North Western Road Car Co. Stockport, (268)	12/1958	6/1961
16	DDB 269	Bristol L5G	71.054	Windover	C32F	4/1949	Ex North Western Road Car Co. Stockport, (269)	12/1958	1962
37	ETA 967	Bristol GO5G	GO5G.202	Eastern Coach Works (1949)	L27/28R	1937	Ex Western National O C. Exeter. (242)	4/1959	1968
41	RC 4627	AEC Regent	06615066	Willowbrook (7/1948)	L27/28R	3/1937	Ex Trent Motor Transport, Derby (1331)	1959	1960
42	RC 4630	AEC Regent	06615069	Willowbrook (7/1948)	L27/28R	3/1937	Ex Trent Motor Transport, Derby (1334)	1959	1960

47	RC 4633	AEC Regent	0615072	Willowbrook (7/1948)	L27/28R	3/1937	Ex Trent Motor Transport, Derby (1335)	1959	1960
8	MUX 794	Leyland Tiger Cub PSUC1/2	553444	Burlingham 'Seagull' Rebuilt by Silcox	C41F to DP41F (3/65)	1/1956	Ex J T Whittle & Son. Highley, Salop.	3/1959	7/1969
32	GHN 189	Bristol K5G	57.029	Eastern Coach Works (1949) ex HN 9019 in 1954	L27/26R	6/1942	Ex United Automobile Services. Darlington. (BGL29)	4/1959	1969
31	HUF 299	Leyland Tiger PS1	471102	Park Royal	C32R	3/1948	Ex Southdown M S, Brighton (1299)	5/1959	by 2/1970
30	HUF 300	Leyland Tiger PS1	471074	Park Royal	C32R	3/1948	Ex Southdown M S, Brighton (1300)	by 6/1959	by 2/1970
49	GDE 834	Leyland Titan PD1A	460540	Burlingham	L27/28R	7/1946	Ex Morrison. Tenby, via Greens Motors, and Western Welsh O C, Cardiff (987)	6/1959	by 4/1960
28	GNO 693	Bristol K5G	45.142	Eastern Coach Works	L27/28R	7/1938	Ex Eastern National O C. Chelmsford, Essex. (1016)	by 7/1959	1960
17	BJA 442	Bristol L5G	63.035	Eastern Coach Works	B35R	5/1947	Ex North Western Road Car Co. Stockport. (142)	7/1959	1961
14	DDB 270	Bristol L5G (See notes of 702 RDE below)	71.055	Windover (See notes of 702 RDE below)	C35F	4/1949	Ex North Western Road Car Co. Stockport. (270)	by 5/1959	1962
10	DDB 278	Leyland Tiger PS2/3	495762	Windover	C32F	5/1950	Ex North Western Road Car Co. Stockport. (278)	by 7/1959	by 12/1959
11	DDB 279	Leyland Tiger PS2/3	495763	Windover	C32F	4/1950	Ex North Western Road Car Co. Stockport. (279)	by 7/1959	12/1962
40	LAL 691	Leyland Titan PD1A	492030	Burlingham	L27/26R	3/1950	Ex Wass Bros. Mansfield, Nottingham (24) via: East Midland No 8 (not operated).	9/1959	6/1968
48	GUF 685	Leyland Titan PD1	460814	Park Royal	H28/26R	8/1946	Ex Southdown M S, Brighton (285)	1/1960	12/1965
49	UTB 550	AEC Reliance	MU3RV199	Plaxton 'Venturer III'	C41C	11/1954	Ex Y. Helliwell & Sons, Nelson, Lancs.	4/1960	9/1966
50	LDE 600	Guy Arab III 6LW	FD36209	Barnard	L27/26R	8/1949	Ex Greens Motors. Haverfordwest, Pembs. via: Western Welsh O C, Cardiff (382)	3/1960 lic 4/60	8/1967
51	LDE 601	Guy Arab III 6LW	FD36208	Barnard	L27/26R	9/1949	Ex Greens Motors. Haverfordwest, Pembs. via: Western Welsh O C, Cardiff (383)	4/1960 lic 6/60	1962
52	GNN 134	Guy Arab II 5LW	FD26699	Roe (4/1954)	L27/28R	5/1944	Ex East Midland M S. Chesterfield. (D34)	4/1960	1973
53	GAL 433	Guy Arab II 5LW	FD26078	Roe (4/1954)	L27/26R	8/1943	Ex East Midland M S. Chesterfield. (D33)	4/1960	by 2/1972
54	NBX 310	Guy Arab LUF	LUF73081	Burlingham	B44F	7/1956	Ex West Wales Motors. Tycroes, Carmarthenshire (38)	4/1960	1972
55	SVX 233	Leyland Royal Tiger PSU1/11	510029	Windover Rebuilt by Silcox	C37C to DP41C	7/1951	Ex F R Harris. Grays, Essex. via: F A Laker. Southend-on-Sea, Essex.	1960	1964
56	ACU 215	Leyland Tiger Cub PSUC1/2	584472	Duple 'Donington'	C41F	6/1958	Ex Hall Bros. South Shields.	by 1/1961	by 5/1975

Fleet No.	Reg.	Chassis	Chassis No.	Body	Into service	Prev. owner / New	Date	Withdrawn
57	LTG 268	Leyland Royal Tiger PSU1/15	520841	Leyland (re-seated from C41C in 6/61)	DP45C before entry -	4/1952 - to service	Ex Rhondda Transport Co. Porth, Glam (328)	6/1961	8/1969
58	120 LDE	Austin LDO5AR	44065	Austin (Silcox conversion)	B14F	5/1961	New	7/1961	1973
59	CRC 512	Leyland Royal Tiger PSU1/15	512772	Leyland (re-seated from C41C in 4/62)	DP45C before entry -	5/1951 - to service	Ex Trent M T, Derby (202)	12/1961 lic 4/62	11/1969
61	50 NDE	Leyland Leopard L2	612695	Duple 'Britannia'	C45F to DP45F	1/1962	New	1/1962	3/1981
63 / 18	JNU 120	Guy Arab II 6LW	FD27177	NCME (Rebuilt by Bond in 1/1955) Rebuilt by Silcox in 6/1962.	H30/26R	11/1944	Ex Midland General O C, Langley Mill (29)	6/1962 lic 11/62	1/1967
60 / 20	PVO 622	Leyland Tiger Cub PSUC1/2	543369	Burlingham 'Seagull'	C41C	7/1954	Ex East Midland M S, Chesterfield. (C22)	6/1962	by 2/1972
63	FJA 615	Leyland Royal Tiger PSU1/15	530196	Leyland	C41C	4/1953	Ex North Western Road Car Co. Stockport. (615)	7/1962	1971
62	734 PDE	Leyland Leopard PSU3/3R	621650	Willowbrook	C51F	9/1962	New	10/1962	8/1978
65 / 64	702 RDE	Bristol / Silcox LL/SX/5G	LL/SX/65/1962	Marshall (1962)	FDP39F	10/1962	Rebuilt chassis in 1962 with parts mainly off Bristol L5G, DDB 270 (14) and re-bodied.	10/1962 lic 4/63	9/1973
65	635 SDE	Leyland Leopard PSU3/3R	L00098	Duple Northern 'Alpine Continental'	C51F	5/1963	New	5/1963	8/1979
66	KRR 70	Leyland Titan PD2/1	494507	Leyland	L27/26R	3/1950	Ex East Midland M S. Chesterfield. (D70)	4/1963	2/1969
67	CRN 219	Leyland Titan PD2/3	492066	Leyland	L27/26R	6/1949	Ex Ribble M S. Preston, Lancs (2720)	6/1963	6/1969
68	LEH 759	Leyland Titan PD2/1	480855	Northern Counties	L27/26R	1948	Ex Potteries M T. Stoke-on-Trent (L351)	6/1963	by 4/1969
10	PRE 731	Leyland Tiger PS1/1	472978	Weymann (1949) fitted in 1954, ex NEH 468	B39F	6/1948	Ex Potteries M T. Stoke-on-Trent (S365)	4/1963	4/1966
-	PRE 732	Leyland Tiger PS1/1	473183	Weymann (1949) fitted in 1954, ex NEH 453	B39F	6/1948	Ex Potteries M T. Stoke-on-Trent (S366)	4/1963	Not operated
2	PRE 735	Leyland Tiger PS1/1	481860	Weymann (1949) fitted in 1955, ex NEH 457	B39F	7/1948	Ex Potteries M T. Stoke-on-Trent (S369)	6/1963	1967
11	LEH 42	Leyland Tiger PS1/1	461153	Weymann (1949) fitted in 1954, ex NEH 455	B39F	5/1947	Ex Potteries M T. Stoke-on-Trent (S328)	4/1963	1967
14	GUF 135	Guy Arab II 5LW	FD27095	Northern Counties	H28/26R	9/1944	Ex Southdown M S. Brighton (435)	7/1963 lic 11/63	11/1967
15	GUF 158	Guy Arab II 5LW	FD27413	Northern Counties	H28/26R	2/1945	Ex Southdown M S. Brighton (458)	7/1963 lic 11/63	11/1967
16	GUF 118	Guy Arab II 5LW	FD27123	Northern Counties	H28/26R	10/1944	Ex Southdown M S. Brighton (418)	7/1963 lic 11/63	by 8/1967

	Reg.	Chassis	Chassis No.	Body	Seating	Date	History	Acquired	Withdrawn
44 / 17	FUH 412	Leyland 'Olympic' HR44	511468	Weymann	B44F	6/1951	Ex Western Welsh O C. Cardiff. (412)	2/1964	1970
20 / 60	PVO 624	Leyland Tiger Cub PSUC1/2	543371 Re-bodied-	Burlingham 'Seagull' / Plaxton 'Panorama I'	C41C / C43F (2/67)	7/1954	Ex East Midland M S. Chesterfield (C24)	4/1964	7/1996
26	FUH 426	Leyland Royal Tiger PSU1/13	511112	Weymann	B44F	9/1951	Ex Western Welsh O C. Cardiff (426)	9/1964	2/1969
69	614 XDE	Leyland Leopard PSU3/3RT	L20689	Duple 'Commander'	C51F to DP51F -/80	9/1964	New Exhibited at the 1964 Commercial Motor Show, Earls Court, London	10/1964	11/1981
70	VGT 328	Leyland Tiger Cub PSUC1/2	584960	Harrington 'Wayfarer IV'	C41F	5/1958	Ex George Ewer (Grey-Green Coaches) London. N16.	1/1965 lic 4/65	1972-4
71	VGT 330	Leyland Tiger Cub PSUC1/2	584993	Harrington 'Wayfarer IV'	C41F	6/1958	Ex George Ewer (Grey-Green Coaches) London. N16.	1/1965 lic 4/65	by 12/1973
72	HUH 47	Leyland Tiger Cub PSUC1/1T	534621	Weymann 'Hermes'	B44F	1/1954	Ex Western Welsh O C. Cardiff. (1047)	12/1965	5/1976
73	664 WDE	Austin LD05AR	59286	Austin (Silcox conversion)	B14F	6/1964	Ex Private owner, (Non PSV) Pembroke.	licenced 6/1966	1972-4
74	DDE950D	Leyland Tiger Cub PSUC1/12T	L53946	Plaxton 'Panorama'	C45F	2/1966	New	2/1966	3/1974
75	FDE282D	Leyland Tiger Cub PSUC1/12T	L53947	Plaxton 'Panorama'	C45F	6/1966	New	6/1966	2/1974
76	HUH 25	Leyland Tiger Cub PSUC1/1T	534373	Weymann 'Hermes'	B44F	12/1953	Ex Western Welsh O C. Cardiff. (1025) via: S. Eynon & Sons. Trimsaran, Carms.	9/1966	1976
77	HCU 962	Leyland Leopard L2	623653	Duple 'Commander'	C43F	6/1963	Ex Hall Brothers. South Shields.	10/1966	2/1973
78	URR 346	Leyland Tiger Cub PSUC1/1	564612	MCCW	B44F	12/1956	Ex East Midland M S. Chesterfield. (R346)	5/1967	1973
79	URR 349	Leyland Tiger Cub PSUC1/1	564702	MCCW	B44F	12/1956	Ex East Midland M S. Chesterfield. (R349)	5/1967	1973
80	HDE903E	Leyland Leopard PSU3/3R	700552	Plaxton 'Derwent'	B62F 3+2 seating	7/1967	New	7/1967	c 8/1988
1 / 2	DCN 845	Leyland Tiger Cub PSUC1/1	535166	Saunders-Roe	B44F	7/1954	Ex Northern General Transport. Gateshead, Tyne/Wear (1545)	4/1968	1/1975
2	OUP 660	Leyland Tiger Cub PSUC1/1T	542934	Saunders-Roe	B44F	9/1954	Ex Sunderland District Omnibus Co. Sunderland, Tyne/Wear (263)	4/1968	5/1976
81	MDE914F	Leyland Leopard PSU3/3RT	800869	Plaxton 'Panorama I'	C51F	5/1968	New	5/1968	4/7/1975
82	NDE440F	Leyland Leopard PSU3/3R	800942	Plaxton 'Derwent'	B62F 3+2 seating	6/1968	New	7/1968	8/1992
-	SVT 952	Leyland Tiger Cub PSUC1/1	534712	Weymann 'Hermes'	B44F	1953	Ex Potteries M T. Stoke-on-Trent (S552) via: unidentified owner (as caravan).	by 4/1969	Not operated
83	KDB 647	Leyland Tiger Cub PSUC1/1	555040	Weymann 'Hermes'	B44F	4/1956	Ex North Western Road Car Co, Stockport. (647)	1/1969	1972-3

No.	Reg	Chassis		Body	Seating		History		
84	KDB 648	Leyland Tiger Cub PSUC1/1	555041	Weymann 'Hermes'	B44F	3/1956	Ex North Western Road Car Co, Stockport. (648)	4/1969 lic 5/69	6/1976
85	KDB 656	Leyland Tiger Cub PSUC1/1T	564007	Weymann 'Hermes'	B44F	4/1956	Ex North Western Road Car Co, Stockport. (656)	4/1969 lic 5/69	1976/7
86	HAP 985	Bristol KSW6G	98.052	Eastern Coach Works	H33/28R	7/1953	Ex Brighton Hove & District O C (447) via: Southdown M S, Brighton (447) not op.	5/1969	12/1978
87	RDE659G	Bristol LH6L	LH251	Plaxton 'Derwent'	DP43F	7/1969	New	7/1969	4/1982
88	RDE660G	Bristol LH6L	LH252	Plaxton 'Derwent'	DP43F	7/1969	New	7/1969	10/1981
89	VFM 587	Bristol LD6B - 6LW unit fitted by Crosville	104.077	Eastern Coach Works	H33/25RD	5/1955	Ex Crosville M S, Chester (DLB722)	10/1969	1/1977
90	SFM 8	Bristol LD6B - 6LW unit fitted by Crosville	100.193	Eastern Coach Works	H33/25R	5/1955	Ex Crosville M S, Chester (DLB719)	10/1969	c9/1978
91	RFM 457	Bristol LD6B - 6LW unit fitted from LDE 949, 1969	100.153	Eastern Coach Works	H33/25R	5/1955	Ex Crosville M S, Chester (DLB712)	by 11/69 lic 1970	1972-3
92	KDB 637	Leyland Tiger Cub PSUC1/1	554789	Weymann 'Hermes'	B44F	4/1956	Ex North Western Road Car Co, Stockport. (637)	1/1970	1972-3
93	KDB 632	Leyland Tiger Cub PSUC1/1	554743	Weymann 'Hermes'	B44F	4/1956	Ex North Western Road Car Co, Stockport. (632)	1/1970	1972-4
94	WHN 122	Bristol LS5G	105.123	Eastern Coach Works	B45F	4/1955	Ex United Automobile Services. Darlington, (2122)	6/1970	11/1975
-	NFM 72	Bristol KSW6B	90.011	Eastern Coach Works	H32/28R	1952	Ex Crosville M S, Chester (DKB440) via: W G Anderton. Birmingham (for spares).	by 8/1970	Not operated
95	PHN 836	Bristol LS5G	89.041	Eastern Coach Works	B45F	10/1952	Ex United Automobile Services. Darlington, (U7) via: Smyth. London SW4.	9/1970	9/1977
96	OHY 984	Bristol KSW6G	98.030	Eastern Coach Works	H32/28R	8/1953	Ex Bristol Omnibus Co. (C8127)	9/1970	3/1978
97	XHW 404	Bristol LS5G	117.108	Eastern Coach Works	B45F	12/1956	Ex Bristol Omnibus Co. (2888)	9/1970	12/1978
98 99	OFM 690	Bristol LS6G	93.013	Eastern Coach Works	C39F	2/1953	Ex Crosville M S. Chester (CUG318)	10/1970	1/1976
99 98	OFM 670	Bristol LS6G	89.034	Eastern Coach Works	C39F	7/1952	Ex Crosville M S. Chester (CUG298)	by 10/1970	1975-6
100	XHW 402	Bristol LS5G	117.106	Eastern Coach Works	B45F	11/1956	Ex Bristol Omnibus Co. (2886)	9/1970 lic 10/70	1978
101	VDE873J	Leyland Leopard PSU3A/4R	7001171	Plaxton 'Panorama Elite Express II'	C53F	12/1970	New	12/1970	3/1976
102	VDE874J	Leyland Leopard PSU3A/4R	7001231	Plaxton 'Panorama Elite Express II'	C53F	12/1970	New	12/1970	3/1976
103	XFM 180	Bristol LD6B - 6LW unit fitted by Crosville.	108.065	Eastern Coach Works (See note A, page 283)	H33/27RD	5/1955	Ex Crosville M S. Chester (DLB769) (See note A. page 283)	8/1970 lic 4/71	1978

	Reg	Chassis	Serial	Body	Type	Date	History	In	Out
104	OTT 63	Bristol LS5G	101.153	Eastern Coach Works	B41F to B45F	3/1954	Ex Western National O C. Exeter. (1709)	11/1971	1978
105	KDB 646	Leyland Tiger Cub PSUC1/1	554969	Weymann 'Hermes'	B44F	4/1956	Ex North Western Road Car Co. Stockport. (646)	1/1972	12/1976
106	LTA 990	Bristol LS5G	93.071	Eastern Coach Works	B41F to B45F	1953	Ex Western National O C. Exeter. (1693)	2/1972	11/1976
107	OTT 50	Bristol LS5G	97.139	Eastern Coach Works	B41F to B45F	5/1953	Ex Western National O C. Exeter. (1696)	2/1972 lic 3/72	1/1979
108	LTA 997	Bristol LS6G	93.095	Eastern Coach Works	C39F	1953	Ex Southern National O C. Exeter (1341) via: Bates (Non PSV) Sale, Cheshire.	by 2/1972	9/1976
109	OAH 753	Bristol LS6B	97.081	Eastern Coach Works	C39F	4/1954	Ex Eastern Counties O C. Norwich (LE753)	4/1972	11/76
110	WVX 445	Bristol LS5G	101.009	Eastern Coach Works	B45F	2/1954	Ex Eastern National O C. Chelmsford (4223) via: Eastern Counties O C. Norwich (LS927)	4/1972	1/1977
111	OAH 751	Bristol LS6B	97.032	Eastern Coach Works	C39F	7/1953	Ex Eastern Counties O C. Norwich (LE751)	4/1972 lic 5/72	12/1976
112	OAH 752	Bristol LS6B	97.033	Eastern Coach Works	C39F	8/1953	Ex Eastern Counties O C. Norwich (LE752)	4/1972 lic 5/72	1/1976
113	XHW 418	Bristol LS5G	119.005	Eastern Coach Works	B45F	3/1957	Ex Bristol Omnibus Co. (2902)	5/1972	5/1972
114	MAX 111	Bristol LS6G	101.022	Eastern Coach Works	B45F	7/1954	Ex Red & White Services. Chepstow (U1154) via: Eastern Counties O C. Norwich (LM590)	4/1972 lic 5/72	7/1976
115	SNG 763	Bristol LS5G	107.011	Eastern Coach Works	DP39F	5/1955	Ex Eastern Counties O C. Norwich (LE763)	4/1972 lic 6/72	3/1977
-	VHN 897	Bristol LS5G	105.076	Eastern Coach Works	B45F	1/1955	Ex United Automobile Services. Darlington. via: H M Smith, Stonnall, Staffs.	5/1972	Not operated
116	PHW 927	Bristol LS5G	97.154	Eastern Coach Works	B45F	2/1954	Ex Bristol Omnibus Co. (2837)	8/1972	1/1977
117	XHW 411	Bristol LS5G	117.133	Eastern Coach Works	B45F	1/1957	Ex Bristol Omnibus Co. (2895)	2/1973	late 1979
118	XHW 422	Bristol LS5G	119.069	Eastern Coach Works	B45F	5/1957	Ex Bristol Omnibus Co. (2906)	-/1972 lic 2/73	by 10/1979
119	GDE374L	Bristol LH6L	LH-658	Plaxton 'Panorama Elite Express III'	C45F	2/1973	New	2/1973	7/1981
120	GDE375L	Bristol LH6L	LH-659	Plaxton 'Panorama Elite Express III'	C45F	2/1973	New	2/1973	1/1978
121	OTT 49	Bristol LS5G	97.138	Eastern Coach Works	B45F	1953	Ex Western National O C. Exeter (1695) via: Creamline Services. Tonmawr, W-Glam.	3/1973	1-9/1977
122	OTT 56	Bristol LS5G	97.191	Eastern Coach Works	B45F	1953	Ex Western National O C. Exeter (1702) via: Creamline Services. Tonmawr, W-Glam.	3/1973	12/1978
123	OTT 52	Bristol LS5G	97.150	Eastern Coach Works	B45F	1953	Ex Western National O C.Exeter (1698) via: Creamline Services. Tonmawr, W-Glam.	3/1973	3/1978

No.	Reg	Chassis	Chassis No	Body	Seating	Date	Notes	In	Out
124	OTT 59	Bristol LS5G	101.002	Eastern Coach Works	B45F	1953	Ex Western National O C. Exeter (1705) via: Creamline Services. Tonmawr, W-Glam.	3/1973	4/1978
125	MAX 105	Bristol LS6G	97.182	Eastern Coach Works	B45F	6/1954	Ex Red & White Services. Chepstow (U554) via: Crosville M S. Chester (SUG288)	5/1973	10/1978
126	RWW 985	Bristol LS5G	117.053	Eastern Coach Works	B45F	7/1956	Ex West Yorkshire R C C. Harrogate via: Simpson. (Pennine M S) Gargrave.	9/1973	7/1979
127	NDE803M	Austin-Morris 250JU	52040	B L M C	12 to 7 (1980)	10/1973	New Converted to Non PSV in 1980.	10/1973	1/1981
128	OO 9548	Bristol MW6G	195.028	Eastern Coach Works	C34F	5/1962	Ex Eastern National O C. Chelmsford (562) via: Tillings Travel. Chelmsford (9360)	late 1973	5/1981
129	YHY 77	Bristol LS5G	119.115	Eastern Coach Works	B45F	9/1957	Ex Bristol Omnibus Co. (2919) via: John Lewis. Morriston, West Glam.	c3/1974	4/1979
130	PDE570M	Leyland Leopard PSU3B/4R	7204738	Plaxton 'Panorama Elite Express II'	C51F	1973	New This was a diverted order from: Tillingbourne Bus Co. Cranleigh, Surrey.	2/1974	by 9/1997
131	RDE567M	Bristol LHL6L	LHL-214	Plaxton 'Panorama Elite Express III'	C51F	6/1974	New	6/1974	by 9/1983
132	RDE876M	Bristol LHL6L	LHL-229	Plaxton 'Panorama Elite Express III'	C51F	7/1974	New	7/1974	by 9/1983
133	HBX190N	Bristol LHL6L	LHL-236	Plaxton 'Panorama Elite Express III'	C51F	4/1975	New	1/5/1975	9/1983
134	HDE250N	Leyland Leopard PSU3C/4R	7500798	Duple 'Dominant'	B65F 3+2 seating	5/1975	New	6/1975	3/2000
135	HDE611N	Leyland Leopard PSU3C/4R	7503191	Duple 'Dominant' Express	C53F to DP53F (3/93)	6/1975	New	7/1975	by 10/1998
136	HDE612N	Leyland Leopard PSU3C/4R	7501667	Plaxton 'Panorama Elite Express III'	C53F to DP53F(10/97)	6/1975	New	6/1975	by 10/1998
137	HDE617N	Leyland Leopard PSU3C/4R	7501668	Plaxton 'Panorama Elite Express III'	C53F	6/1975	New	6/1975	by 5/1997
138	LDE163P	Leyland Leopard PSU3C/4R	7601283	Duple 'Dominant' Express	C53F to DP53F (8/95)	5/1976	New	6/1975	by 6/1997
139	LDE164P	Leyland Leopard PSU3C/4R	7601284	Duple 'Dominant' Express	C53F	5/1976	New	5/1976	by 6/1997
140	LDE165P	Bristol LH6L	LH-1254	Duple 'Dominant'	B47F	5/1976	New	5/1976	5/1997
141	LDE166P	Bristol LH6L	LH-1256	Duple 'Dominant'	B47F	5/1976	New	5/1976	5/1997
142	LDE167P	Bristol LH6L	LH-1255	Duple 'Dominant Express'	C45F	5/1976	New	5/1976	by 12/1982
7	923 AHY	Bristol MW5G	135.021	Eastern Coach Works	B45F	2/1958	Ex Bristol Omnibus Co. (2997)	by 9/1976	7/1979
6	928 AHY	Bristol MW5G	139.049	Eastern Coach Works	B45F	9/1958	Ex Bristol Omnibus Co. (2998)	5/1976 lic 6/76	by 8/1981

3	936 AHY	Bristol MW5G	139.084	Eastern Coach Works	B45F	10/1958	Ex Bristol Omnibus Co. (2946)	1/1976	10/1980
4	939 AHY	Bristol MW5G	139.087	Eastern Coach Works	B45F	10/1958	Ex Bristol Omnibus Co. (2949)	2/1976 lic 4/76	8/1981
8	982 EHY	Bristol MW5G	152.038	Eastern Coach Works	B45F	9/1959	Ex Bristol Omnibus Co. (2938)	9/1976	by 8/1980
1	519 JHU	Bristol MW5G	164.099	Eastern Coach Works	B45F	10/1960	Ex Bristol Omnibus Co. (2933)	5/1976 lic 6/76	5/1980
2	520 JHU	Bristol MW5G	164.100	Eastern Coach Works	B45F	10/1960	Ex Bristol Omnibus Co. (2970)	5/1976 lic 6/76	5/1980
5	134 AMW	Bristol MW6G	204.027	Eastern Coach Works	B45F	4/1963	Ex Wilts & Dorset M.S. Salisbury (722) via: Hants & Dorset M.S. Bournemouth (832)	5/1976	5/1980
9	HLJ 915G	Bristol MW5G	233.134	Eastern Coach Works	B43F	11/1966	Ex Hants & Dorset M.S. Bournemouth (859)	9/1976	5/1981
143 r/r	NDE 86R 9195 PU	Leyland Leopard PSU3C/4R	7505578	Duple 'Dominant'	B65F 3+2 seating	2/1977	New Re-registered: 9195 PU in 12/2000 Re-reg: PWN 807R after w/drawn in 3/2004	2/1977 lic 4/77	3/2004
144	NDE998R	Leyland Leopard PSU3C/4R	7505579	Duple 'Dominant' Express	C53F	12/1976	New	1/1977	9/1986
145	NDE999R	Leyland Leopard PSU3C/4R	7505792	Duple 'Dominant' Express	C53F	12/1976	New	1/2/1977	9/1986
15	HEL390D	Bristol MW5G	233.086	Eastern Coach Works	B43F	8/1966	Ex Hants & Dorset M.S. Bournemouth (856)	5/1977 lic 9/77	6/1981
10	HEL 391D	Bristol MW5G	233.087	Eastern Coach Works	B43F to B45F	9/1966	Ex Hants & Dorset M.S. Bournemouth (857)	1/1977	6/1981
11	HEL 392D	Bristol MW5G	233.088	Eastern Coach Works	B43F to B45F	9/1966	Ex Hants & Dorset M.S. Bournemouth (858)	12/1976	6/1981
12	HLJ 916D	Bristol MW5G	233.135	Eastern Coach Works	B43F to B45F	12/1966	Ex Hants & Dorset M.S. Bournemouth (860)	1/1977	7/1981
18	EMR299D	Bristol MW6G	233.039	Eastern Coach Works	DP41F	6/1966	Ex Wilts & Dorset M.S. Salisbury (724) via: Hants & Dorset M.S. Bournemouth (834)	1977	5/1982
14	EMR300D	Bristol MW6G	233.040	Eastern Coach Works	B41F to B45F	6/1966	Ex Wilts & Dorset M.S. Salisbury (725) via: Hants & Dorset M.S. Bournemouth (835)	2/1977	by 3/1984
16	EMR302D	Bristol MW6G	233.042	Eastern Coach Works	B41F to B45F	7/1966	Ex Wilts & Dorset M.S. Salisbury (727) via: Hants & Dorset M.S. Bournemouth (837)	5/1977	by 4/1985
17	EMR304D	Bristol MW6G	233.092	Eastern Coach Works	B41F to B45F	9/1966	Ex Wilts & Dorset M.S. Salisbury (812) via: Hants & Dorset M.S. Bournemouth (839)	10/1977	10/1980
146	RDE298S	Bristol LH6L	LH-1260	Plaxton 'Supreme' Express	C45F	1/1978	New	1/1978	9/1982
147	RDE772S	Leyland Leopard PSU3E/4R	7704207	Duple 'Dominant' Express	C53F	2/1978	New	2/1978 lic 4/78	1986
19	ETD 949B	Daimler Fleetline CRG6LX	60720	Northern Counties	H43/31F	11/1964	Ex Lancashire United Transport. Atherton, Manchester (179)	by 4/1978 lic 6/78	5/1980

Fleet	Registration	Chassis	Chassis no.	Body	Seating	Date	History	In	Out
20 r/r	538 OHU ABX172A	Bristol Lodekka FLF6G	199.195	Eastern Coach Works	H38/32F	12/1962	Ex Bristol Omnibus Co. (7075) Re-registered: ABX 172A in 3/1987	4/1978	8/1987
21	839 SUO	Bristol RELH6G	212.066	Eastern Coach Works	C45F	6/1964	Ex Western National O C. (Royal Blue) Exeter (2353)	4/1978 lic 6/78	1/1980
22	BHU 976C	Bristol Lodekka FLF6B 6LW unit fitted by Bristol	224.148	Eastern Coach Works	H38/32F	2/1965	Ex Bristol Omnibus Co. (C7176)	by 4/1978	by 8/1986
23	LTE 261C	Leyland Leopard PSU3/3R	L23377	Marshall	B50F	4/1965	Ex Lancashire United Transport. Atherton, Manchester (208)	4/1978	1/1982
24	YNG 784	Bristol MW5G	139.001	Eastern Coach Works	C39F	6/1958	Ex Eastern Counties O C (LS 784) via: Tally Ho Coaches. Kingsbridge. Devon.	c 9/1978 lic 10/78	6/1981
25	7793 NG	Bristol MW5G	164.017	Eastern Coach Works	C39F	3/1960	Ex Eastern Counties O C (LS 793) via: Tally Ho Coaches. Kingsbridge. Devon.	c 9/1978 lic 10/78	2/1981
26	842 SUO	Bristol RELH6G	212.070	Eastern Coach Works	C45F	6/1964	Ex Western National O C Royal Blue (2362) via: Tally Ho Coaches. Kingsbridge. Devon.	by10/1978 lic 1/79	1/1980
31	JDW 301F	Bristol RESL6L	RESL-5-131	Eastern Coach Works	B44F	9/1967	Ex Newport B T. (101)	11/1978 lic 1/79	1/1981
34	JDW 304F	Bristol RESL6L	RESL-5-135	Eastern Coach Works	B44F	9/1967	Ex Newport B T. (104)	11/1978 lic 1/79	1/1981
-	JDW 305F	Bristol RESL6L	RESL-5-136	Eastern Coach Works	B42F	9/1967	Ex Newport B T. (105)	11/1978	Not operated
37	JDW 307F	Bristol RESL6L	RESL-5-138	Eastern Coach Works	B42F	9/1967	Ex Newport B T. (107)	1/1979 lic 3/79	11/1979
27	JHK 456C	Bristol MW6G	213.218	Eastern Coach Works	DP43F to DP45F	1/1965	Ex Eastern National O C. Chelmsford (1432)	1/1979	by 8/1986
28	HFM 590D	Bristol MW6G	233.127	Eastern Coach Works	B45F	12/1966	Ex Crosville M S. Chester. (SMG 590)	1/1979	1/1981
29 r/r	804 SHW ADE146A	Bristol Lodekka FLF6B (fitted 6LW unit by 7/84)	210.086	Eastern Coach Works	H38/32F	10/1963	Ex Bristol Omnibus Co. (C7111) Re-registered: ADE 146A by 7/1989	1/1979	by 3/1990
30	1216 FM	Bristol MW6G	195.137	Eastern Coach Works	B45F	1/1963	Ex Crosville M S. Chester. (SMG 438)	4/1979 lic 1/7/79	11/1980
37 39	1218 FM	Bristol MW6G	195.139	Eastern Coach Works	B43F	1/1963	Ex Crosville M S. Chester. (SMG 440)	by 2/1979 lic 3/79	11/1980
38 40	1225 FM	Bristol MW6G	195.181	Eastern Coach Works	B43F	5/1963	Ex Crosville M S. Chester. (SMG 446)	by 2/1979 lic 3/79	1/1981
32	JDW 302F	Bristol RESL6L	RESL-5-132	Eastern Coach Works	B42F	9/1967	Ex Newport B T. (102)	3/1979	11/1979 to 2/1980
33	JDW 303F	Bristol RESL6L	RESL-5-134	Eastern Coach Works	B42F	9/1967	Ex Newport B T. (103)	3/1979 lic 6/79	9/1979
148	WBX 870T	Leyland Leopard PSU3E/4R	7805075	Duple 'Dominant II' Express	C53F	2/1979	New	3/1979	by 11/1999
149 r/r	WBX 871T 538 OHU	Leyland Leopard PSU3E/4R	7805367	Duple 'Dominant II' Express	C53F	4/1979	New Re-registered: 538 OHU by 5/2000 Returned to WBX 871T upon withdrawal.	4/1979	3/2004

Fleet No	Registration	Chassis	Chassis No	Body	Seating	Date	Notes	Date(s)	Disposal
39	1231 FM	Bristol MW6G	213.004	Eastern Coach Works	B45F	6/1963	Ex Crosville M S. Chester. (SMG 451)	5/1979	1/1982
40 / 42	MRU124F	Bristol RELH6G	RELH4/121	Duple 'Commander III'	C49F	6/1968	Ex Hants & Dorset M S. Bournemouth (1053)	4/1979 lic 5/79	4/1980
41 / 43	MRU126F	Bristol RELH6G	RELH4/123	Duple 'Commander III'	C49F	6/1968	Ex Hants & Dorset M S. Bournemouth (1054)	4/1979 lic 5/79	1/1980
44	1222 FM	Bristol MW6G	195.178	Eastern Coach Works	B41F	4/1963	Ex Crosville M S. Chester. (SMG 443)	6/1979 lic 1/7/79	4/1982
46	1246 FM	Bristol MW6G	213.090	Eastern Coach Works	B45F	2/1964	Ex Crosville M S. Chester. (SMG 465)	6/1979 lic 1/7/79	1/1982
47	1247 FM	Bristol MW6G	213.091	Eastern Coach Works	B45F	3/1964	Ex Crosville M S. Chester. (SMG 466)	by 8/1979 lic 10/79	by 4/1982
150 r/r	YBX608V 804 SHW	Leyland Leopard PSU5C/4R	7900384	Duple 'Dominant II'	C57F	7/1979	New. Re-registered 804 SHW by 7/1989 and re-registered CDE 391V upon sale 12/2000	8/1979	12/2000
48	JMY122N	Bedford YRT	EW45J908	Willowbrook '008'	C49F	7/1975	Ex National Travel (South East)	11/1979 lic 1/1/80	9/1982
49	SWY334L	Bedford YRT	2T475849	Willowbrook '001'	B55F	11/1972	Ex Wigmore, Dinnington, South Yorkshire.	c9/1979 lic 4/80	9/1982
50	109 CUF	Leyland Leopard PSU3/1RT	L01997	Marshall	B51F	12/1963	Ex Southdown M S. Brighton (109) via: Western National (25) & NPSV @ Warrington	c11/1979 lic 1/2/80	by 10/1985
51	115 CUF	Leyland Leopard PSU3/1RT	L02013	Marshall	B51F	12/1963	Ex Southdown M S. Brighton (115) via: Western National O C. Exeter (29)	c11/1979 lic 1/2/80	by 8/1985
45	1232 FM	Bristol MW6G	213.005	Eastern Coach Works	B45F	6/1963	Ex Crosville M S. Chester (SMG 452)	by 2/1980 lic 3/80	10/1981
32	KDD283E	Leyland Leopard PSU3/3RT	L65224	Plaxton 'Panorama I'	C47F	6/1967	Ex Black & White. Cheltenham, Glos. (283) via: Elsworth. Blackpool.	3/1980	11/1980
33	KDD289E	Leyland Leopard PSU3/3RT	700050	Plaxton 'Panorama I'	C47F	7/1967	Ex Black & White. Cheltenham, Glos. (289) via: Marshall. Blackpool.	3/1980	5/1982
151 r/r	BBX915V SIL 9611	Leyland Leopard PSU3E/4R	7903439	Duple 'Dominant II' Express	C53F	3/1980	New. Re-registered SIL 9611 in 7/2000	3/1980	10/2003
152 r/r	BDE140V SIL 9612	Leyland Leopard PSU3E/4R	7903334	Duple 'Dominant'	B63F 3+2 seating	4/1980	New. Re-registered SIL 9612 in 8/2000	5/1980	9/2003
153 r/r	BDE143V SIL 9613	Leyland Leopard PSU3E/4R	7903453	Duple 'Dominant II' Express	C53F	4/1980	New. Re-registered SIL 9613 by 5/2000	4/1980	12/2001
52	LAE890L	Bedford YRT	CW452116	Duple 'Dominant'	C53F	3/1973	Ex Wessex. Bristol. via: National Travel (SW) Ltd (490)	by 4/1980 lic 5/80	9/1982
91	UTD291H	Bristol LH6L	LH-263	Northern Counties	B39D	1/1970	Ex Lancashire United Transport (328)	by 4/1980 lic 5/80	by 7/1985
19	RWC942D	Bristol Lodekka FL6G	231.220	Eastern Coach Works	H38/32F	9/1966	Ex Eastern National O C. Chelmsford (2870) via: Alexander (Midland) Falkirk, Scotland.	5/1980 lic 10/80	11/1980
76	KCK976H	Leyland Leopard PSU4A/4R	903543	Plaxton 'Panorama Elite I'	C36F to C42F	3/1970	Ex Ribble M S. Preston, Lancs (976) via: National Travel (South West) 416	7/1980 lic 1/81	by 12/1996

267

No.	Reg.	Chassis	Body	Seating	Date	History / Notes	Acquired	Withdrawn
77	KCK977H	Leyland Leopard PSU4A/4R	903544	Plaxton 'Panorama Elite I'	C36F	3/1970	Ex Ribble M S. Preston, Lancs (977) via: National Travel (South West)	9/1980 lic 12/80	by 7/1986
86	KCK987H	Leyland Leopard PSU4A/4R	903662	Plaxton 'Panorama Elite I'	C36F	4/1970	Ex Ribble M S. Preston, Lancs (987) via: National Travel (South West) 417	7/1980 lic 12/80	by 3/1991
89	KCK989H	Leyland Leopard PSU4A/4R	903820	Plaxton 'Panorama Elite I'	C36F	4/1970	Ex Ribble M S. Preston, Lancs (989) via: National Travel (South West) 419	7/1980 lic 12/80	9/1982
19	FLJ 154D	Bristol Lodekka FLF6G	231.055	Eastern Coach Works	H38/32F	2/1966	Ex Hants & Dorset M S. Bournemouth (1234)	9/1980 lic 10/80	by 8/1988
103	LPT 903P	Leyland Leopard PSU3C/4R	7503350	Willowbrook	B55F	8/1975	Ex Trimdon M S. Trimdon Grange, Durham.	by10/1980 lic 12/80	8/1987
104	LPT 904P	Leyland Leopard PSU3C/4R	7503733	Willowbrook	B55F	8/1975	Ex Trimdon M S. Trimdon Grange, Durham.	by10/1980 lic 12/80	8/1987
108	NLJ 518M	Bristol LH6L	LH-841	Eastern Coach Works	B43F	10/1973	Ex Hants & Dorset M S. Bournemouth (3518)	12/1980 lic 3/81	by 12/1988
109	NLJ 519M	Bristol LH6L	LH-877	Eastern Coach Works	B43F	10/1973	Ex Hants & Dorset M S. Bournemouth (3519)	12/1980 lic 6/81	9/1990
127	JHD 377J	Leyland Leopard PSU3B/4R	7100651	Plaxton 'Panorama Elite II'	C47F to DP47F	7/1971	Ex Hebble M S. Halifax (455) via: National Travel (East)	1/1981	7/1992
119	SPK 119M	Bristol LHS6L	LHS-152	Eastern Coach Works	B35F	10/1973	Ex London Country B S. (BL19)	1/1981	by 4/1996
120	SPK 120M	Bristol LHS6L	LHS-153	Eastern Coach Works	B35F	10/1973	Ex London Country B S. (BL20)	1/1981	9/1985
116	SPK 116M	Bristol LHS6L	LHS-149	Eastern Coach Works	B35F	9/1973	Ex London Country B S. (BL16)	by 8/1981	9/1985
3	OWT783M	Bristol LH6L	LH-815	Eastern Coach Works	B45F	12/1973	Ex West Yorkshire Road Car Co (1177)	8/1981 lic 12/81	7/1987
4	OWT784M	Bristol LH6L	LH-816	Eastern Coach Works	B45F	2/1974	Ex West Yorkshire Road Car Co (1178)	by 8/1981 lic 10/81	7/1987
5	OWT785M	Bristol LH6L	LH-817	Eastern Coach Works	B45F	2/1974	Ex West Yorkshire Road Car Co (1179)	6/1981 lic 10/81	7/1987
6	OWT786M	Bristol LH6L	LH-827	Eastern Coach Works	B45F	2/1974	Ex West Yorkshire Road Car Co (1180)	6/1981 lic 10/81	7/1987
7	OWT787M	Bristol LH6L	LH-828	Eastern Coach Works	B45F	2/1974	Ex West Yorkshire Road Car Co (1181)	by 8/1981 lic 10/81	7/1987
8	OWT788M	Bristol LH6L	LH-829	Eastern Coach Works	B45F	2/1974	Ex West Yorkshire Road Car Co (1182)	by 8/1981 lic 10/81	7/1987
9	TCK 469	Leyland Leopard PSU3/1R	629367	Marshall	B53F	6/1963	Ex Ribble M S. Preston, Lancs (469) via: Marchwood. Haverfordwest, Pembs.	by10/1981	9/1982
154	JDE972X	Leyland Tiger TRCTL11/3RH	8101069	Plaxton 'Supreme VI' Express	C57F	2/1982	New	2/1982 lic 3/82	by 10/1985
155	JDE973X	Leyland Tiger TRCTL11/3RH	8101070	Plaxton 'Supreme VI' Express	C57F	2/1982	New	2/1982 lic 3/82	9/1985

No.	Reg.	Chassis	Serial	Body	Seating	Date	History	In service	Withdrawn
156	JDE 189X	Leyland Tiger TRCTL11/2R	8101758	Duple 'Dominant IV' Exp. incorporating SBG front end	C53F	3/1982	New	3/1982 lic 4/1982	2/1985
63	BNE 763N	Bristol LH6L	LH-922	Eastern Coach Works	B43F	11/1974	Ex Greater Manchester PTE (1320)	9/1982	by 12/1987
66	BNE 766N	Bristol LH6L	LH-925	Eastern Coach Works	B43F	11/1974	Ex Greater Manchester PTE (1323)	by 8/1982 lic 11/82	9/1983
67	BNE 767N	Bristol LH6L	LH-926	Eastern Coach Works	B43F	11/1974	Ex Greater Manchester PTE (1324)	by 8/1982 4/1983	10/1987
157	NDE 147Y	Leyland Tiger TRCTL11/2R	8201143	Plaxton 'Paramount 3200' Express	C53F	2/1983	New	2/1983	9/1985
158	NDE 748Y	Leyland Tiger TRCTL11/2R	8201070	Plaxton 'Paramount 3200' Express	C49F	2/1983	New	2/1983	9/1985
159	NDE 749Y	Leyland Tiger TRCTL11/2R	8200982	Plaxton 'Paramount 3200' Express	C49F	2/1983	New	2/1983	9/1985
146 r/r	AJD 162T 538 OHU	Leyland Leopard PSU4E/4R	7800429	Plaxton 'Supreme IV'	C45F	3/1979	Ex Bicknell, Godalming, Surrey. Re-registered 538 OHU in 3/1987.	11/1983	c4/2000
131 r/r r/r	WFH170S KSU 409 WFH170S	Leyland Leopard PSU3E/4R	7703388	Plaxton 'Supreme'	C53F	2/1978	Ex Hants & Dorset M.S. Bournemouth (3030) Re-registered: KSU 409 in 5/1988 Re-registered: WFH170S (Not op) 5/2005	11/1983	5/2005
132 r/r	AFH 182T 817 FKH	Leyland Leopard PSU3E/4R	7801922	Plaxton 'Supreme'	C53F	9/1978	Ex South Wales Transport. Swansea (151) Re-registered 817 FKH in 9/1987	11/1983	2/2003
133	DAD258T	Leyland Leopard PSU5C/4R	7806361	Plaxton 'Supreme IV'	C57F	4/1979	Ex National Travel South West (258) via: South Wales Transport (153)	11/1983	8/1988
142	DAD 254T	Leyland Leopard PSU5C/4R	7802797	Plaxton 'Supreme IV'	C57F	2/1979	Ex National Travel South West (254) via: Hants & Dorset, Bournemouth (3037)	by 2/1984 lic 3/1984	by 8/1990
160	A53 VGD	Mercedes Benz L608D	310327-20-528264	Coachcraft	C21F	3/1984	Ex Keenan, Coalhall, Strathclyde.	by 7/1984	by 1/1988
163 r/r	817 FKH B386YDE	DAF SB2300DHS585	242665	Plaxton 'Paramount 3200'	C55F	2/1985	New. Re-registered: B386 YDE in 8/1987.	2/1985	8/1987
161	KAD346V	Leyland Leopard PSU5C/4R	7904664	Plaxton 'Supreme IV'	C57F	3/1980	Ex National Travel South West (346) via: Black & White Motorways, Cheltenham	3/1985	by 8/1987
162	KAD348V	Leyland Leopard PSU5C/4R	7905025	Plaxton 'Supreme IV'	C57F	3/1980	Ex National Travel South West (348) via: Black & White Motorways, Cheltenham	3/1985	8/1987
164 r/r 109	B538XDE PVO 624 A9 WLS	DAF SB2300DHS585	245871	Plaxton 'Paramount 3200'	C53F	6/1985	New Re-registered: PVO 624 in 7/1986 Re-registered: A9 WLS in 12/1992	6/1985	6/1997
165	B222 NUT	DAF SB2300DHS585	243673	Plaxton 'Paramount 3200'	C53F to C57F	2/1985	Ex Yeates (dealer) Loughborough (former demonstration vehicle)	6/1985 lic 7/85	8/1987
31	OCA 631P	Bristol LH6L	LH-1214	Eastern Coach Works	B43F	3/1976	Ex Crosville M.S. Chester (SLL 631) via: NCB Rotherham (Non PSV)	7/1985 lic 9/85	by 9/1990
34	OCA 634P	Bristol LH6L	LH-1228	Eastern Coach Works	B43F	3/1976	Ex Crosville M.S. Chester (SLL 634) via: NCB Rotherham (Non PSV)	7/1985 lic 9/85	by 8/1990

No	Reg	Chassis	Body	Seating	Date	History	Date	Withdrawn
40	KTT 40P	Bristol LH6L	LH-1137	Eastern Coach Works	B43F to B45F	10/1975	Ex Western National O.C. Exeter (110) via: NCB Rotherham (Non PSV)	7/1985 lic 9/85	by 5/1997
166	115 CUF	DAF SB2300DHS585	246250	Plaxton 'Paramount 3200'	C53F	9/1985	New	9/1985	8/1990
167 rfr rfr	C429 ADE 587 NCG	DAF SB2300DHS585	246263	Plaxton 'Paramount 3200'	C55F	9/1985	New Re-registered: 587 NCG c/1986	9/1985	5/1993
168 rfr rfr	C392 CDE 109 CUF A7 WLS	DAF SB2300DHS585	245987	Plaxton 'Paramount 3200'	C49FT to C55F by 1/98	4/1986	New Re-registered: 109 CUF c 6/1986 Re-registered: A7 WLS in 3/1992 Returned to C392 CDE in 9/1998	4/1986	9/1998
169 111 rfr	VAW 527 A11 WLS C358DBX	DAF SB2300DHS585	246215	Plaxton 'Paramount 3200'	C55F	3/1986	New Re-registered: A11 WLS in 10/1994 Re-registered: C358 DBX in 2/2001	3/1986	3/2001
11	WHN411G	Bristol VRTSL 6G	VRT/SL/164	Eastern Coach Works	H39/31F	7/1969	Ex United Automobile Services (601) via: South Wales Transport, Swansea (902)	4/1986	by 4/1997
24	WCD524K	Bristol VRTSL2 6G	VRT/SL2/233	Eastern Coach Works	H39/31F	11/1971	Ex Southdown M.S. Brighton (524) via: South Wales Transport, Swansea (524)	8/1986	by 6/1997
70 77	OCD770G	Bristol VRTSL 6G	VRT/SL/163	Eastern Coach Works	H39/31F	3/1969	Ex Southdown M.S. Brighton (100) via: Brighton & Hove (2100)	8/1986	by 9/1996
111	UUF 111J	Bristol VRTSL 6G	VRT/SL2/178	Eastern Coach Works	H39/31F	4/1971	Ex Southdown M.S. Brighton (511)	8/1986	6/1991
154	WRK 3X	DAF MB200DKTL600	216718	Jonckheere 'Bermuda'	C57F	3/1982	Ex Randall. London, NW10 via: Roman City. Bath, Somerset.	9/1986	9/1988
170	D192 HDE	DAF SB2300DHS585	275658	Duple 340	C57F to C53FT	3/1987	New	3/1987	7/1992
128	YTG 138H	Leyland Leopard PSU3A/4R	7001491	Plaxton 'Panorama Elite I'	C53F to DP53F	4/1970	Ex Creamline. Tonmawr, West Glamorgan.	3/1987	by 5/1993
129 9	HPT 320H	Leyland Leopard PSU3A/4R	903447	Plaxton 'Derwent'	B55F	2/1970	Ex Trimdon M.S. Trimdon Grange. Durham. via: Creamline. Tonmawr. West Glamorgan.	3/1987	by 5/1994
10	HPT 321H	Leyland Leopard PSU3A/4R	903607	Plaxton 'Derwent'	B55F	2/1970	Ex Trimdon M.S. Trimdon Grange. Durham. via: Creamline. Tonmawr. West Glamorgan.	3/1987	by 5/1992
-	LJD 926K	Leyland Leopard PSU3B/4R	7200975	Plaxton 'Panorama Elite II' rebodied 8/1973	C53F	6/1972	Ex Ebdon. Sidcup, Kent. via: Creamline. Tonmawr. West Glamorgan.	3/1987	Not operated
71 4	JOV 713P	Bristol VRTSL2 6LXG	VRT/SL2/1153	Metro-Cammell-Weymann	H43/33F	11/1975	Ex West Midlands PTE (4713) via: Crosville M.S. Chester (HVG 967)	5/1987	by 10/1993
95	VUB395H	Leyland Leopard PSU3A/4R	7001211	Plaxton 'Panorama Elite I'	C53F to DP53F	3/1970	Ex Wallace Arnold. Leeds. via: Martindale. Ferryhill. Durham.	3/1987 lic 6/87	4/1993
1 61	VCW 1 L KDE 161L	Leyland Leopard PSU3B/4R	7300922	Duple 'Dominant' Express	C49F	6/1973	Ex Burnley Colne & Nelson (1). via: Worthington. Collingham, Notts. Re-registered: KDE 161L by 3/1991	7/1987	by 4/1997
171 rfr rfr	D901HBX A3 WLS D45 KDE	Duple 425	SDA1512/032	Duple 425	C59F	7/1987	New Re-registered: A3 WLS by 12/1992 Re-registered: D45 KDE c10/1994	7/1987	10/1994

Fleet No	Registration	Chassis	Body	Chassis/Body No	Seating	Date	Notes	In	Out
18	AJA 418L	Bristol VRTSL2 6G	Eastern Coach Works	VRT/SL2/515	H43/32F	7/1973	Ex. S E L N E C PTE (418) via: Stevenson. Uttoxeter, Staffs (48)	8/1987	by 9/1997
21	AJA 421L	Bristol VRTSL2 6G	Eastern Coach Works	VRT/SL2/559	H43/32F	7/1973	Ex. S E L N E C PTE (421) via: Stevenson. Uttoxeter, Staffs (51)	8/1987	by 9/1997
30	MHX 530P	Leyland Leopard PSU3C/4R	Duple 'Dominant'	7601750	C53F	6/1976	Ex R A C S. London SE18 (K128) via: J A Evans. Tregaron, Cardigan.	8/1987	by 5/1999
37	SJA 370J	Leyland Leopard PSU3A/4R	Plaxton 'Panorama Elite II'	7004415	C49F to C53F	7/1971	Ex North Western Road Car Co (370) via: Berresford. Cheddleton, Staffs.	8/1987	by 4/1992
41	AAW411K	Leyland Leopard PSU3B/4R	Plaxton 'Panorama Elite II' Express	7200889	C51F	7/1972	Ex Brown. Trench, Salop.	8/1987	by 4/1996
43	AUA 431J	Leyland Leopard PSU3B/4R	Plaxton 'Panorama Elite II' fitted 'Supreme IV' front end	7100690	C53F to DP53F	3/1971	Ex Wallace Arnold. Leeds. via: Morgan. Nantyglo, Gwent.	10/1987	by 4/1994
172 102 r/r	E522 MDE A2 WLS E522 MDE	Duple 425	Duple 425	SDA1512/058	C55FT to C57F by4/2000	3/1988	New Re-registered: A2 WLS by 10/1992 Re-registered: E522 MDE in 2/2003	3/1988	2/2003
-	VCW 2 L	Leyland Leopard PSU3B/4R	Duple 'Dominant' Express	7302062	DP56F Bus seats	6/1973	Ex Burnley Colne & Nelson (2) Loan ex Wacton (dealer) Bromyard	6/1988	6/1988
70 3	JOV 700P	Bristol VRTSL2 6LXG	Metro-Cammell-Weymann	VRT/SL2/1140	H43/33F	10/1975	Ex West Midlands PTE (4700) via: Chartercoach. Gt Oakley. Essex.	8/1988	by 10/1993
54	OKY 54R	Leyland Leopard PSU3D/4R (DAF engine)	Willowbrook 'Crusader' (1989)	7606000	C51F	2/1977	Chassis acquired from National Travel (East), Sheffield c 6/88. Overhauled / fitted DAF unit by Silcox before re-bodying by Willowbrook.	licenced 4/1989	12/1992 (returned) (4/1993)
7	F77 TDE	Mercedes Benz 609D	P M T	668063-20-852258	B24F	10/1988	New	10/1988	10/1994
8	F78 TDE	Mercedes Benz 609D	P M T	668063-20-861543	B24F	10/1988	New	10/1988	10/1994
9 55	F559 UDE	Mercedes Benz 709D	P M T 'Bursley'	669063-20-868476	C25F	5/1989	New	5/1989	3/1996
-	LAG 287F	Leyland Leopard PSU3/3R	Northern Counties	800132	B53F	6/1968	Loan ex Wacton (dealer) Bromyard (H&W)	5/1989	7/1989
-	TBU 740G	Bristol LH6L	Plaxton 'Panorama Elite I'	LH-243	DP45F Bus seats	4/1969	Loan ex Martin Perry. Bromyard (H&W)	5/1989	7/1989
-	GKE 458L	Leyland Leopard PSU4B/4R	Marshall	7200349	B52F	1/1973	Loan ex Martin Perry. Bromyard (H&W)	5/1989	7/1989
19	MHS 19P	Leyland Leopard PSU3/3R	Alexander 'AYS'	7600176	B53F	3/1976	Ex M Perry. Bromyard, Hereford/Worcester.	5/1989	by 10/1997
-	G739 ADE	Leyland-DAF 400	Leyland-DAF		B16F	3/1990	New Operated as Non-PSV	3/1990 NPSV	?
-	G68 CDE	Leyland-DAF 400	Leyland-DAF	CN873834	B16F	3/1990	New	3/1990 lic by 5/91	?
-	RUB 362G	Leyland Leopard PSU3A/4R	Plaxton 'Panorama Elite I'	900817	C49F	1969	Ex Wallace Arnold. Leeds. via: Stourport Swimming Club, H&W (NPSV)	by 4/1990	Not operated

67	GNJ 567N	Bristol VRTSL2 6LX	VRT/SL2/902	Eastern Coach Works	H43/31F	12/1974	Ex Southdown M S. Brighton (567) via: Williams. Camborne, Cornwall.	8/1990	10/1993
6	H736 EDE	Mercedes Benz 709D	669003-2P-039892	Dormobile 'Routemaker'	B29F to B27F	8/1990	New	8/1990	8/2010
3	H743 EDE	Mercedes Benz 709D	669003-2P-039891	Dormobile 'Routemaker'	B29F to B27F	8/1990	New	8/1990	8/2007
4	H754 EDE	Mercedes Benz 709D	669003-2P-040568	Dormobile 'Routemaker'	B29F to B27F	8/1990	New	8/1990	by 9/2005
2	H227 GDE	Mercedes Benz 811D	670303-2P-055835	Dormobile 'Routemaker'	B33F to B31F	1/1991	New	1/1991	by 2/2010
22	OSJ 622R	Leyland Leopard PSU3C/3R	7602742	Alexander 'AY'	B53F	12/1976	Ex Western S M T (2623) via: United Automobile Services (1203)	4/1991	by 9/1997
23	OSJ 623R	Leyland Leopard PSU3C/3R	7603088	Alexander 'AY'	B53F	12/1976	Ex Western S M T (2623) via: Minsterley. Stipperstones, Salop.	4/1991	by 9/1997
83	GNL 839N	Leyland Leopard PSU3C/4R	7501744	Alexander 'AY'	DP62F 3+2 seating	4/1975	Ex Tyne & Wear PTE (839) via: Minsterley. Stipperstones, Salop.	4/1991 lic 5/91	12/1997
84	GNL840N	Leyland Leopard PSU3C/4R	7501745	Alexander 'AY'	DP62F 3+2 seating	7/1975	Ex Tyne & Wear PTE (840) via: Crump. Malvem, Worcester.	4/1991 lic 5/91	by 9/1997
-	E110 UEJ	Freight Rover 250D	827661	Freight Rover	12	5/1988	Ex J M Morgan. (Meurig's Coaches) Lampeter. Cardigan.	by 7/1990 lic by 6/91	by 11/1991
173 rtr rtr	D753 APK GSK 676 A4 WLS	LAG Panoramic (Integral)	G3552140	LAG 'Panoramic'	C49FT	1/1987	Ex Hogg. Boston, Lincs. Re-reg: GSK 676 in 10/91 to A4 WLS -11/92 Re-registered: D980 NCV in 1/1994	8/1991	1/1994
174 rtr	D218 XPK A6 WLS	LAG Panoramic (Integral)	G350Z107	LAG 'Panoramic'	C49FT	10/1986	Ex Berryhurst. London, SE11. Re-reg: A6 WLS in 11/1992 to D218 XPK in 6/1993	8/1991	6/1993
59 rtr	LMA 59P PVO 624	Leyland Leopard PSU3C/4R	7503348	Plaxton 'Panorama Elite III'	C53F	8/1975	Ex Stephenson. Rochford, Essex. Re-registered: PVO 624 by 12/1992	1/1992	6/2004
12	BUR 712S	Leyland Leopard PSU3E/4R	7800197	Duple 'Dominant'	C53F to DP53F	5/1978	Ex Stephenson. Rochford, Essex. Previously: FIL 6784 originally: XWX169S	1/1992 lic 2/92	by 9/1997
66 rtr rtr rtr	WFH166S 115 CUF 9195 PU TDE 708S	Leyland Leopard PSU5C/4R	7705024	Duple 'Dominant'	C57F	3/1978	Ex National Travel (SW) 166 via: Stephenson. Rochford, Essex. Re-reg:115 CUF in 6/1992 to 9195 PU in 8/1992 to TDE 708S in 12/2000	1/1992	12/2000
112 rtr rtr	9195 PU A12 WLS A81 VDE	DAF SB2300DHS585	245878	Plaxton 'Paramount 3500'	C53F	5/1984	Ex Travelfar. Henfield (Originally: A263BTY) Re-registered: A12 WLS in 8/1992 Re-registered: A81 VDE in 6/1997	1/1992	6/1997
114 rtr rtr	B722 MBC A14 WLS B89 ADE	Volvo B10M-61	7960	Caetano 'Algarve'	C49FT to C53F	1/1985	Ex Ageneralink. Dundee, Tayside. Re-registered: A14 WLS in 4/1992 Re-registered: B89 ADE in 1/1998	1/1992	1/1998
5	J387 ODE	Mercedes Benz 811D	670303-2P-017717	Crystals (Whittaker frame)	B31F	4/1992	New	4/1992	12/2007

Fleet	Registration	Make / Model	Chassis No.	Body	Seating	New	History	In	Out
28 r/r r/r	NGV288M 109 CUF CDE110M	Leyland Leopard PSU5/4R	7201110	Willowbrook 'Warrier' (1988)	B61F 3+2 seating	8/1973	Ex Glyn Williams. Cross Keys, Gwent (1) Re-registered: 109 CUF in 1/1993 Re-registered: CDE110M in 3/1999	7/1992	by 10/1998
79	HWY719N	Leyland Leopard PSU3B/4R	7500026	Willowbrook 'Warrier' (1988)	B55F	3/1975	Ex West Riding (379) via: Glyn Williams. Cross Keys, Gwent (7)	7/1992	12/1998
72 r/r	HWY720N GSK 676	Leyland Leopard PSU3B/4R	7500128	Willowbrook 'Warrier' (1988)	B55F	3/1975	Ex Glyn Williams. Cross Keys, Gwent (11) Re-reg GSK 676-1/93 to HWY720N-1/99	7/1992	1/1999
115 r/r	E167OMD A15 WLS	Volvo B10M – 61	16959	Plaxton 'Paramount 3200'	C57F	2/1988	Ex Frames / Rickards. Brentford, Middex. Re-reg A15 WLS-12/92 to E167OMD-4/99	12/1992	4/1999
175 r/r r/r	J47 SNY A11 WLS J328PDE	Leyland Tiger TRCL10/3ARZM	TR00815	Plaxton '321' (Duple '320' body built by Plaxton after merger).	C53F	8/1991	Ex Bebb. Llantwit Fardre, Mid-Glam. Re-registered: A15 WLS in 12/1992 Re-registered: J328 PDE in 9/1994	12/1992	9/1994
105 r/r	G994 FVV A 5 WLS	LAG Panoramic (Integral)	G355Z388	LAG 'Panoramic'	C49FT	8/1989	Ex Henderson. Crewe, Cheshire. Re-reg: A5 WLS in 1/1993 to G994 FVV in 4/1999	12/1992	4/1999
108 r/r	F628 SRP A 8 WLS F628 SRP	LAG Panoramic (Integral)	G355Z263	LAG 'Panoramic'	C49FT	11/1988	Ex Berryhurst. London, SE11. Re-registered: A8 WLS in 1/1993 Re-registered: F628 SRP in 2/2000	1/1993	2/2000
54 r/r	OKY 54R VAW 527	Leyland Leopard PSU3D/4R (DAF engine)	7606000	Willowbrook 'Crusader' (1989)	C51F	2/1977	Re-acquired from dealer in 4/1993 Re-reg: VAW 527 in 3/1995 to OKY 54R by 9/2003	4/1993	9/2002
9	K651 TDE	Mercedes Benz 814D	670313-2N-010451	Crystals	B31F to B33F	6/1993	New	6/1993	6/2010
70	CWG707V	Leyland Atlantean AN68A/1R	7903336	Alexander 'AL type'	H45/29D	2/1980	Ex South Yorkshire PTE (1707) via: Camms. Nottingham (170)	8/1993	7/1998
171	CWG712V	Leyland Atlantean AN68A/1R	7903205	Alexander 'AL type'	H45/29D	2/1980	Ex South Yorkshire PTE (1712) via: Camms. Nottingham (171)	8/1993	by 9/1997
75	CWG759V	Leyland Atlantean AN68A/1R	7902446	Roe	H45/29D	11/1979	Ex South Yorkshire PTE (1759) via: Camms. Nottingham (174)	8/1993	by 9/1997
106 r/r r/r	B170 BFE A 6 WLS B48 ADE	Auwaerter 'Neoplan' N122/3	84 99 27	Auwaerter 'Skyliner'	CH57/20CT to CH57/17CT	8/1984	Ex Amberline. Speke, Liverpool. Re-registered: A6 WLS in 8/1993 Re-registered: B48 ADE by 8/1996	8/1993	by 8/1996
116 r/r r/r	H75 HAW A16 WLS H59 JDE	Toyota Coaster HDB30R	0001130	Caetano 'Optimo II'	C21F	3/1991	Ex Harry Shaw. Bedworth, Coventry. Re-registered: A16 WLS in 10/1993 Re-registered: H59 JDE by 4/1996	10/1993	4/1996
104 r/r r/r	F866 XJX A4 WLS F866 XJX	Volvo B10M-60	21431	Van Hool 'Alizee' T8	C49FT	5/1989	Ex Berkeley. Paulton, Avon. Re-registered: A4 WLS in 3/1994 Re-registered: F866 XJX in 1/2002	1/1994	1/2002
17	M174BDE	Dennis Dart 9.8 SDL	3040/2073	East Lancashire	B40F	8/1994	New Purchased directly from coachbuilder. Cancelled order from Derby City Transport.	8/1994	10/1996
1	M361CDE	Mercedes Benz 709D	669003-2N-022657	Wadham Stringer 'Wessex II'	B29F to B27F	8/1994	New	8/1994	by 9/2005
8	M368CDE	Mercedes Benz 709D	669003-2N-025132	Mellor	B27F	11/1994	New	11/1994	5/2013

Fleet No	Reg	Chassis No	Chassis	Body	Seating	Date	History	In	Out
-	L416 PAR	3035/1882	Dennis Dart 9.8 SDL	Marshall 'SPV C37'	B40F	4/1994	Demonstrator on loan from Marshall Bus, Cambridge.	9/1994	9/1994
29	EHW294W	13872	Volvo B58-61	Duple 'Dominant II'	C55F	4/1981	Ex Kerricabs. Newport, Gwent.	9/1994	8/1999
7	M674CDE	669003-2N-025159	Mercedes Benz 709D	Mellor	B27F	11/1994	New	licenced 12/1994	8/2013
16	M16 SMC	3053/2210	Dennis Dart 9 SDL	Marshall 'C36'	DP31F	11/1994	New	11/1994	5/2005
17	M17 SMC M385 EBX	3053/2211	Dennis Dart 9 SDL	Marshall 'C36'	DP31F	11/1994	New Re-registered: M385 EBX in 3/2012	11/1994	3/2012
18	M18 SMC	3053/2219	Dennis Dart 9 SDL	Marshall 'C36'	DP31F	11/1994	New	11/1994	by 8/2013
103 rtr rtr	F552TMH A 3 WLS F552TMH	20189	Volvo B10M-60	Van Hool 'Alizee' T8	C53F	3/1989	Ex Travellers. Hounslow, London. Re-registered: A3 WLS in 11/1994 Re-registered: F552TMH in 2/1998	11/1994	2/1998
-	GJI 9328	7101395	Leyland Leopard PSU5/4R	Chassis only acquired		8/1971	Ex Burnett. Smethwick, West Midlands. Previously BMS526K, 4193AT, XJH430K	1/1995	Not operated
31	GNF 13V	T71	Leyland Titan TNTL11/1RF	Park Royal	H47/26F	2/1980	Ex Capital Citybus. London (100)	3/1995	7/1998
-	K507 RDE		LDV 400	Pearl	16	by 7/1993	Ex Kennings Vehicle Hire (Non PSV)	by 3/1996	by 9/1997
11	D859 CKV	2641	Fiat / Iveco Daily 49.10	Robin Hood 'City Nippy'	B21F	12/1986	Ex Stagecoach Midland Red (South) 859	4/1996	3/1999
12	F865 PAC	5842	Fiat / Iveco Daily 49.10	Robin Hood 'City Nippy'	B21F	9/1988	Ex Stagecoach Midland Red (South) 865	4/1996	1/1999
10	F580 OOU	5948	Fiat / Iveco Daily 49.10	Dormobile	B23F	8/1988	Ex Bristol City Line (7580)	4/1996	3/1999
13 15	F585 OOU	5951	Fiat / Iveco Daily 49.10	Dormobile	B23F	8/1988	Ex Bristol City Line (7585)	4/1996	12/1998
106 rtr rtr	G903WAY A 6 WLS G903WAY	22099	Volvo B10M-60	Caetano 'Algarve'	C49FT to C53F	1/1990	Ex Thompson. Uxbridge, London. Re-registered: A6 WLS in 4/1996 Re-registered: G903 WAY in 1/2001	4/1996	1/2001
96 207 rtr	D578 DPM A 11 WLS D578 DPM	8600266	Leyland Tiger TRCTL11/3LZ	Plaxton 'Derwent II'	DP54F	2/1987	Ex Ministry of Defence, 82 KF 37 Re-registered: A11 WLS in 3/2002. Re-registered: D578 DPM in 11/2013	12/1996 lic 6/97	11/2013
94 205 rtr	D576 DPM A 6 WLS D390 HHN	8600207	Leyland Tiger TRCTL11/3LZ	Plaxton 'Derwent II'	DP54F	12/1986	Ex Ministry of Defence, 82 KF 20 Re-registered: A6 WLS in 3/2002. Re-registered: D390 HHN in 6/2016.	by 3/1997 lic 5/97	by 3/2016
220 rtr	D577 DPM A 8 WLS	8600265	Leyland Tiger TRCTL11/3LZ	Plaxton 'Derwent II'	DP54F to B71F	1/1987	Ex Ministry of Defence, 82 KF 35 Re-registered: A8 WLS in 3/2002	by 3/1997 lic 4/98	11/2014
217	A 16 WLS	8600264	Leyland Tiger TRCTL11/3LZ	Plaxton 'Derwent II'	DP54F to B71F	12/1986	Ex Ministry of Defence, 82 KF 33	by 3/1997 lic 1/1998	10/2014

Fleet No / Reg	Chassis	Chassis No	Body	Seating	New	History	In service	Withdrawn
95 206 r/r D146 KDE 804 SHW D146 KDE	Leyland Tiger TRCTL11/3LZ	8600197	Plaxton 'Derwent II'	DP54F to B54F to B71F	1/1987	Ex Ministry of Defence, 82 KF 14 Re-registered: 804 SHW in 3/2002 Re-registered: D146 KDE in 9/2010	by 3/1997 lic 6/1997	9/2010
89 200 r/r E98 LLP SIL 9613 E98 LLP	Leyland Tiger TRCTL11/3LZ	TR00048	Plaxton 'Derwent II'	DP54F	10/1987	Ex Ministry of Defence, 87 KF 43 Re-registered: SIL 9613 in 2/2003 Re-registered: E98 LLP in 4/2011	by 3/1997 lic 3/1997	4/2011
90 201 E628WWD A 2 WLS	Leyland Tiger TRCTL11/3LZ	TR00022	Plaxton 'Derwent II'	DP54F	9/1987	Ex Ministry of Defence, 87 KF 28 Re-registered: A2 WLS in 5/2004	by 3/1997 lic 3/1997	8/2014
91 202 r/r E125 ODE KSU 409 E125 ODE	Leyland Tiger TRCTL11/3LZ	TR00021	Plaxton 'Derwent II'	DP54F	9/1987	Ex Ministry of Defence, 87 KF 27 Re-registered: KSU 409 by 9/2005 Re-registered: E125 ODE in 10/2012	by 3/1997 lic 3/1997	by 7/2012
92 203 r/r E672WWD 9195 PU E672WWD	Leyland Tiger TRCTL11/3LZ	TR00063	Plaxton 'Derwent II'	DP54F	10/1987	Ex Ministry of Defence, 64 KG 06 Re-registered: 9195 PU in 2/2004 Re-registered: E672 WWD in 5/2012	by 3/1997 lic 5/1997	6/2012
204 r/r E673WWD 538 OHU E673WWD	Leyland Tiger TRCTL11/3LZ	TR00012	Plaxton 'Derwent II'	DP54F	9/1987	Ex Ministry of Defence, 87 KF 18 Re-registered: 538 OHU in 3/2004 Re-registered: E673 WWD in 6/2012	by 3/1997 lic 5/1997	6/2014
97 208 E133 ODE	Leyland Tiger TRCTL11/3LZ	TR00026	Plaxton 'Derwent II'	DP54F	9/1987	Ex Ministry of Defence, 87 KF 32	by 3/1997 lic 6/1997	3/2014
209 E137 ODE	Leyland Tiger TRCTL11/3LZ	TR00045	Plaxton 'Derwent II'	DP54F	10/1987	Ex Ministry of Defence, 64 KG 03	by 3/1997 lic 7/1997	7/2014
210 E138 ODE	Leyland Tiger TRCTL11/3LZ	TR00019	Plaxton 'Derwent II'	DP54F	9/1987	Ex Ministry of Defence, 87 KF 25	by 3/1997 lic 7/1997	6/2013
211 E139 ODE	Leyland Tiger TRCTL11/3LZ	TR00018	Plaxton 'Derwent II'	DP54F	9/1987	Ex Ministry of Defence, 87 KF 24	by 3/1997 lic 7/1997	c 7/2013
212 r/r r/r E141 ODE A 4 WLS E141 ODE	Leyland Tiger TRCTL11/3LZ	TR00046	Plaxton 'Derwent II'	DP54F	10/1987	Ex Ministry of Defence, 87 KF 46 Re-registered: A4 WLS in 6/2010 Re-registered: E141 ODE in 9/2011	by 3/1997 lic 9/1997	c 9/2011
214 E144 ODE	Leyland Tiger TRCTL11/3LZ	TR00014	Plaxton 'Derwent II'	DP54F to B71F	9/1987	Ex Ministry of Defence, 87 KF 20	by 3/1997 lic 9/1997	8/2013
215 E145 ODE	Leyland Tiger TRCTL11/3LZ	TR00042	Plaxton 'Derwent II'	DP54F to B71F	9/1987	Ex Ministry of Defence, 87 KF 40	by 3/1997 lic 10/97	10/2014
216 E149 ODE	Leyland Tiger TRCTL11/3LZ	TR00029	Plaxton 'Derwent II'	DP54F to B71F	9/1987	Ex Ministry of Defence, 87 KF 35	3/1997 lic 11/97	8/2014
218 A 14 WLS to -2-	Leyland Tiger TRCTL11/3LZ	TR00013	Plaxton 'Derwent II'	DP54F to B69F	9/1987	Ex Ministry of Defence, 87 KF 19 Re-registered ? 10/2014.	by 3/1997 lic 2/98	10/2014
219 A 12 WLS	Leyland Tiger TRCTL11/3LZ	TR00044	Plaxton 'Derwent II'	DP54F to B69F	9/1987	Ex Ministry of Defence, 87 KF 38	by 3/1997 lic 2/98	12/2014
221 r/r NSV 324 D956 BMV	Leyland Tiger TRCTL11/3LZ	8600292	Plaxton 'Derwent II'	DP54F to B54F	2/1987	Ex Ministry of Defence, 82 KF 41 Re-registered: D956 BMV in 9/2013	5/1998 lic 9/1998	8/2013
222 r/r A 3 WLS E818 AKU	Leyland Tiger TRCTL11/3LZ	TR00023	Plaxton 'Derwent II'	DP54F to B69F	9/1987	Ex Ministry of Defence, 87 KF 29 Re-registered: E818 AKU in 6/2016	5/1998 lic 10/98	6/2016

No.	Registration	Chassis	Body	Serial	Seating	New	Notes	Acquired	Withdrawn
223	E183 ODE	Leyland Tiger TRCTL11/3LZ	Plaxton 'Derwent II'	TR00064	DP54F to B69F	10/1987	Ex Ministry of Defence, 64 KG 04	by 3/1997 lic 1/99	7/2014
224 rfr	A 7 WLS E81 EFJ	Leyland Tiger TRCTL11/3LZ	Plaxton 'Derwent II'	TR00028	DP54F to B54F	9/1987	Ex Ministry of Defence, 87 KF 44 Re-registered: E81 EFJ in 11/2013	5/1998 lic 1/99	11/2013
225 rfr	109 CUF SIL 6637	Leyland Tiger TRCTL11/3LZ	Plaxton 'Derwent II'	TR00020	DP54F	9/1987	Ex Ministry of Defence, 87 KF 26 Re-registered: SIL 6637 in 9/2009	5/1998 lic 3/99	-/2014 XXX
226	E194 ODE	Leyland Tiger TRCTL11/3LZ	Plaxton 'Derwent II'	TR00040	DP54F B54F	9/1987	Ex Ministry of Defence, 87 KF 39	5/1998 lic 4/99	7/2014
179 rfr rfr	P779WDE 9195 PU P779WDE	Dennis Javelin 12m	Caetano 'Algarve II'	SFD731BR3 TGJ31964	C51FT to C49FT	5/1997	New Re-registered: 9195 PU in 5/2013 Re-registered: P779 WDE in 6/2016	5/1997	3/2016
180	P780WDE	Dennis Javelin 12m	UVG S320	SFD721BR3 VGJ22008	C53F	7/1997	New	7/1997	9/2015
24	NSV 324	Leyland Leopard PSU5/4R	Plaxton 'Panorama Elite III'	7300439	C57F	3/1974	Ex M J Evans. Bristol (Previously: AND14M) Re-registered: -?- in 9/1998	9/1997	by 10/1998
181	R530 HDE	Volvo B10M-62	Caetano 'Algarve II'	46492	C49FT	1/1998	New	1/1998	3/2007
182	R531 HDE	Dennis Javelin 12m	Marcopolo 'Explorer 2'	SFD731BR3 VGJ52042	C53F	3/1998	New	3/1998	6/2016
183	R532 HDE	Dennis Javelin 12m	Plaxton 'Premiere 320'	SFD721BR3 TGJ21541	C53F	3/1998	New	3/1998	6/2016
184	S224 BDE	Dennis Javelin 12m	Marcopolo 'Explorer 2'	SFD721BR3 VGJ51963	C53F	9/1998	New	9/1998	12/2005
230	K721 UDE	Dennis Javelin 10m	Wadham Stringer 'Vanguard II'	10SDA 2120/780	C40F to C48F	4/1993	Ex Ministry of Defence (Army) 15 KL 44 via: J Stone. Leigh, Gtr. Manchester.	12/1998	4/2006
231	K722 UDE	Dennis Javelin 10m	Wadham Stringer 'Vanguard II'	10SDA 2120/785	C40F to C48F	4/1993	Ex Ministry of Defence (Army) 15 KL 51 via: J Stone. Leigh, Gtr. Manchester.	12/1998	4/2006
12 81	H681 YGO	Optare Metro-Rider MR03	Optare	VN 1088	B26F	7/1991	Ex London Buses MRL181 via: Richmond. Epsom, Surrey.	2/1999	12/2001
14 89	H689 YGO	Optare Metro-Rider MR03	Optare	VN 1096	B26F	7/1991	Ex London Buses MRL189 via: Richmond. Epsom, Surrey.	2/1999	12/2001
10	D603 MKH	Fiat 49-10	Robin Hood 'City Nippy'	003413	B25F	1/1987	Ex Kingston upon Hull C T (603) via: PJ Rixon. Porthcawl, Mid Glam.	3/1999	12/2000
227 rfr	A 5 WLS E406 ODE	Leyland Tiger TRCTL11/3LZ	Plaxton 'Derwent II'	TR00065	DP54F to B54F	9/1987	Ex Ministry of Defence, 87 KF 45 Re-registered: E406 ODE in 5/2012	by 4/1999 lic 5/1999	5/2012
228 rfr	A 15 WLS C59 TJC	Leyland Tiger TRCTL11/3LZ	Plaxton 'Derwent II'	8600198	DP54F to B54F	1/1987	Ex Ministry of Defence, 82 KF 15 Re-registered: C59 TJC in 8/2013	by 4/1999 lic 6/1999	7/2014
229	GSK 676	Leyland Leopard PSU5D/5L	Wadham Stringer 'Vanguard'	8201125	B54F	12/1983	Ex Ministry of Defence (RAF) 51 AC 03 This vehicle's cherished registration number was lost when the vehicle was withdrawn.	by 4/1999 lic 8/1999	by 12/2004
185	T141 RDE	Dennis Javelin 12m	Caetano 'Enigma'	SFD721BR4 WGJB2135	C49FT	4/1999	New	4/1999	9/2010

Fleet No	Reg	Chassis	Chassis No	Body	Seating	Date	Notes	Date	Date
186 r/r	T142 RDE / M18 SMC	Dennis Javelin 12m	SFD731BR4 VGJ22130	SCC 'Cutlass' Salvador Caetano Coachworks	C53F to C70F	4/1999	New Re-registered M18 SMC in 3/2014	4/1999	6/2016
187	T143 RDE	MAN 18.310HOCLR	WMAA5116 89W035546	Marcopolo 'Continental 340'	C49FT	6/1999	New	6/1999	1/2005
188	W108NDE	Dennis Javelin 12m	SFGD731BR 4WGJ42193	Berkhof 'Axial 50'	C51FT	3/2000	New	3/2000	6/2016
189	W109NDE	Dennis Javelin 12m	SFD731BR4 YGJ52298	Marcopolo 'Continental 340'	C53F	5/2000	New	5/2000	6/2016
190	K780 UDE	Dennis Javelin 12m	12SDA 212L/750	Wadham Stringer	B54F to C70F	1/1993	Ex Ministry of Defence, 75 KK 29	11/1999 lic 3/2000	12/2004
191	K726DWN	Dennis Javelin 12m	12SDA 212L/758	Wadham Stringer	B54F to C70F	1/1993	Ex Ministry of Defence, 75 KK 36	11/19999 lic 4/2000	2005
192	N356MDE	Dennis Javelin 12m	SFD723BL3 TGJ21584	UVG 'Unistar'	B54F to DP55F	12/1996	Ex Ministry of Defence, D-GF-25 (converted from LHD)	11/1999 lic 5/2000	3/2003
11	H172 RBO	Optare Metro-Rider MR01	VN 1080	Optare	B31F	7/1991	Ex Cardiff Bus (172)	10/2000	8/2001
15	H173 RBO	Optare Metro-Rider MR01	VN 1081	Optare	B31F	7/1991	Ex Cardiff Bus (173)	10/2000	8/2001
19	L784 SEJ	Mercedes Benz 709D	6690032-NO-09524	Eurocoach	B23F	11/1993	Ex Dublin Bus (ME1) 93-D-10001	12/2000 lic 3/2001	6/2013
20	L632 XBX	Mercedes Benz 709D	6690032-NO-09513	Eurocoach	B23F	12/1993	Ex Dublin Bus (ME6) 93-D-10006	12/2000 lic 6/2001	2/2007
193	Y199 JDE	Dennis Javelin 12m	SFD731BR4 WGJ92214	Berkhof 'Axial 50'	C51FT	3/2001	New	3/2001	3/2010
21	Y201 JDE	Dennis Dart SLF	SFD322BR1 YGW14482	SCC 'Compass'	B38F	3/2001	New	3/2001	6/2016
22	V675 FPO	Dennis Dart SLF	SFD322BR1 WGW12927	SCC 'Compass'	B40F	12/1999	Ex White Rose. Thorpe, Surrey.	9/2001	2/2005
194	Y733 OBE	Mercedes Benz Atego 1223L	WD8970258 2K514882	Optare-Ferqui 'Solera'	C35FT	4/2001	Previously a demonstration vehicle with Optare, Cross Gates, Leeds (dealer).	9/2001	7/2002
-	Y198 KNB	Optare Solo M850	VN 6556	Optare	B29F	4/2001	Demonstrator; operated on hire for 1 week from Optare, Cross Gates, Leeds (dealer).	10/2001	10/2001
195	CU51 HVS	Dennis R410	SFD112BR 11GC10146	Plaxton 'Paragon'	C49FT	2/2002	New	2/2002	4/2008
196	CV02 HBN	Dennis Javelin 12m	SFD731BR4 XGJD2288	Caetano 'Enigma'	C53F	3/2002	New	3/2002	7/2011
23	CV02 HBP	Dennis Dart SLF	SFD212BR11 GW16006	SCC 'Compass'	B33F to B31F	4/2002	New	4/2002	5/2016
24	CV02 HBO	Dennis Dart SLF	SFD212BR11 GW16007	SCC 'Compass'	B33F to B31F	4/2002	New	4/2002	6/2016
232	A153 VDE	Leyland Tiger TRCTL11/3R	8300185	Marshall 'Campaigner'	B54F to B68F	1/1984	Ex Ministry of Defence, 20 KB 58	3/2002 lic 4/2002	12/2010

	Reg	Type	Chassis No.	Body	Seating	Date	Notes	In service	Not operated
-	L464 XOU	Dennis Javelin 12m	12SDA 2124L/760	Wadham Stringer	C53F to C70F	1/1993	Ex Ministry of Defence, 00 23 65. Previously BI-NV-568, originally 75 KK 38	7/2002 reg: 3/03	Not operated 6/2010
233	D264 ROH	Leyland Tiger TRCTL11/3R	8500537	Plaxton 'Paramount 3200'	C53F to C70F	3/1987		7/2002	6/2010
r/r	A 4 WLS						Previously: HBZ4299, D385ENV, MIW5794. Originally: D704RAK. Re-registered A4WLS in 2/03, returning to D264 ROH in 6/2010.		
r/r	D264 ROH								
194	FY02WHD	Mercedes Benz 'Atego' 1223L	WDB9702582K729484	Optare/Ferqui 'Solera'	C39F	4/2002	New	8/2002	6/2016
-	V956 HEB	Mercedes Benz 412D 'Sprinter'	9044632P 979208	Eurocoach	B14L	by 1/2000	Demonstrator on hire 7-8/2002	7/2002	8/2002
197	FY02 YHF	Mercedes Benz 413CDi 'Sprinter'	9046632R 386986	Optare 'Scirocco'	16	8/2002	New	8/2002	11/2006
25	RIL 1476	Mercedes Benz 811D	670303-2P-000339	L. H. E. 'Traveller'	C24FL to DP16FL	by 7/1990	Originally registered G445 LEP. Ex Patterson. Birmingham (PO9) Re-reg: G445 LEP after withdrawal 10/2011	6/2003	10/2009
r/r	G445 LEP								
234	D372 UVL	Leyland Tiger TRCTL11/3R	8400156	Duple 'Caribbean II'	C53F	10/1986	Ex James Bros. Llangeitho, Cardigan. Re-registered: VAW 527 in 9/2003.	6/2003 lic 9/2003	2/2009
r/r	VAW 527								
-	N966 DWJ	Volvo B10M-62	43798	Plaxton 'Premiere 350'	C53F	5/1996	Ex Snaith. Otterburn, Northumberland. Dealer loan ex Transbus, Anston.	9/2003	9/2003
235	A649 YOX	Leyland Tiger TRCTL11/3R	8300149	Marshall 'Campaigner'	B57F	10/1983	Ex Ministry of Defence. 20 KB 47 via: First Somerset & Avon (2217)	10/2003 lic 3/2004	6/2006
26	YN 04 LXJ	Optare 'Alero'	SAB210000-00000386	Optare	B14F	4/2004	New	4/2004	2/2006
27	R414 VCC	Mercedes Benz 410D Sprinter	9044632P-754107	Mellor	B14FL	3/1998	Ex Wrexham C B C (Non PSV) Re-registered: 817 FKH in 5/2004 Re-registered: R414 VCC in 6/2016	4/2004	6/2016
r/r	817 FKH								
r/r	R414 VCC								
28	CU04AUW	Transbus Dart SLF 8.5m	SFD6BACR44GW17720	Transbus 'Mini Pointer'	B29F	5/2004	New	5/2004	6/2016
-	R704 MEP	L D V Convoy	DN018986	L D V	16	8/1997	Ex Morris. (Netherwood House School) Saundersfoot, Pembs.	5/2004	5/2004
-	S351 CDE	L D V Convoy	DN029993	L D V	16	9/1998	Ex Morris. (Netherwood House School) Saundersfoot, Pembs.	5/2004	8/2004
32	S352 CDE	L D V Convoy	DN038182	L D V	16	9/1998	Ex Morris. (Netherwood House School) Saundersfoot, Pembs.	5/2004	?
29	V229 DDE	L D V Convoy	DN049706	L D V	16	11/1999	Ex Morris. (Netherwood House School) Saundersfoot, Pembs.	5/2004	10/2011
10	L865 LFS	Mercedes Benz 711D	669003-2N-015819	Plaxton 'Beaver'	B25F	1/1994	Ex Coakley Bus. Motherwell, Strathclyde.	10/2004	3/2007
11	L867 LFS	Mercedes Benz 711D	669003-2N-015287	Plaxton 'Beaver'	B25F	2/1994	Ex Coakley Bus. Motherwell, Strathclyde.	10/2004	6/2007
198	CU54KWS	Volvo B12B	YY3R8F81X3A001656	Caetano 'Enigma'	C53FT to C49FT	2/2005	New	2/2005	6/2016

Fleet No.	Reg.	Chassis	Chassis No.	Body	Seating	Date new	Notes	Date in	Date out
30	CU05DME	MAN 14.200	WMAA66ZZX4H003294	MCV 'Evolution'	B40F	3/2005	New	3/2005	6/2016
14	YC51HAO	Optare Solo M920	190000000-00740	Optare	B34F	11/2001	Ex Geoff Amos. Eydon, Daventry, Northampton (109)	4/2005	5/2009
15	YC51HAE	Optare Solo M920	190000000-00739	Optare	B33F	11/2001	Ex Geoff Amos. Eydon, Daventry, Northampton (108)	4/2005	3/2011
-	F722 FDV	Mercedes Benz 709D	669003-20-901096	Reeve-Burgess 'Beaver'	B25F	11/1988	Ex Devon General / Stagecoach Devon. via: Howard. Halstead, Essex.	5/2005	Not operated
-	D106 GHY	Volvo B10M-61	14787	Alexander 'PS'	DP53F	5/1987	Ex Badgerline. via: First Somerset & Avon (66506)	10/2005	Not operated
-	D109 GHY	Volvo B10M-61	14790	Alexander 'PS'	DP53F	5/1987	Ex Badgerline. via: First Somerset & Avon (66509)	10/2005	Not operated
16	CV55AXW	Optare Solo M920	SAB1900000-0002206	Optare	B34F to B33F	1/2006	New	2/2006	6/2016
26	CV55 BAU	Optare Solo M780SL	SAB1900000-0002079	Optare	B22F	2/2006	New	2/2006	c3/2010
199	CV55 AZN	Volvo B12B	YV3R8G120-5A104435	Caetano 'Enigma'	C49FT	2/2006	New	2/2006	6/2016
184	CU06 ANP	Volvo B12B	YV3R8G120-5A104418	Caetano 'Enigma'	C49FT	4/2006	New	4/2006	3/2016
12	S862 BHR	Mercedes Benz 410D Sprinter	WDB904463-2P857150	G & M Coachbuilders	B16FL	1/1999	Ex Seend Community Bus. Seend, Wilts.	6/2006	5/2016
178 r/r r/r	H613UWR NSV 324 H613UWR	Volvo B10M-60	YV31M2A15-MA026428	Plaxton 'Paramount 3500' Mk III (Rebuilt in 2007 by Blackpool Coach Services)	C46FT to C50F	3/1991	Ex Wallace Arnold Tours. via: First Western National (2258) Re-reg: NSV 324 in 9/2014 to H613UWR in 6/2016	10/2006 lic 7/2007	6/2016
235	D113 GHY	Volvo B10M-56	YV31MGC-19HA014816	Alexander 'PS'	B54F	5/1987	Ex Badgerline. via: First Somerset & Avon (66513)	2/2007	1/2009
181	WA53WSY	Volvo B12M	YV3R9F81X-3A001220	Berkhof 'Axial 50'	C51FT	1/2004	Ex P Kavanagh. Urlingford, Co Kilkenny (EI) Previously registered: 04 KK 4.	3/2007	3/2012
20	MX07 BCE	Optare Solo M950	SABFWJAE-07R192603	Optare	B33F	3/2007	New	3/2007	6/2016
22	MX07 BAO	Optare Solo M950	SABFWJAE-06R192581	Optare	B34F to B30F	3/2007	New	3/2007	6/2016
197	YX07 AWV	Mercedes Benz 1323L Atego	WDB970268-2L123796	Optare/Ferqui 'Solera 2'	C37FT	3/2007	New This vehicle was originally allocated the registration number:- YX56 AFV	3/2007	6/2016
11	N952 NAP	Mercedes Benz 709D	669003-2N-040156	Alexander 'Sprint'	B23F	2/1996	Ex Stagecoach East Kent. via: Munden. Bristol.	5/2007	2014
10	MX04 VLT	Optare Solo M850	SAB1900000-0001310	Optare	B29F to B27F	4/2004	Ex Stagecoach Devon. via: Hutt. Finstock, Oxfordshire.	6/2007	c11/2015
177	P384 YHT	Dennis Javelin 12m	SFD723BR3-TGJ21939	U V G 'S320'	C70F to C71F	3/1997	Ex Ministry of Defence (Royal Navy) Previously: 17 RN 09, P539 SUS, 17 RN 09	8/2007	6/2016

Fleet	Registration	Make/Model	Chassis No.	Body	Seating	Date	History	Acquired	Withdrawn
33	CU07 HVK	Renault Master	VF1FDB1H6-3790622		M5L	8/2007	New	8/2007	6/2016
34	SN08 AAJ	Alexander-Dennis Enviro 300	SFD141AR2-7GG10305	ADL 'Enviro 300'	B55F to B47F	3/2008	New	3/2008	6/2016
100	WA08 JVX	VDL Bova Futura FHD 127.365	XL9AA38R-833003847	VDL 'Bova Futura 2'	C53FT	4/2008	New	4/2008	6/2016
101	YN08 NKJ	Alexander-Dennis Javelin 12m	SFD755BR6-8GJ22609	Plaxton 'Profile'	C53F	5/2008	New	5/2008	6/2016
35	MX09 HHS	Alexander-Dennis Enviro 200	SFD361AR2-8GY10968	ADL 'Enviro 200'	B37F	5/2009	New	5/2009	6/2016
-	CV57HMU	Ford Transit		Ford	16	9/2007	Hired from Day's Rental, Swansea.	6/2009	7/2009
-	CV58 XBU	Ford Transit		Ford	16	-/2008	Hired from Day's Rental, Swansea.	6/2009	7/2009
-	CV09 EFE	Ford Transit		Ford	16	-/2009	Hired from Day's Rental, Swansea.	6/2009	7/2009
-	CV09 EFF	Ford Transit		Ford	16	-/2009	Hired from Day's Rental, Swansea.	6/2009	7/2009
-	CV09 YGH	Ford Transit		Ford	16	-/2009	Hired from Day's Rental, Swansea.	6/2009	7/2009
102	WA04EWT	Volvo B12M	YV3R9F810-2A000396	Van-Hool 'Alizee'	C49FT to C53F	3/2004	Ex Astra, Andoversford, Gloucestershire.	3/2010	6/2016
36	YJ10 EXU	Optare Solo M710SE	SABCN2AB-OAL193557	Optare	B23F	4/2010	New Owned by Pembrokeshire C.C.	4/2010	6/2016
37	YJ10 EXV	Optare Solo M710SE	SABCN2AB-OAL193616	Optare	B23F	4/2010	New Owned by Pembrokeshire C.C.	4/2010	6/2015
38 r/r r/r	P901 CTO / SIL 9613 / P901 CTO	Dennis Dart SLF	SFD222BR1-TGW10322	Plaxton 'Pointer'	B40F	10/1996	Ex Trent-Barton. Derby (901) Re-registered: SIL 9613 in 4/2015, returning to P901 CTO after withdrawal 6/2016	5/2010	5/2015
39	T430 KAG	Dennis Dart SLF	SFD322AR1-WGW12864	Plaxton 'Pointer'	B34D to B35F	2/1999	Ex London United (DP30) via: Transdev London.	6/2010	c5/2015
40	XIL 9100	Mercedes Benz 811D	WDB670303-2N030413	U V G 'Citi-star'	DP33F	1/1996	Ex Chalkwell. Sittingbourne, Kent. Previously: N133 RAP, 5752 AP	6/2010	8/2015
-	617 DDV	Bristol MW6G	164.034	Eastern Coach Works	C39F	6/1960	Owned by Bluestone Holiday Pk, Narberth. Operated & maintained by Silcox staff.	6/2010	by 2013
-	573 UVX	Bristol MW6G	184.057	Eastern Coach Works	C39F	6/1961	Owned by Bluestone Holiday Pk, Narberth. Operated & maintained by Silcox staff.	6/2010	by 2013
236	RLZ 1670	Bova Futura FHD 12.370	XL9AA18CG-19003020	Bova 'Futura'	C49FT to C70F	6/2001	Ex Dealtop. Clyst St Mary, Devon. Previously: Y14 DLC	9/2010	6/2016
237 r/r r/r	P771 BJF / 804 SHW / P771 BJF	Dennis Javelin 12m	SFD721BR3-TGJ21753	Caetano 'Algarve'	C70F	1/1997	Ex Tilley. Wainhouse Corner, Cornwall. Re-registered: 804SHW in 5/2012, returning to P771BJF in 6/2016	10/2010	6/2016

No.	Reg	Chassis	Chassis No.	Body	Seats	New	Notes	Acquired	Withdrawn
238	S488 UAK	Dennis Javelin 12m	SFD721BR4-VGJ21974	Plaxton 'Premiere 320'	C57F	1/1999	Ex Jones. Burley Gate, H'ford & Worcester.	10/2010	by 5/2016
41	YJ60 LRL	Optare Solo M710SE	SABDN2AB-OAL193723	Optare	B26F	12/2010	New. Owned by Pembrokeshire C.C.	12/2010	6/2016
42	YJ60 LRN	Optare Solo M710SE	SABDN2AB-OAL193724	Optare	B26F	12/2010	New. Owned by Pembrokeshire C.C.	12/2010	6/2016
-	YJ60 KFP	Optare Solo M710SE	SABCN2AB-OAL193692	Optare	B23F	9/2010	Demonstrator on hire from Optare. Leeds.	4/2011	4/2011
43 r/r r/r	S103 EGK / A4 WLS / S103 EGK	Dennis Dart SLF	SFD212BR1-WGW12728	Plaxton 'Pointer'	B29D to B29F	12/1998	Ex London General (LDP103). Re-registered: A4 WLS in 5/2012. Re-registered: S103 EGK in 6/2016	11/2011	6/2016
44 r/r r/r	S107 EGK / A5 WLS / S107 EGK	Dennis Dart SLF	SFD212BR1-WGW12732	Plaxton 'Pointer'	B29D to B29F	12/1998	Ex London General (LDP107). Re-registered: A5 WLS in 7/2012. Re-registered: S107 EGK in 6/2016	11/2011	6/2016
45 r/r r/r	S113 EGK / A15 WLS / S113 EGK	Dennis Dart SLF	SFD212BR1-WGW12750	Plaxton 'Pointer'	B29D to B31F	12/1998	Ex London General (LDP113) acquired via Metrobus (387). Re-registered: A15 WLS in 8/2015, returning to S113 EGK in 6/2016	3/2012	6/2016
46 r/r r/r	S638 JGP / KSU 409 / S638 JGP	Dennis Dart SLF	SFD212BR1-WGW12690	Plaxton 'Pointer'	B29D to B29F	12/1998	Originally registered WLT 990. Ex London General (LDP 90). Acquired via: Metrobus London (388). Re-registered: KSU 409 in 10/2014. Re-registered: S638 JGP in 6/2016	3/2012	c5/2015
103	WA08GPO	VDL Bova Futura FHD12.340	XL9A38R8-3303783	VDL Bova 'Futura 2'	C48FT to C50FT	3/2008	Ex Rover European. Horsley, Gloucester. Previously: TO08 DRH, orig: WA08 GPO	c2/2012 lic 3/2012	6/2016
239 r/r r/r	R708 NJH / RIL 1476 / R708 NJH	Dennis Javelin 12m	SFD731BR3-TGJ41798	Berkhof 'Axial'	C53F	9/1997	Ex Bodman. Worton, Wiltshire. Re-registered: RIL 1476 in 10/2012. Re-registered: R708 NJH in 6/2016	6/2012	6/2016
240 r/r r/r	R50 TGM / 538 OHU / R50 TGM	Volvo B10M-62	YV31MA614-VA047453	Plaxton 'Premiere 320'	C57F	5/1998	Ex Bodman. Worton, Wiltshire. Re-registered: 538 OHU in 6/2013. Re-registered: R50 TGM in 6/2016	6/2012	6/2016
241 r/r	XUD 367 / P883 FMO	Dennis Javelin 12m	SFD731BR3-TGJ41853	Berkhof 'Axial'	C53F	4/1997	Ex Bodman. Worton, Wiltshire. Previously: P883 FMO, 1760 VC, P883FMO. Re-registered: P883 FMO in 6/2016	6/2012	6/2016
242 r/r	M308 SHN / M17 SMC	Dennis Javelin 12m	12SDA 2125/1028	Plaxton 'Premiere 350'	C70F	2/1995	Ex Mc Leans Coaches. Witney, Oxford. Previously: HIL 7540, M308 SHN. Re-registered: M17 SMC in 10/2012	8/2012	6/2016
47	Y619 GFM	Dennis Dart SLF	SFD322BR1-YGW14974	Marshall 'Capital'	B41F	3/2001	Ex Warrington B T(19)	4/2013	6/2016
243	Y235 BAW	Dennis Javelin	SFD721BR4-YGJ22325	Plaxton 'Premiere 320'	C57F	5/2001	Ex Ministry of Defence	8/2013 lic 9/2013	6/2016
244 r/r	Y126 BPB / Y237 BAW	Dennis Javelin	SFD721BR4-YGJ22328	Plaxton 'Premiere 320'	C57F	5/2001	Ex Ministry of Defence. Re-registered: Y237 BAW in 9/2013	9/2013	6/2016

Fleet	Reg	Chassis	Chassis No.	Body	Seating	Date	Notes	Date	Date
245 r/r	Y158 RLC / Y252 XHH	Dennis Javelin	SFD721BR4-YGJ22324	Plaxton 'Premiere 320'	C57F	2001	Ex Ministry of Defence / Re-registered Y252 XHH in 9/2013	9/2013	6/2016
246 r/r	SX02WDS / CT02 NAE	Dennis Javelin	SFD721BR4-YGJ22408	Plaxton 'Premiere 320'	C57F	by 8/2002	Ex Ministry of Defence / Re-registered CT02 NAE in 10/2013	10/2013	6/2016
104	BN63 NYD	King-Long XMQ6130Y	LA6R1MSU-8DB103307	King-Long	C57FT	10/2013	New	10/2013	6/2016
48	V723 GGE	Mercedes Benz 0814 Vario	WDB670374-2N084294	Plaxton 'Beaver 2'	B33F	9/1999	Ex Bakerbus. Biddulph, Staffs / via: Guideissue. Knypersley, Staffs (183).	11/2013	5/2016
247	YN06 CFZ	Scania K114EB6	YS2K6X200-01854471	Irizar	C65FL	8/2006	Ex Excalibur. Peckham, London.	12/2013	by 2/2015
248 r/r	Y124 PLT / Y139 YSO	Dennis Javelin 12m	SFD721BR4-YGJ22322	Plaxton 'Premiere 320'	C57F	4/2001	Ex Ministry of Defence / Re-registered Y139 YSO in 3/2014	2/2014 lic 3/2014	6/2016
249 r/r	Y183 SRK / Y154 EBY	Dennis Javelin 12m	SFD721BR4-YGJ22326	Plaxton 'Premiere 320'	C57F	4/2001	Ex Ministry of Defence / Re-registered Y154 EBY in 7/2014	1/2014 lic 2/2014	6/2016
250	RUI 6748	Dennis Javelin 12m	12SDA 2159/1500	Berkhof 'Excellence 1000'	C53F	5/1996	Ex Edwards Bros. Tiers Cross, Pembs. / Previously: N865 XMO, EUI 656, N865XMO.	2/2014	6/2016
105	BK63 ZTB	King-Long XMQ6127	LA621K25S-DB103302	King-Long	C49FT	11/2013	Ex Guideissue. Knypersley, Staffs (284).	2/2014	6/2016
251	R114 SBD	Dennis Javelin 12m	SFD721BR3-VGJ22036	U V G 'S320'	C69F	1/1998	Originally registered: R20 BUS / Ex West. South Woodford, London. / Re-registered: A11 WLS in 11/2014 / Re-registered: R114 SBD in 6/2016	5/2014	6/2016
r/r r/r	A11 WLS R114 SBD								
49	AE08 KTK	MAN 14.240	WMAA66ZZ-87CO10245	MCV 'Evolution'	B27F	7/2008	Ex Airparks. Crawley, West Sussex.	7/2014	10/2014
50	AE09 DJU	MAN 14.240	WMAA66ZZ-X8CO11107	MCV 'Evolution'	B27F	8/2009	Ex Airparks. Crawley, West Sussex. / via: Guideissue. Knypersley, Staffs (277).	6/2014	10/2014
51	AE09 DJV	MAN 14.240	WMAA66ZZ-08CO11133	MCV 'Evolution'	B27F	8/2009	Ex Airparks. Crawley, West Sussex.	7/2014	10/2014
52	AE09 DJO	MAN 14.240	WMAA66ZZ-57CO10252	MCV 'Evolution'	B27F	8/2009	Ex Airparks. Crawley, West Sussex. / via: Guideissue. Knypersley, Staffs (276).	7/2014	10/2014
53	KX06 LYP	Enterprise Plasma EBO1	TS9EBO1G-S5P130013	Plaxton 'Primo'	B28F	4/2006	Ex Bakerbus. Biddulph, Staffs. / Owned by King-Long (Island Fortitude)	by 12/2014	1/2015
54	Y178 CFS	Dennis Dart SLF	SFD467BR-11GW45855	Plaxton 'Pointer 2'	B42F	8/2001	Ex Leven Valley. Stockton on Tees (48).	5/2015	5/2016
55	W793VMV	Dennis Dart SLF	SFD612BR-1XGW14468	Plaxton 'Pointer 2'	B29F	5/2000	Ex Leven Valley. Stockton on Tees (93).	5/2015	6/2016
56	W794VMV	Dennis Dart SLF	SFD612BR-1XGW14455	Plaxton 'Pointer 2'	B29F	5/2000	Ex Leven Valley. Stockton on Tees (94).	5/2015	6/2016
99	MX54 KYJ	Optare Solo M920	SAB19000-000001376	Optare	B33F	1/2005	Ex Jackett. Gunnislake, Cornwall. / via: Hazell Rental. Exeter.	5/2015	c3/2016
57	MX12 DYN	Alexander-Dennis E20D Enviro 200	SFD1D1AR-6BGY12931	Alexander-Dennis	B28F	5/2012	Ex TLC Travel, West Bowling, Bradford, W Yorks. (12931)	7/2015	6/2016

58	MX12 DZK	Alexander-Dennis E20D Enviro 200	SFD1D1AR-6BGY12930	Alexander-Dennis	B28F	5/2012	Ex TLC Travel. Bradford W Yorks. (12930) via: Spirit Buses. Rothbury, Northants.	7/2015	6/2016
59	YJ58 FFN	VDL SB200	XMGDEO2F-SOHO15868	Plaxton 'Centro'	B45F	9/2008	Ex Tellings-Golden-Miller Group. London. Vehicle owned by Pembrokeshire C.C.	11/2015	6/2016
-	R401 FWT	Volvo B10M-62	YV31MA611-WA048755	Plaxton 'Premiere 350'	C48FT	3/1998	Ex D Caney, Bartley Green, W Midlands. Previously registered: DEN 83D, R401 FWT	2/2016	6/2016
60	SN16 OGV	Alexander-Dennis E20D Enviro 200	SFD7E1AR-6FGY15345	Alexander-Dennis	B39F	4/2016	New	4/2016	6/2016
61	SN16 ORS	Alexander-Dennis E20D Enviro 200	SFD8E1AR-6FGY15298	Alexander-Dennis	B33F	4/2016	New	4/2016	6/2016
62	SN16 ORU	Alexander-Dennis E20D Enviro 200	SFD8E1AR-6FGY15299	Alexander-Dennis	B33F	4/2016	New	4/2016	6/2016
-	BL14 LSO	Volvo B11RT	YV3T2T12-6EA168656	Sunsundegui 'SC7'	C61FL	8/2014	Ex Excalibur. Peckham, London. via: Barnard. Kirton in Lindsey, Lincs.	4/2016	6/2016
-	BL14 LSV	Volvo B11RT	YV3T2T12-7EA168665	Sunsundegui 'SC7'	C61FL	8/2014	Ex Excalibur. Peckham, London.	4/2016	6/2016
-	BL14 LSU	Volvo B11RT	YV3T2T12-XEA168658	Sunsundegui 'SC7'	C61FL	8/2014	Ex Excalibur. Peckham, London. via: A P Travel. Cowbridge, Vale of Glam.	5/2016	6/2016
-	BX62 BKV	King-Long XMQ6130Y	LA6R1MSU-1CB103390	King-Long	C57FT	2/2013	Ex Excalibur. Peckham, London. via: A P Travel. Cowbridge, Vale of Glam.	5/2016	6/2016
-	BN63 NYU	King-Long XMQ6129Y	LA6A1LBS-8DB102846	King-Long	C53FT	10/2013	New to King-Long. Coventry. Ex Excalibur. Peckham, London.	5/2016	5/2016

A grand total of 579 vehicles.

Note A: Bristol LD6B, XFM 180 had its roof modified by Silcox before entering service. The curved upper deck cove panels and roof vents were removed and replaced with flat panels giving it extra clearance to negotiate Bubbleston Bridge near Tenby.

VEHICLE DISPOSALS

5	DE 7244	Sold to unidentified Staffordshire owner 2/1942, probably Sir Alexander Gibb (Contractor).
1	DE 7985	Scrapped in 1936.
6	DE 8384	Sold to unidentified Staffordshire owner 2/1942, probably Sir Alexander Gibb (Contractor) void 4/1943
2	DE 8595	Sold to unidentified Staffordshire owner 2/1942, probably Sir Alexander Gibb (Contractor) void 4/1943
8	GT 9498	Last licenced to Silcox 12/1942. Scrapped 1942.
3	DM 7628	Last licenced to Silcox 9/1938. Scrapped 1938.
7	DE 9151	Scrapped in 1937.
4	DE 9301	Derelict remains still at garage in 6/1951.
-	HS 5800	Last licenced to Silcox in 1938. No further trace.
9	BDE 96	Derelict remains still in existence at garage 8/1950.
10	BDE 238	No further trace. Registration void by 27/11/1959.
11	CDE 259	Sold to Hussey, Egan & Pickmere (Contractors) Birmingham 6/1956 (non PSV).
12	CDE 732	Sold to P D Smart & Sons. Cwmcarn, Monmouthshire by 6/1948.
7	DDE 222	Sold to T W Rogers. Cwmduad, Carmarthen by 8/1950.
1	DDE 963	Sold to T M Daniel. Cardigan 6/1949.
3	EDE 16	Sold to D T Jones. Trelech, Carmarthen 5/1950.
14	EDE 734	Scrapped in 1951.
15	EDE 735	In use as a paint store by 6/1959, still there 4/1964.
16	EDE 773	Scrapped in 1951.
17	AET 456	In use as a store shed by 6/1959, remains still in existence at depot 7/1968.
18	DYN 291	Sold to Price, Crickhowell, Brecon by 3/1948
19	FXT 824	De-licenced by 8/1950.
-	GJ 2086	Returned to London Transport 'off hire' 2/1943.
-	GJ 2097	Returned to London Transport 'off hire' 2/1943.
-	GK 1009	Returned to London Transport 'off hire' 2/1943.
20	FDE 215	Derelict at depot 9/1961.

Above The derelict remains of Silcox's **DE 9301** a Guy bodied Guy 'Conquest' on waste land near Waterloo Garage in July 1950.

2	FDE 404	Sold to H E Clarke. Capel Ivan, Newcastle Emlyn, Carmarthenshire 1/1950.
5	FDE 410	Sold to Owen Williams, Central Garage, Cardigan 9/1949
21	FDE 447	Sold to J M Morgan, Henllan, Cardiganshire, 8/1949. To Morris Bros. Swansea 1/1951.
6	FDE 448	Sold to J M Morgan, Henllan, Cardiganshire 8/1949
28	FDE 517	Sold to Frank Cowley (dealer) Salford, Manchester by 3/1959 & scrapped 2/1962.
22	FDE 530	Sold to T C Herbert, Maenclochog, Pembrokeshire 8/1949
23	FDE 531	Sold to A G Reed, Bridgend, Glamorganshire, 2/1949. Scrapped 10/1952.
24	FDE 534	Sold to A G Reed, Bridgend, Glamorganshire, 2/1949. To Glasgow owner 2/1955.
25	FDE 535	Sold to D & W V Doolan, Bridge St, Neath, Glam. 1947, via unknown dealer at Bridgend.
26	FDE 536	Sold to Mitchell. Glyncorrwg, Glam. 6/1949 & withdrawn 9/1951.
27	FDE 537	Sold to R Parkhouse. Penclawdd, Swansea 4/1950 & scrapped 11/1953.
29	FDE 609	No further trace.
30	FDE 733	Scrapped 1959.
31	GDE 124	Scrapped 1959.
32	GDE 235	Sold to Frank Cowley (dealer) Salford, Manchester 12/1959 & scrapped.
39	JDE 43	Sold to Baxter. Hanley, Staffs 11/1953. To Potteries M T, Stoke on Trent 12/1958.
33	JDE 426	Sold to Butterworth (dealer) Bury, Lancs 1960 & scrapped by 12/1960.
34	JDE 427	Sold to T J Harries & Sons (Prendergast Motors) Haverfordwest 11/1958.
35	JDE 428	Scrapped by 4/1959.
36	JDE 429	Converted to breakdown truck 4/1963; out of use by 4/1971, scrapped at depot 6-8/1972.
37	JDE 430	Sold to T J Harries & Sons (Prendergast Motors) Haverfordwest 1/1959.
38	JDE 431	Sold to Hussey, Egan & Pickmere (Contractors) Pembroke & Birmingham 6/1960.
-	ADE 903	Sold to Purnell. Rogerston, Monmouthshire 12/1948.
4	FDE 964	Sold to E D Jones. Coed-y-bryn, Llandyssul, Cardiganshire 8/1949.
8	LDE 340	Sold to Harper Bros. Heath Hayes, Staffs (14) 4/1953. Fitted with Harper B37F body in 2/1959.
9	LDE 630	Sold to Jones Omnibus Services (57) Aberbeeg, Monmouthshire 12/1953.
21	LDE 850	Dismantled for spare parts by 2/1970, remains cut up for scrap.

Above: One of Silcox's withdrawn 1947 Strachan bodied Bristol L5Gs was converted into a tow truck/recovery vehicle in 1963. This picture shows the home made conversion to bus number **36, JDE 429** which was operated on garage trade plates – **0139DE** in 1964.

22	LDE 949	Dismantled for spare parts by 2/1970, remains scrapped. Engine fitted to RFM 457 ex Crosville M S.
23	LDE 950	Derelict in yard 5/1972. Probably scrapped on site.
1	MDE 530	Sold to J R Daniel (t/a T M Daniel) Cardigan, 7/1953.
2	MDE 531	Sold to Hughes (dealer) Mirfield, Yorkshire, 1952. To Unknown owner at Darlington 7/1953.
7	MDE 532	Sold to G Patterson. Beadnell, Northumberland, 3/1954.
3	NDE 330	Sold to W Way & Co (scrap dealer) Cardiff, 5/1967.
4	NDE 331	Sold to W Way & Co (scrap dealer) Cardiff, 10/1967.
5	NDE 332	Sold to Martin (dealer) Middlewich, Cheshire, 4/1973.
6	NDE 616	Scrapped 12/1964.
42	FOP 349	No further trace.
40	FOP 353	No further trace.
41	FOP 366	Sold to F Cowley (dealer) Salford, Manchester 4/1959. To Threlfalls Brewery, Salford (NPSV) 4/59.
26	FOP 380	Sold to F Cowley (dealer) Salford, Manchester 11/1958. To Sherwood Paints, Bury (NPSV) 2/1959.
27	FOP 403	Sold to F Cowley (dealer) Salford, Manchester 4/1960.
24	ODE 401	Derelict in yard 5/1972. (Note - the original MCCW body was derelict in yard 9/1961).
25	ODE 402	Derelict in yard by 8/1967, still there 7/1969. Used for spares, remains cut up on site.
12	ODE 600	Sold with no further trace.
18	LYL 725	Sold to Gleave (dealer) Audlem, Cheshire 7/1959. To Marshalls Coaches. London N16, in 1959.
19	KAB 338	Sold by 12/1972 with no further trace.
2	LYL 722	Sold to M Davies (Timperley Coaches) Timperley, Altringham 4/1958.
9	SDE 400	Scrapped on site between 5/1974 – 8/1975.
39	SDE 450	Sold to Martin (dealer) Weaverham, Cheshire 1969.
7	KWW541	Sold to W Way & Co (scrap dealer) Cardiff 5/1967 for scrap.
41	MRH 226	Derelict remains still at depot 5/1972.
-	NJW 300	Returned to Guy Motors, Wolverhampton off hire -/1955
46	WDE 343	Scrapped 11/1969
44	ACK 871	Derelict in yard by 9/1961, being scrapped 12/1961.
45	ACK 875	No further trace.
30	MDE 333	Sold to F Cowley (dealer) Salford, 1959. To: Monty, Moreton. Nuneaton 5/1959, scrapped 10/1963.
35	ODE 1	Sold to Arlington Motors (dealer) Cardiff 9/1966. To: W Way & Co (scrap dealer) Cardiff 11/1966.
29	UDE 111	Sold to Green Bus Co. Rugeley, Staffs 9/1970, for spares.
43	YDE 444	Sold to unknown dealer by 6/1970.
34	OHA 298	Sold to Arlington Motors, Cardiff 5/1967. To: W Way & Co (scrap dealer) Cardiff 6/1967.
15	DDB 268	Used for spare parts by 11/1963, later cut up for scrap.
16	DDB 269	Derelict at depot by 4/1963, and still there 4/1964.
37	ETA 967	No further trace.
41	RC 4627	Body transferred to LDE 949 fleet no 22, 9/60 - 5/61, chassis presumed scrapped.
42	RC 4630	Body transferred to ODE 401 fleet no 24, by 9/1961, chassis presumed scrapped.
47	RC 4633	Body transferred to LDE 950 fleet no 23, by 6/1961, chassis presumed scrapped.
8	MUX 794	No further trace.
32	GHN 189	Sold for preservation to M Banks; P Battersby & G Holt. Kingston upon Hull, 5/1969.
31	HUF 299	Sold to unknown dealer 2-6/1970. No further trace.
30	HUF 300	Sold to A Barraclough (dealer) Barnsley, for scrap 5/1970.
49	GDE 834	Sold to F Cowley (dealer) Salford, Manchester 4/1960.
28	GNO 693	Sold to Showman at Carmarthen by 4/1961. To Hitchcock (scrap dealer) Llanelli, 5/1965.
17	BJA 442	Sold to F Cowley (dealer) Salford 12/1961.To Midway Haulage. Golborne, Lancs (caravan) 9/1962.
14	DDB 270	Body scrapped 7/1962. Chassis frame used in the construction of **702 RDE** fleet no 65, **'new'** in 1963
10	DDB 278	Sold to J M Daniel (t/a T M Daniel) Cardigan 12/1959.
11	DDB 279	Used for spares, partially dismantled 2/1963, derelict remains still at depot 8/1967.
40	LAL 691	No further trace.
48	GUF 685	Derelict at depot 8/1966, later cut up for scrap.
49	UTB 550	Sold to J Kelleher. Boherbue, Co Cork, Ireland, 8/1967 re-registered DZK 494.
50	LDE 600	No further trace.

51	LDE 601	Used for spares by 11/1962, remains later cut up for scrap.
52	GNN 134	Sold by 12/1973. To W Way & Co (scrap dealer) Cardiff by 1/1977 for scrap.
53	GAL 433	Sold by 12/1972. No further trace.
54	NBX 310	Sold to Martin (dealer) Middlewich, Cheshire by 7/1972.
55	SVX 233	Sold to Arlington Motors (dealer) Cardiff 12/1964. Believed later to W Way (scrap dealer) Cardiff.
56	ACU 215	Out of use by 5/1975, being dismantled for spares 8/75 - 5/76 and scrapped on site.
57	LTG 268	Sold to North (dealer) Sherburn in Elmet, N Yorkshire 1969.
58	120 LDE	Sold to unidentified Non PSV operator, at Warrington, Lancs. 6/1973.
59	CRC 512	Sold to unknown dealer by 6/1970.
61	50 NDE	Sold to Martin (dealer) Middlewich, Cheshire 4/1981.
18	JNU 120	No further trace.
20	PVO 622	Derelict in yard 5/1972.
63	FJA 615	Derelict in yard 8/1972.
62	734 PDE	No further trace.
64	702 RDE	Sold to Martin (dealer) Middlewich 4/1973. Reported also to W Way (scrap dealer) Cardiff 9/1973.
63	635 SDE	Withdrawn 8/1979. Scrapped on site.
66	KRR 70	No further trace.
67	CRN 219	No further trace.
68	LEH 759	No further trace.
10	PRE 731	Derelict at depot 8/1967-7/1968. No further trace.
-	PRE 732	Not operated, used for spares, remains to R Askin (dealer) Barnsley, for scrap 12/1963
2	PRE 735	No further trace.
11	LEH 42	Sold to W Way & Co (breaker) Cardiff 10/1967 for scrap.
14	GUF 135	Sold to Hartwood Finance (dealer) Barnsley, for scrap by 1/1968.
15	GUF 158	Sold to Johnson (dealer) Goldthorpe, Yorkshire 11/1967.
16	GUF 118	Derelict at depot 8/1967, later broken up.
17	FUH 412	No further trace.
60	PVO 624	Original Burlingham body scrapped at depot 1967. The re-bodied vehicle scrapped at depot 2-5/1992
26	FUH 426	No further trace.
64	614 XDE	No further trace.
70	VGT 328	No further trace.
71	VGT 330	To Martin (dealer) Middlewich by 12/73. To unidentified scrap dealer, Carlton by 2/74 & cut up 1977.
72	HUH 47	Sold to Ribble Preservation Group by 8/1976 to provide spares for FCK 865 & JRN 41.
73	664 WDE	Converted to a NPSV company personnel carrier & tow truck 6/1974. Scrapped 1977.
74	DDE950D	Sold to Letheren. Lydney, Gloucestershire 4/1974.
75	FDE282D	Sold to J M Crookes (Wenallt Coaches) Rhiwbina, Cardiff 2/1974.
76	HUH 25	Sold by 8/1976. No further trace.
77	HCU 962	To Arlington (dealer) Cardiff 2/73, hired to Humphreys 2/73, sold to M E Thacker, Cowbridge c11/73.
78	URR 346	Sold to Lister (dealer) Bolton 12/73. To Morris & Stevens. Wigan, Lancs 4/1974.
79	URR 349	Sold by 12/1973. No further trace.
80	HDE903E	Sold to Rallybeam. Debach, Suffolk 8/1988.
2	DCN 845	Dismantled for spares 1/1975. Scrapped at depot 4-8/1976.
1	OUP 660	Derelict by 8/1976, sold for scrap by 12/1976.
81	MDE914F	Sold to Arlington (dealer) Cardiff 7/1975. To Ferris. Radyr, Glam 7/1975.
82	NDE440F	Scrapped at depot by 9/1996.
-	SVT 952	Not operated. Acquired for spares only, presumed broken up at depot.
83	KDB 647	Sold to Martin (dealer) Middlewich by 6/1973. To Evans (Archway Motors) Shifnal, Salop 10/1973.
84	KDB 648	No further trace.
85	KDB 656	Used for spares 7/1976. Remains to unidentified scrap dealer at Barnsley 2/1977.
86	HAP 985	Sold to P Ticehurst & J Shorten, Brighton Transport Society for preservation by 2/1979.
87	RDE659G	Body scrapped & chassis dumped in yard by 12/1983.
88	RDE660G	Sold 5-8/1983. No further trace.
89	VFM 587	Sold to unknown scrap dealer 1977.

90	SFM 8	Sold to Martin (dealer) Middlewich 1977.
91	RFM 457	Sold to Martin (dealer) Middlewich by 10/1973.
92	KDB 637	Derelict at depot by 6/1973. Sold for scrap by 12/1973.
93	KDB 632	No trace.
94	WHN 122	Derelict at depot by 4/1976.
-	NFM 72	Acquired for spares, remains to Martin (dealer) Middlewich by 9/1970, scrapped by 9/1971.
95	PHN 836	Scrapped by 12/1977.
96	OHY 984	To Eastern Counties Omnibus Society for spares. Remains to Rollinson, Carlton (breaker) 4/1978.
97	XHW 404	No trace.
98	OFM 670	Used for spares by 4/1976, sold for scrap by 12/1976.
99	OFM 690	Sold by 8/1976. No further trace.
100	XHW 402	Scrapped by 12/1977.
101	VDE873J	Sold to Morris Travel. Pencoed, Mid-Glamorganshire 3/1976.
102	VDE874J	Sold to Letheren. Lydney, Gloucestershire 2/1976.
103	XFM 180	Sold to T Goodwin (scrap dealer) Carlton, W Yorkshire, by 12/1978.
104	OTT 63	Sold to T Goodwin (scrap dealer) Carlton by 10/1978.
105	KDB 646	No trace.
106	LTA 990	Sold to T Goodwin (breaker) Carlton 11/76; to Bowell Bros (breaker) Cundy Cross, Barnsley 11/1976.
107	OTT 50	Sold to T Wigley (breaker) Carlton, W Yorks. 1/1979.
106	LTA 997	Sold by12/1976. No further trace.
109	OAH 753	Sold to T Goodwin (breaker) Carlton 11/76. To Bowell Bros (breaker) Cundy Cross, 1/1977.
110	WVX 445	Sold to unknown scrap dealer early 1977.
111	OAH 751	Sold by 12/1976. No further trace.
112	OAH 752	Sold to unknown dealer by 8/1976. To Bowell Bros (breaker) Cundy Cross, 1/1977 for scrap.
113	XHW 418	Sold to T Goodwin (breaker) Carlton by 2/1979.
114	MAX 111	Being used for spares by 8/1976, remains broken up at depot by 12/1976.
115	SNG 763	Sold to unidentified breaker at Carlton 4/1977, for scrap.
-	VHN 897	Acquired for spares only. Derelict at depot 4/1976, broken up by 8/1976.

Above: This 1955 Bristol LS5G, **VHN 897** was purchased in May1972 to provide spares for the other LSs in the fleet. It's seen here in 1974 being use as a seat store. Note the 'Regent' petrol tanker lorry in the backdrop. Silcox had a maintenance contract with the nearby Regent (Texaco) refinery at Glebe Cross, to service and repair their locally based fleet. Additionally, the workshops carried out work for many other transport businesses.

116	PHW 927	Sold to Bowell Bros (breaker) Cundy Cross, Barnsley 1/1977 for scrap.
117	XHW 411	Sold to unknown dealer by 10/79. To T Goodwin (breaker) Carlton by 10/1979.
118	XHW 422	Sold to unknown dealer by 12/78. To T Goodwin (breaker) Carlton by 23/12/1978.
119	GDE374L	Sold to unknown dealer 7/1981. To Martin. St Columb Major, Cornwall 10/1981.
120	GDE375L	Sold to Pioneer Coaches. Laugharne, Carmarthenshire 1/1978.
121	OTT 49	Gone by 12/77. To Jenkins & Davies Engineering. Pembroke Dock by 4/1978. To caravan by 4/82.
122	OTT 56	Sold to unknown dealer by 1/1979. To T Goodwin (breaker) Carlton by 3/2/1979.
123	OTT 52	Sold to T Goodwin (breaker) Carlton 3/1978.
124	OTT 59	Sold to Martin (dealer) Middlewich 4/1978. To T Goodwin (breaker) Carlton 4/1978.
125	MAX 105	Sold to unknown dealer 10/1978. To T Goodwin (breaker) Carlton by 11/1978.
126	RWW 985	Sold to Martin (dealer) Middlewich 7/1979. To T Goodwin (breaker) Carlton by 8/1979.
127	NDE803M	Used as Non PSV 1980. Being scrapped at the depot 2/1981.
128	OO 9548	Sold by 3/1982. No further trace.
129	YHY 77	Sold to T Goodwin (breaker) Carlton 4/1979.
130	PDE570M	Sold to G Ripley (dealer) Carlton by 9/1997 for scrap.
131	RDE567M	Sold to Kirkby (dealer) South Anston by 10/1983. No further trace.
132	RDE876M	Sold to Sean Hayes. Cobh, Ireland 3/1984.
133	HBX190N	Sold to BRD & MG Hawkins (t/a: Barrie's Coaches) Haverfordwest by 11/1983.
134	HDE250N	Scrapped on site 8/2003.
135	HDE611N	Scrapped on site by 10/1999.
136	HDE612N	Scrapped on site by 10/1999.
137	HDE617N	Sold to G Ripley (dealer) Carlton by 5/1997 for scrap.
138	LDE163P	Sold to G Ripley (dealer) Carlton by 6/1997, To Wigley (breaker) Carlton for scrap by 9/1997.
139	LDE164P	Sold to G Ripley (dealer) Carlton by 6/1997. To Wigley (breaker) Carlton for scrap by 9/1997.
140	LDE165P	Sold to G Ripley (dealer) Carlton by 5/1997.
141	LDE166P	Scrapped on site 8/2003.
142	LDE167P	Sold to Williams (Bryncelyn Coaches) Betws, Ammanford, Carmarthenshire 9/1983
7	923 AHY	Sold to Martin (dealer) Middlewich 7/1979. To T Goodwin (breaker) Carlton by 8/1979.
6	928 AHY	Sold by 2/1983. No further trace.
3	936 AHY	Sold by 3/1982. No further trace.
4	939 AHY	Sold to Laverack, (PVS Ltd) dealer, Carlton 9/1981.
8	982 EHY	Derelict at depot by 27/9/1984.
1	519 JHU	Sold to Martin (dealer) Middlewich 5/1980. To T Goodwin (breaker) Carlton by 30/5/1980.
2	520 JHU	Static playbus at White Horse P H, Kilgetty by 4/81. To Broadmoor Nurseries, Jeffreyston c12/1982.
5	134 AMW	Sold to unknown dealer. To T Goodwin (breaker) Carlton by 9/7/1980.
9	HLJ 915D	Sold by 3/1982. No further trace.
143	NDE 86R	Re-registered: (9195 PU / PWN807R). Scrapped on site 11/2010.
144	NDE998R	Sold to 'D Coaches' Morriston, Swansea 9/1986.
145	NDE999R	Sold to 'D Coaches' Morriston, Swansea 9/1986.
15	HEL390D	No trace.
10	HEL391D	Sold by 3/1982. No further trace.
11	HEL392D	Sold by 3/1982. No further trace.
12	HLJ 916D	Sold to Laverack (PVS Ltd) dealer, Carlton 9/1981.
18	EMR299D	Sold to Lister (dealer) Bolton 8/1982. To J Sykes (dealer) Carlton for scrap 8/1982.
14	EMR300D	Scrapped on site 3/1984.
16	EMR302D	Sold to Wacton Trading (dealer) Bromyard 10/1986. To A J S (dealer) Carlton for scrap 3/1987.
17	EMR304D	Stolen from Milford Haven 26/10/80, crashed 15ft into a river at Blackbridge, Neyland, Pembs. Sold to Arnold (scrap dealer) Johnston, Pembrokeshire 1/11/1980 for scrap.
146	RDE298S	Sold to Arlington (dealer) by 12/1983. To Williams, Cwmdu, Brecon, 3/1985. Exported to Malta 8/1996, To J Xuereb of Mellieha, Malta 8/1986, re-registered Y-0611, later EBY-611.
147	RDE772S	Sold to 'Pride of The Road'. Royston, S Yorks. 2/1987.
19	ETD949B	Sold to Martin (dealer) Middlewich. To T Goodwin (breaker) Carlton by 9/7/1980.
20	538 OHU	Re-reg: (ABX 172A). Gone by 9/1987. To Reed School of Motoring (npsv) Hyde, Manchester 12/1987.

21	839 SUO	Sold to Hardwick (A J S Salvage) Carlton for scrap by 9/1984.
22	BHU976C	Sold to Wacton Trading (dealer), Bromyard 8/1986. To Stagecoach. Perth, Scotland 8/1986.
23	LTE 261C	No trace.
24	YNG 784	No trace.
25	7793 NG	Sold to Martin (dealer) Middlewich 4/1981. To P V S (breaker) Carlton by 5/8/1981.
26	842 SUO	Sold to Martin (dealer) Middlewich c3/1980. To T Goodwin (breaker) Carlton by 15/3/1981.
31	JDW301F	No trace.
34	JDW304F	Sold to unknown dealer by 4/1981.
-	JDW305F	Acquired for spares only.
37	JDW307F	Sold to Martin (dealer) Middlewich 11/1979. To scrap dealer at Carlton by 25/11/1979.
27	JHK 456C	Sold to Wacton Trading (dealer) Bromyard 8/1986. To A J S (breaker) Carlton 3/1987.
28	HFM590D	Sold to unknown dealer 2/1981. To T Goodwin (breaker) Carlton by 1/3/1981.
29 r/r	804 SHW ADE146A	Re-reg: (**ADE 146A**). To Wacton (dealer) Bromyard, Hereford 3/1990. To Ireland (dealer) Hull 3/1990, To Top Deck Travel. Horsell, Surrey 5/1990, re-registered KGH 891A & exported 12/1996.
30	1216 FM	No trace.
37	1218 FM	Sold to T Goodwin (breaker) Carlton by 1/11/ 1980.
40	1225 FM	Sold to unknown dealer 2/1981. To T Goodwin (breaker) Carlton by 21/2/1981.
32	JDW302F	Sold to Martin (dealer) Middlewich by 11/1979. To T Goodwin (breaker) Carlton by 25/11/1979.
33	JDW303F	Dismantled for spares & derelict at depot by 4/1980.
148	WBX870T	Dismantled for spares, remains cut up on site – 8/2003.
149	WBX871T	Re-registered: (**538 OHU, WBX 871T**). Scrapped on site by 12/2004.
39	1231 FM	No trace.
40	MRU124F	Sold to Martin (dealer) Middlewich by 10/1980.
41	MRU126F	Sold to Martin (dealer) Middlewich by 10/1980.
44	1222 FM	Sold to Lister (dealer) Bolton by 8/1982. To J Sykes (breaker) Carlton 8/1982.
46	1246 FM	No trace.
47	1247 FM	Sold to unknown dealer -/1982. To unknown farm Scotland 10/1982.
150	YBX 608V	Re-registered: (**804 SHW, CDE 391V**). Sold to Irish Ferries. Pembroke Dock (Non PSV) 12/2000.
48	JMY122N	Sold to Arlington Motors (dealer) by 3/1983. To Willis. Bodmin, Cornwall by 5/1983.
49	SWY334L	Sold to Grenville. Troon, Cornwall 9/1982.
50	109 CUF	Scrapped by 1993.
51	115 CUF	No trace.
45	1232 FM	Sold to Lister (dealer) Bolton by 8/1982. To unknown scrap dealer at Barnsley 8/1982.
32	KDD 283E	Cannibalised for spares, remains sold for scrap 2-8/1983.
33	KDD 289E	Sold to Lister (dealer) Bolton by 8/1982. To unknown scrap dealer at Barnsley 8/1982.
151	BBX 915V	Re-registered: (**SIL 9611**) Scrapped on site by 12/2004.
152	BDE 140V	Re-registered: (**SIL 9612**) Scrapped on site by 12/2004.
153	BDE 143V	Re-registered: (**SIL 9613**) Scrapped on site by 11/2001.
52	LAE 890L	Sold to Arlington Motors (dealer) Potters Bar by 12/1982. No further trace.
91	UTD 291H	Broken up on site by 7/1985.
19	RWC942D	No trace.
76	KCK 976H	Scrapped on site by 9/1996.
77	KCK 977H	Scrapped on site late-1990.
86	KCK 987H	Withdrawn by 3/1991 after accident. Broken up at depot 3/1993.
89	KCK 989H	Scrapped on site by 9/1996.
19	FLJ 154D	Sold to Wacton (dealer) Bromyard 8/1988. To Country Bus. Cheltenham dealer 6/1989 & exported.
103	LPT 903P	Sold to Wacton (dealer) Bromyard 8/1987. To Lister (dealer); to Thornes. Bubwith, Humber 8/1987.
104	LPT 904P	Sold to Wacton (dealer) Bromyard 8/1987. To Trimdon M S. Trimdon Grange, Durham 10/1987.
108	NLJ 518M	Fire damaged by 12/1988. Scrapped 2-5/1992.
109	NLJ 519M	Sold to Irwell Valley Coaches. Eccles, Gtr. Manchester 9/1990.
127	JHD 377J	Broken up at depot 3/1993.
119	SPK119M	Used for spares, remains to Ripley (dealer) Carlton for scrap by 6/1997.
120	SPK120M	Sold to Edgecombe Coaches. Sidmouth, Devon 9/1985.

116	SPK116M	Sold to unknown dealer 9/1985, To North Mymms Coaches. Potters Bar, Herts. 2/1986.
3	OWT783M	Sold to Wacton Trading (dealer) Bromyard 7/87. To Trimdon M S. Trimdon Grange, Durham 8/1987.
4	OWT784M	Sold to Wacton Trading (dealer) Bromyard 7/87. To Trimdon M S. Trimdon Grange, Durham 8/1987.
5	OWT785M	Sold to Wacton Trading (dealer) Bromyard 7/87. To Trimdon M S. Trimdon Grange, Durham 8/1987.
6	OWT786M	Sold to Wacton Trading (dealer) Bromyard 7/87. To Trimdon M S. Trimdon Grange, Durham 8/1987.
7	OWT787M	Sold to Wacton Trading (dealer) Bromyard 7/87. To Trimdon M S. Trimdon Grange, Durham 8/1987.
8	OWT788M	Sold to Wacton Trading (dealer) Bromyard 7/87. To Trimdon M S. Trimdon Grange, Durham 8/1987.
9	TCK 469	Sold to A Barraclough (dealer) Carlton, for scrap by 1/1983.
154	JDE 972X	Sold to dealer by 10/1985. To Shirley. Walsall, West Midlands by 6/1986.
155	JDE 973X	Sold to Yeates (dealer) 9/1985. To Arlott Bros. Aldermaston Wharf, Berks (14) c2/1986.
156	JDE 189X	Sold to Tillingbourne Bus Co. Cranleigh, Surrey, by 7/1985.
63	BNE 763N	Sold to Trimdon M S. Trimdon Grange, Durham 12/1987.
66	BNE 766N	Sold to Williams (Bryncelyn Coaches) Betws, Ammanford. Carmarthenshire. 9/1983.
67	BNE 767N	Sold to Wacton Trading (dealer) Bromyard 10/87. To Trimdon M S. Trimdon Grange, Durham 11/87.
157	NDE 147Y	Sold to Yeates (dealer) 9/1985. To Horlock's Coaches. Northfleet, Kent. 2/1986.
158	NDE 748Y	Sold to dealer 9/85. To Nottingham C T (778) 12/1985. To Guide Friday, Stratford upon Avon 11/88.
159	NDE 749Y	Sold to dealer 9/85. To Nottingham C T (777) 12/1985.
146	AJD 162T	Re-registered: (**538 OHU, AJD 162T**). Scrapped on site 8/2003.
131	WFH170S	Re-regd: (**KSU 409, WFH 170S**). Sold for scrap 2/2006.
132	AFH 182T	Re-registered: (**817 FKH, AFH 182T**). Scrapped on site 8/2003.
133	DAD 258T	Sold to Islwyn Borough Transport (57). Pontllanfraith, Gwent. 8/1988.
142	DAD 254T	Sold to James Bros. (Cenarth Coaches), Cenarth, Cardigan by 8/1990. Scrapped by 8/2003.
160	A53 VGD	No trace.
163	817 FKH	Re-registered: (**B386 YDE**) Sold to Wacton (dealer) Bromyard 8/1987. To Bennett. Gloucester 9/1987
161	KAD 346V	Sold to Millington. Kenfig Hill, Mid-Glamorgan by 8/1987.
162	KAD 348V	Sold to London Buses (LP2) 8/1987.
164	B538 XDE	Re-regd: (**PVO 624, A9 WLS**) Renumbered **109**. Written off in accident 6/97. Sold for scrap 10/1997.
165	B222 NUT	Sold to Wacton (dealer) 8/1987. To Yeates (dealer) 10/87. To Moon. Warnham, W Sussex by 2/1988.
31	OCA631P	Sold by 9/1990. To Irwell Valley Coaches. Eccles, Gtr. Manchester 12/1990.
34	OCA634P	Sold to Wacton (dealer) Bromyard by 8/1990.
40	KTT 40P	Used for parts by 5/97. Sold to G Ripley (dealer) Carlton 6/97. To PVS, Cudworth for scrap by 9/97.
166	115 CUF	Sold to G Price. Trimsaran, Carms, 8/1990. Cherished registration mark returned to Silcox in 6/1992.
167	C429 ADE	Re-regd: (**587 NCG**) Sold to Wilson (dealer) Ratby, Leics, c/w cherished registration number in 12/92.
r/r	587 NCG	Re-acquired 4/93; returned to Wilson by 5/93, to Litchfield. Stevington, Bedfordshire 6/1993.
168	C392CDE	Re-regd: (**109 CUF, A7 WLS, C392 CDE**). To Wilson (dealer) Ratby 9/98. To Hall. Coventry 1/1999
169	VAW 527	Renumbered **111**. Re-reg: (**A11 WLS, C358 DBX**). Sold to Gemini. Birchgrove, Swansea 3/2001.
11	WHN411G	Sold to G Ripley (dealer) Carlton by 4/1997. To preservationist by 7/1997 where it remains today.
24	WCD524K	Sold to G Ripley (dealer) Carlton for scrap by 6/1997.
70	OCD770G	Renumbered **77** by 5/1989. Scrapped by 9/1996.
111	UUF 111J	Scrapped by 6/1995.
154	WRK 3X	Sold to Islwyn Borough Transport, Pontllanfraith, Gwent (59) 9/1988 & re-registered IIB 1825.
170	D192 HDE	Sold to dealer 7/1992. To Powner Travel. Hinckley, Leicestershire 10/1992.
128	YTG 138H	Broken up by 9/1996.
129	HPT 320H	Renumbered **9** by 11/1990. No further trace.
10	HPT 321H	No further trace.
-	LJD 926K	Not operated. Acquired for spares & remains broken up at depot.
71	JOV 713P	Renumbered **4**. Scrapped at depot by 10/1993.
95	VUB 395H	Scrapped by 9/1996.
1	VCW 1L	Re-registered: (**KDE 161L**) & re-numbered **61** by 3/1991. Scrapped at depot by 4/1997.
171	D901HBX	Re-registered: (**A3 WLS, D45 KDE**). Sold to Oxenham. Goldsithney, Cornwall 10/1994.
18	AJA 418L	Sold to G Ripley (dealer) Carlton for scrap by 9/1997.
21	AJA 421L	Sold to G Ripley (dealer) Carlton for scrap by 9/1997.
30	MHX530P	Scrapped on site 5/1999.

37	SJA 370J	Scrapped on site 3/1993.
41	AAW411K	Sold to G Ripley (dealer) Carlton by 9/1996. To Expert-point Ltd. Stratford upon Avon 5/1997.
43	AUA 431J	Scrapped on site by 9/1996.
172	E522MDE	Re-regd: (**A2 WLS, E522 MDE**) & *renumbered* **102** by 10/92. To Steele. Sandown I O W, 2/2003.
-	VCW 2L	*Returned to Wacton (dealer) Bromyard off loan 6/1988.*
70	JOV 700P	*Renumbered* **3**. Sold by 10/1993. To South Pembrokeshire Playbus (Non PSV) 11/1993.
54 r/r	OKY 54R VAW527	Sold to A Wilson (dealer) Ratby 12/1992, & re-acquired 4/1993. Re-registered: (**VAW 527**) in 3/95; withdrawn 9/2002, returning to (**OKY 54R**) by 9/2003. Scrapped on site by 12/2004.
7	F77 TDE	Sold to dealer 10/1994. To Castle Garage. Llandovery, Carmarthenshire by 3/1995.
8	F78 TDE	Sold to Patel. Leicester 10/1994.
9	F559 UDE	*Renumbered* **55**. Sold to Houston Ramm (dealer) Heywood 3/1996, to Squirrel. Hitcham, Suffolk 3/96
-	LAG 287F	Returned to Wacton (dealer) Bromyard off loan 7/1989.
-	TBU 740G	Returned to Wacton (dealer) Bromyard off loan 7/1989.
-	GKE 458L	Returned to Wacton (dealer) Bromyard off loan 7/1989.
19	MHS 19P	Sold to G Ripley (dealer) Carlton by 10/1997. To Goodwin Farms Ltd. Wakefield (NPSV) 1/1998.
-	G739 ADE	Operated as non-PSV. No further trace.
-	G68 CDE	Sold to private owner, non-PSV use.
-	RUB 362G	Not operated. Acquired for spares, remains cut up 2-5/1992.
67	GNJ 567N	Written off after accident 10/1993, to Haven Auto-breakers, Pembroke Dock for scrap by 7/1995.
6	H736 EDE	Scrapped on site by 12/2011.
3	H743 EDE	Scrapped on site 7/2008.
4	H754 EDE	Sold for scrap by 4/2007.
2	H227 GDE	Scrapped on site 2/2010.
22	OSJ 622R	Sold to G Ripley (dealer) Carlton for scrap by 9/1997.
23	OSJ 624R	Sold to G Ripley (dealer) Carlton for scrap by 9/1997.
83	GNL 839N	Used for spares, remains sold to Bus Parts (dealer) Winchester, Hants. 1/1998.
84	GNL 840N	Sold to G Ripley (dealer) Carlton by 9/1997, to Goodwin Farms Ltd. Wakefield, W-Yorks (NPSV) 1/98.
-	E110 UEJ	Sold to private owner, non-PSV use.
173 r/r	D753 APK A4 WLS	Re-regd: (**GSK676, A4 WLS**) Sold to Moseley (dealer) Taunton 1/94, re-regd; D980 NCV by Moseley in 1/1994. Sold to Ford. Gunnislake, Cornwall 2/1994. Registration **A4 WLS** returned to Silcox.
174	D218 XPK	Re-regd: (**A6 WLS**). Burnt out in 6/1993. Registration A6 WLS transferred to B170 BFE in 8/1993.
59	LMA 59P	Re-regd: (**PVO 624**), Scrapped on site by 5/2005. Registration number presumed sold.
12	BUR 712S	Sold to G Ripley (dealer) Carlton for scrap by 9/1997.
66	WFH166S	Re-regd: (**115 CUF, 9195 PU, TDE 708S**). Used for spares, remains scrapped on site 8/2003.
112	9195 PU	Re-regd: (**A12 WLS, A81 VDE**). Sold to Caetano (dealer) 6/97. To R & N Lyles. Batley, W Yorks 7/1997.
114	B722MBC	Re-regd: (**A14 WLS, B89 ADE**) Sold to Caetano (dealer) 1/98. To Allenway & Barnes. Stratford (LN) 3/99.
5	J387 ODE	Scrapped on site 5/2009.
28	NGV288M	Re-registered: (**109 CUF, CDE 110M** - 3/99). W/drawn by 10/1998, scrapped on site 8/2003.
79	HWY719N	Scrapped on site by 10/1999.
72	HWY720N	Re-registered: (**GSK 676, HWY 720N**). Scrapped on site 8/2003.
115	E167OMD	Re-registered: (**A15 WLS, E167 OMD**). Sold to M Hogan. Thurles, Co Tipperary, 7/1999.
175 r/r	J47 SNY A11 WLS	Re-registered: (**A11 WLS, J328 PDE**) Sold to Central (dealer) Frooms Hill 9/1994, to Wealden (dealer) Five Oaks Green 1/1995. Exported to Canco Supreme. Zetjun, Malta 1/1995, registered Y-0934.
105	G994 FVV	Re-regd: (**A5 WLS, G994 FVV**). Sold to Caetano (dealer) Heather, Leics. 4/1999. No further trace.
108	F628 SRP	Re-regd: (**A8 WLS, F628 SRP**). To AMC (dealer) Shepshed 2/2000.To Harrison. Alfreton, Derby 5/2001.
54	OKY 54R	Re-regd: (**VAW 527, OKY 54R**). Scrapped on site by 12/2004.
9	K651 TDE	Scrapped on site 11/2010.
70	CWG707V	Sold to Gemini Travel. Birchgrove, Swansea 9/1998.
171	CWG712V	Sold to G Ripley (dealer) Carlton for scrap by 9/1997.
75	CWG759V	Sold to G Ripley (dealer) Carlton for scrap by 9/1997.
106	B170 BFE	Re-registered: (**A6 WLS, B48 ADE**). Sold to Glenvic Coaches. Nailsea, Bristol by 8/1996.
116 r/r	H75 HAW A16 WLS	Re-registered: (**A16 WLS, H59 JDE**). Sold to Houston Ramm (dealer) Sudden 4/1996. To Fitzpatrick Coaches. Drumree, Co Meath, Eire 6/1996. Re-registered 94-MH-3218.

104	F866 XJX	Re-regd: **(A4 WLS, F866 XJX)**.To Vale (dealer) Gt Kingshill 1/2002, to Ebdon. Erith, London 2/2002.
17	M174BDE	Sold to Jempson & Bailey. Peasmarsh, East Sussex 10/1996.
1	M361CDE	Sold to M & R Commercials (scrap dealer) Swansea 3/2015.
8	M368CDE	Scrapped on site 6/2013.
-	L416 PAR	Returned ex loan to Marshall of Cambridge (dealer) 11/1994.
29	EHW294W	Sold to AMC (dealer) Shepshed, Leics. 11/1999.
7	M674CDE	Sold for scrap by 5/2015.
16	M16 SMC	Sold to Harris. Fleur-de-Lys, Gwent 5/2005.
17	M17 SMC	Re-registered: **(M385 EBX)** in 3/2012 & withdrawn. Sold for scrap by 5/2015.
18	M18 SMC	Re-registered: (unknown) in 3/2014. Withdrawn by 8/2013. Sold for scrap by 5/2015.
103 r/r	F552TMH A3 WLS	Re-registered: **(A3 WLS, F552 TMH).** Sold to Mid-West (dealer) Staverton, Glos. 2/1998, to Baker, Weston-Super-Mare, Somerset by 4/1998.
-	GJI 9328	Acquired chassis only - for spares, remains scrapped by 4/1997.
31	GNF 13V	Sold to Gemini Travel. Birchgrove, Swansea 9/1998.
-	K507 RDE	Sold by 9/1997. No further trace
11	D859 CKV	W/drawn 3/1999. Used for spares, remains scrapped on site by 12/2000.
12	F865 PAC	W/drawn 1/1999. Used for spares, remains scrapped on site by 12/2000.
10	F580 OOU	W/drawn 3/1999. Used for spares, remains scrapped on site by 12/2000.
13	F585 OOU	Renumbered **15**. Withdrawn 12/1998. Used for spares, Remains scrapped on site 12/2000.
106 r/r	G903WAY A6 WLS	Re-registered: **(A6 WLS, G903WAY).** Sold to Berkhof UK Ltd (dealer) Basingstoke, 1/2001, to Mitchell. Plean, Central Scotland 3/2001.
89 200	E98 LLP SIL 9613	Renumbered **200**. Re-registered: **(SIL 9613, E98 LLP).** W/drawn 4/2011, Out of use @ depot 6/2011
90 201	E628WWD A2 WLS	Renumbered **201**. Re-registered: **(A2 WLS, E628 WWD).** W/drawn 8/2014. Sold to Irish Ferries Ltd, Pembroke Dock (2) 8/2014 as Non PSV. Registration mark A2 WLS not re-used
91 202	E125ODE KSU 409	Renumbered **202**. Re-registered: **(KSU 409, E125 ODE).** Withdrawn by7/2012, scrapped on site 5/2013.
92 203	E672WWD 9195 PU	Renumbered **203**. Re-registered: **(9195 PU, E672 WWD).** Withdrawn 6/2012, scrapped on site 5/2013.
204	E673WWD 538 OHU	Re-registered: **(538 OHU, E673 WWD).** Withdrawn 6/2014.To Charterfields (auctioneers) 6/2016. Sold @ £20.00 to DJ & NW Brown. Builth Wells, Powys 7/2016.
94 205	D576DPM A6 WLS	Renumbered **205**. Re-registered: **(A6 WLS).** Withdrawn by 3/2016. Re-registered **(D390 HHN)** by Charterfields (auctioneers) 6/2016. To D Badham. East Williamston, Pemb, for preservation 6/2016.
95 206	D146 KDE 804 SHW	Renumbered **206**. Re-registered: **(804 SHW, D146 KDE).** Sold to Plaxton (dealer) Anston 10/2010.
96 207	D578DPM A11 WLS	Renumbered **207**. Re-registered: **(A11 WLS, D578 DPM).** Withdrawn 11/2013. Sold to unknown scrap dealer 1/2014.
208	E133 ODE	Originally f/n **97**. Renumbered **208**. Withdrawn 3/2014. Sold for scrap 7/2014.
209	E137ODE	Withdrawn 7/2014. Scrapped 7/2014.
210	E138ODE	Originally f/n **99**. Withdrawn 6/2013. Gone by 7/2014, presumed scrapped.
211	E139ODE	Withdrawn c7/2013. Accident damaged. Sold for scrap by 5/2015.
212	E141ODE	Re-registered: **(A4 WLS, E141 ODE).** Sold 7/2012, probably for scrap.
214	E144ODE	Withdrawn 8/2013. Sold to unidentified scrap dealer 1/2014.
215	E145ODE	Withdrawn 10/2014. Sold by 5/2015. To D Badham. East Williamston for preservation by 6/2016.
216	E149ODE	Sold to Irish Ferries. Pembroke Dock (3) 8/2014. Maintained by Silcox.
217	A16 WLS	Withdrawn 10/2014. Sold 5/15, to D Badham, East Williamston, Pembs, for preservation by 6/2016.
218	A14 WLS	Re-registered: -?- 6/2016. To Charterfields (auctioneers) to unidentified at Merthyr Tydfil 7/2016.
219	A12 WLS	Withdrawn 12/2014. Sold to unidentified preservationist Pembroke Dock 12/2015, as A12 WLS.
220 r/r	D577DPM A8 WLS	Re-registered: **(A8 WLS).** Withdrawn 11/2014, Sold for scrap 4/2015. Probably re-registered **D577 DPM.**
221	NSV 324	Withdrawn 8/2013. Re-reg: **(D956 BMV)** 9/2013. No further trace.
222	A3 WLS	Withdrawn 6/2016 (the last MoD Tiger in service with Silcox). Re-registered: **(E818 AKU)** 6/2016. To Charterfields (auctioneers) to Elliott & Richman. Rode Heath, Cheshire 7/2016.

223	E183ODE	Withdrawn 7/2014, and scrapped 7/2014.
224	A7 WLS	Re-registered: (**E81 EFJ**) in 11/2013. No further trace.
225	109 CUF	Re-registered: (**SIL 6637**) in 9/2009. Withdrawn c2014 and scrapped 7/2014.
r/r	SIL 6637	Personalised registration mark not re-used.
226	E194ODE	Withdrawn 7/2014 and scrapped 7/2014.
227	A5 WLS	Re-registered: (**E406 ODE**) & withdrawn 5/2012. Sold by 7/2014 for scrap.
228	A15 WLS	Re-registered: (**C59 TJC**) 8/2013. Withdrawn 7/2014, sold by 5/2015 for scrap.
229	GSK 676	Withdrawn by 12/2004, broken chassis. Sold for scrap by 6/2007. Cherished registration mark lost.
179	P779WDE	Re-registered (**9195 PU**) 5/2013. Withdrawn 2/2016. To Charterfields (auctioneers) 6/2016 re-registered
r/r	9195 PU	(**P779WDE**) Sold @ £10, to Browns of Builth Wells, Powys for spares, 7/2016.
180	P780WDE	Withdrawn 9/2015. To Charterfields (auctioneers) sold @ £410 to unknown for spares 7/2016,
181	R530 HDE	Sold to Moseley (dealer) Wellington 3/2007. To Warren (Bluebird Coaches) Neath, W Glam. 6/2007.
182	R531 HDE	Withdrawn 6/2016. To Charterfields (auctioneers) sold @ £1,950 to unidentified at N Ireland 8/2016.
183	R532 HDE	Withdrawn 6/2016. To Charterfields (auction) sold @ £2550 to Stanways Cs, Stoke-on-Trent 7/2016.
184	S224 BDE	Sold to Caetano (dealer) Heather, 12/2005. To Reliant. Heather, Leics. 12/2005.
24	NSV 324	Re-reg: -?- in 9/1998, w/drawn by 10/98. Sold to Goodwin Farms. Wakefield (NPSV) 12/1998.
230	K721 UDE	Sold to Construction Engineers, Chicago Bridge & Ironworks. Pembroke Dock (Non PSV) 4/2006.
231	K722 UDE	Sold to Caetano (dealer) Heather, 4/2006.
12	H681YGO	*Renumbered* **81**. Sold to SCC (dealer) Waterlooville, 12/2001. To Nu-Venture. Aylesford, Kent 4/2002.
14	H682YGO	*Renumbered* **89**. Sold to SCC (dealer) Waterlooville, 12/2001. To Nu-Venture. Aylesford, Kent 4/2002.
10	D603MKH	Sold to Brian Isaac Coaches, Morriston, Swansea for spares 12/2000.
185	T141 RDE	Sold to Moseley (dealer) Wellington 9/2010. To Jenkins (Crystal Travel) Milkwall, Glos. -/2010.
186	T142 RDE	Re-registered: (**M18 SMC**) 3/2014. Withdrawn 6/2016. To Charterfields (auctioneers) sold @ £5,550
r/r	M18 SMC	to Llew Jones. Llanrwst, Conwy 7/2016, with the personalised registration mark.
187	T143 RDE	Sold to Caetano (dealer) Heather, 1/2005, to Reliant. Heather, Leics. 2/2005.
188	W108NDE	Withdrawn 6/2016. Sold to Edwards Coaches. Llantwit Fardre, Mid-Glam. 6/2016.
189	W109NDE	Withdrawn 6/2016. Sold to Edwards Coaches. Llantwit Fardre, Mid-Glam. 6/2016.
190	K780 UDE	Sold to Vale (dealer) Great Kingshill 12/2004. To A D Withers (dealer) 1/2005. To Kent C C, Aylesford, Kent 2/2005.
191	K726DWN	Sold to Majestic. Shareshill, Staffordshire 2/2005.
192	N356MDE	Sold to Vale (dealer) Great Kingshill 3/2003, To Harrod. Wormegay, Norfolk 3/2003.
11	H172RBO	Sold to Sullivan Buses. Potters Bar, Herts. 8/2001.
15	H173RBO	Sold to Sullivan Buses. Potters Bar, Herts. 8/2001.
19	L784 SEJ	Withdrawn 7/2013. Sold for scrap 7/2014.
20	L632 XBX	Sold to Mistral (dealer) Knutsford 2/2007.
193	Y199 JDE	Sold to Moseley (dealer) Wellington 3/2010, To Carmel Coaches, Exeter, by 12/2012.
21	Y201 JDE	Withdrawn 6/2016. To Charterfields (auctioneers). Sold @ £1500 to Cainey. Thornbury, Glos 7/2016.
22	V675 FPO	Sold to Southdown PSV (dealer) Copthorne 2/2005, To Cavalier. Long Sutton, Lincs. (5328) 4/2005.
194	Y733 OBE	Completely burnt out in service 7/2002. Scrapped at depot 8/2002.
-	Y198 KNB	Returned to Optare (dealer) Leeds ex loan & demonstration 10/2001.
195	CU51HVS	Sold to Moseley (dealer) Wellington 4/2008, To Taylor. Yeovil, Somerset 5/2008.
196	CV02HBN	W/drawn 7/2011. Sold to Lloyd (dealer) Hixon for scrap 6/12, To Wigley. Carlton for scrap by 4/2015.
23	CV02HBP	Licence expired 5/2016. To G W A (auctioneers) Clitheroe, Lancs. 6/2016. Scrapped 7/2016.
24	CV02HBO	W/drawn 6/2016. To G W A (auctioneers) Clitheroe, 6/2016. Sold – no trace 7/2016.
232	A153 VDE	Withdrawn 12/2010. Sold for scrap 7/2012.
-	L464 XOU	Not operated. Sold to Vale (dealer) Gt Kingshill 3/2003, To Harrod. Wormegay, Norfolk 3/2003.
233	D264ROH	Re-registered: (**A4 WLS**) 2/2003 & returned to (**D264 ROH**) upon withdrawal in 6/2010.
r/r	A4 WLS	Withdrawn 6/2010, derelict at depot 4/2012 & scrapped on site 2012.
r/r	D264ROH	
194	FY02WHD	Withdrawn 6/2016. To GWA (auctioneers) 6/2016, To: Going My Way. Cheadle, Staffs 7/2016.
-	V956 HEB	Demonstration vehicle on loan 7-8/2002. Returned to owner 8/2002.
197	FY02 YHF	Sold to Optare (dealer) Cross Gates, Leeds 11/2006. To Hutchinson. Hutton-Le-Hole -/2007

25	RIL 1476	Re-registered: (**G445 LEP**) in 10/2011.
r/r	G445 LEP	Sold for scrap 7/2012.
234	D372 UVL	Re-registered (**VAW 527**) in 9/2003. Withdrawn 2/2009. Cherished registration number sold off.
r/r	VAW 527	Scrapped on site 11/2010.
235	A649YOX	Sold to Construction Engineers, Chicago Bridge & Ironworks, South Hook, Pembrokeshire 6/2006.
-	N966DWJ	Returned ex loan to Transbus (dealer) Anston 9/2003.
26	YN04LXJ	Sold to Mistral (dealer) Knutsford 2/2006, To Moray Council (A1) by 3/2010.
27	R414 VCC	Re-registered: (**817 FKH**) 5/2004. Mot expired 6/2016. Withdrawn & re-registered (**R414 VCC**) 6/16,
r/r	817 FKH	To Charterfields (auctioneers) sold @ £570 as non-runner to Midlands Trade Centre (dealer) Yardley,
r/r	R414 VCC	West Midlands, 7/2016.
28	CU04AUW	Withdrawn 6/2016. To GWA (auctioneers) Clitheroe. Sold to Pilkington. Accrington, Lancs. 8/2016.
-	R704 MEP	Not operated. Gone by 5/2004.
-	S351 CDE	Probably not operated. Sold to Auto-services (dealer) Pontypool, Gwent 8/2004. To Private Owner.
32	S352 CDE	Sold with no further trace.
29	V229 DDE	Sold to Bluestone Leisure Park (Non PSV). Canaston Wood, Narberth, Pembs. 10/2011.
10	L865 LFS	Sold to Mistral (dealer) Knutsford 3/2007. No further trace.
11	L867 LFS	Withdrawn 2/2007. Sold for scrap 6/2007.
198	CU54KWS	Withdrawn 6/2016. To GWA (auctioneers). Sold 7/2016. No further trace.
30	CU05DME	Withdrawn 6/2016. To GWA (auctioneers). Sold to Autocar. Five Oaks Green, Kent 8/2016.
14	YC51HAO	Sold to Mistral (dealer) Knutsford 5/2009. To Horsburgh, Pumpherston, Nr Edinburgh 10/2012.
15	YC51HAE	Withdrawn 3/2011. Sold to Southdown PSV (dealer) Copthorne 11/2011, but still at Silcox yard 4/12. To Hillier. Foxham, Wilts. 5/2012.
-	F722 FDV	Acquired for spares. Remains sold to scrap dealer at Pembroke Dock 7/2006.
-	D106GHY	Not operated. Sold to Chicago Bridge & Ironworks (NPSV) South Hook, Pembs 11/2005.
-	D109GHY	Not operated. Sold to Chicago Bridge & Ironworks (NPSV) South Hook, Pembs 11/2005.
16	CV55AXW	Withdrawn 6/2016. To GWA (auctioneers), 6/2016, to Go-Goodwins. Eccles, Gtr Manchester 7/2016.
26	CV55BAU	Sold to Chelston Leisure Service. Torquay, Devon 3/2010.
199	CV55AZN	Withdrawn 6/2016. To GWA (auctioneers), 6/2016, to Caney. Bartley Green, W Midlands 7/2016.
184	CU06ANP	Sold to D Caney. Bartley Green, W Midlands 3/2016.
12	S862 BHR	Licence expired 5/2016, To Charterfields (auctioneers) 6/2016, sold @ £310 to Midlands Trade Centre (dealer) Yardley, B'ham in 7/2016.
178	H613UWR	Re-registered: (**NSV 324**) 9/2014. Withdrawn 6/2016. Re-registered (**H613 UWR**) to Charterfields
r/r	NSV 324	(auctioneers) 6/2016. Sold @ £2,450 to unknown dealer in N Ireland in 7/2016.
235	D113GHY	Sold to C A Rees (T/A: D R Travel) Pontyates, Llanelli, Carms. 1/2009.
181	WA53WSY	Sold to Moseley (dealer) Wellington 3/2012. To Keepings. Penrhiwceiber, Mid Glam 4/2013.
20	MX07BCE	Withdrawn 6/2016. To GWA (auctioneers). To Harris. Fleur-de-Lis, Gwent 7/2016.
22	MX07BAO	Withdrawn 6/2016. To GWA (auctioneers) sold 7/2016. To Pickford. Chippenham, Wilts by 1/2017.
197	YX07AWV	Withdrawn 6/2016. To Mason (Narberth Mini Bus Travel). Whitland, Carmarthenshire 8/2016.
11	N952 NAP	Sold to M & R Commercials (scrap dealer) Swansea 3/2015.
10	MX04 VLT	W/drawn c11/2015. To GWA (auctioneers) 6/2016. To Go-Goodwins. Eccles, as non-runner 7/2016.
177	P384 YHT	Withdrawn 6/2016. To Charterfields (auctioneers). Sold @ £4,050.
33	CU07HVK	Withdrawn 6/2016. To Charterfields (auctioneers). To Llew Jones. Llanrwst, Conwy @ £1525, 7/2016
34	SN08 AAJ	Withdrawn 6/2016. To GWA (auctioneers) 6/2016. To Stott. Milnsbridge, West Yorkshire 7/2016.
100	WA08JVX	Withdrawn 6/2016. To GWA (auctioneers) 6/2016. To Going My Way. Cheadle, Staffs 7/2016.
101	YN08 NKJ	Withdrawn 6/2016. To GWA (auctioneers) 6/2016. To TK Travel. Burghfield Common, Berks. 7/2016.
35	MX09HHS	Withdrawn 6/2016. To GWA (auctioneers) 6/2016. To Pickford. Chippenham, Wiltshire 7/2016.
-	CV57HMU	Returned to Day's Rental. Swansea, off hire 7/2009.
-	CV58XBU	Returned to Day's Rental. Swansea, off hire 7/2009.
-	CV09EFE	Returned to Day's Rental. Swansea, off hire 7/2009.
-	CV09EFF	Returned to Day's Rental. Swansea, off hire 7/2009.
-	CV09YGH	Returned to Day's Rental. Swansea, off hire 7/2009.
102	WA04EWT	Withdrawn 6/2016. To GWA (auctioneers) 6/2016. Sold - Exported

36	YJ10EXU	Operated on behalf of owners Pembrokeshire County Council. Withdrawn 6/2016 & returned to PCC, passing to Edwards Bros. Tiers Cross, Pembrokeshire 6/2016 with the PCC supported service.
37	YJ10EXV	Operated on behalf of owners Pembrokeshire County Council. Withdrawn 6/2015 with serious fire damage. Returned to PCC by 6/2016 with no further trace, presumed scrapped.
38	P901 CTO	Re-registered: (**SIL9613**) in 4/2015. Withdrawn 5/2015 with engine failure.
r/r	SIL9613	Re-registered: (**P901 CTO**) by Charterfields (auctioneers) in 6/2016. Sold to M Hayward, Carmarthen
r/r	P901 CTO	@ £10, for scrap 6/2016, to Ammanford Metals, Cross Hands, Carms, for scrap 7/2016.
39	T430 KAG	Withdrawn c5/2015. To Charterfields (auctioneers) 6/2016. Sold to M Hayward. Carmarthen @ £10 for spares 6/2016, to Ammanford Metals, Cross Hands, Carms, for scrap 7/2016.
40	XIL 9100	Withdrawn 8/2015. Sold to M & R Commercials (scrap dealer) Swansea 12/2015.
-	617 DDV	To North Somerset Coaches, Nailsea (74) 11/2013.
-	573 UVX	To Talisman Logistics Ltd, Great Bromley, Essex 9/2013.
236	RLZ 1670	Withdrawn 6/2016. To Charterfields (auction) as non-runner to Llew Jones. Llanrwst, Conwy 7/2016.
237	P771 BJF	Re-registered: (**804 SHW**) 5/2012. Withdrawn 6/2016.
r/r	804 SHW	Re-registered: (**P771 BJF**) 6/2016 by Charterfields (auctioneers), sold @ £3,900 to Richards Bros.
r/r	P771 BJF	Cardigan 7/2016.
238	S488 UAK	Withdrawn by 5/2016. To Charterfields (auctioneers) 6/2016. Sold as spares £675. No further trace.
41	YJ60 LRL	Withdrawn 6/2016. Returned to owners; Pembrokeshire C C in 6/2016. Passed to Edwards Bros. Tiers Cross, with the PCC supported service, 6/2016.
42	YJ60 LRN	Withdrawn 6/2016. Returned to owners; Pembrokeshire C C in 6/2016. Passed to Edwards Bros. Tiers Cross 6/2016, to First Cymru Buses (53711) 7/2016 with the PCC supported service.
-	YJ60 KFP	Returned to dealer ex loan 4/2011.
43	S103 EGK	Re-registered: (**A4 WLS**) 5/2012. Withdrawn 6/2016.
r/r	A4 WLS	Re-registered: (**S103 WLS**) 6/2016 by Charterfields (auctioneers).
r/r	S103 EGK	Sold to unidentified dealer @ £400 (6/2016).
44	S107 EGK	Re-registered: (**A5 WLS**) 7/2012. Withdrawn 6/2016.
r/r	A5 WLS	Re-registered: (**S107 EGK**) 6/2016 by Charterfields (auctioneers).
r/r	S107 EGK	Sold to David Badham. East-Williamston, Pembrokeshire for preservation @ £100, 6/2016.
45	S113 EGK	Re-registered: (**A15 WLS**) 8/2015. Withdrawn 6/2016.
r/r	A15 WLS	Re-registered: (**S113 EGK**) 6/2016 by Charterfields (auctioneers).
r/r	S113 EGK	Sold to David Badham. East-Williamston, Pembrokeshire for preservation @ £850, 6/2016.
46	S638 JGP	Re-registered: (**KSU 409**) 10/2014. Withdrawn c5/2015.
r/r	KSU 409	Re-registered: (**S638 JGP**) 6/2016 by Charterfields (auctioneers).
r/r	S638 JGP	Sold for scrap @ £25. (7/2016).
103	WA08GP0	Withdrawn 6/2016. To GWA (auctioneers) 6/2016. To Watkins Coaches Glyn Neath, W Glam. 8/2016.
239	R708 NJH	Re-registered: (**RIL 1476**) 10/2012. Withdrawn 6/2016.
r/r	RIL 1476	Re-registered: (**R708 NJH**) 6/2016 by Charterfields (auctioneers).
r/r	R708 NJH	Sold @ £2,700 to Elliott & Richman. Rode Heath, Cheshire 6/2016.
240	R50 TGM	Re-registered: (**538 OHU**) 6/2013. Withdrawn 6/2016.
r/r	538 OHU	Re-registered: (**R50 TGM**) 6/2016 by Charterfields (auctioneers).
r/r	R50 TGM	Sold @ £2,500 to Llew Jones. Llanrwst, Conwy 7/2016.
241	XUD 367	Withdrawn 6/2016. Re-registered to original: (**P883 FMO**) in 6/2016 by Charterfields (auctioneers).
r/r	P883FMO	Sold @ £2,100 to M Hayward (dealer) Carmarthen 7/2016, scrapped on site, engine to -?- W Ireland. Cherished registration XUD 367 sold by Charterfields to Ffoshelig Coaches, Carmarthen,
242	M308SHN	Re-registered: (**M17 SMC**) 10/2012. Withdrawn 6/2016. To Charterfields (auctioneers) 6/2016.
r/r	M17 SMC	Sold @ £3,450 to Llew Jones. Llanrwst, Conwy as M17 SMC in 7/2016.
47	Y619GFM	Withdrawn 6/2016. To Charterfields (auctioneers) 6/2016. Sold @ £800 to Bysiau Cwm Taf. Whitland, Carmarthenshire 7/2016, licenced 11/2016.
243	Y235BAW	Withdrawn 6/2016. To Charterfields (auctioneers) 6/2016. Sold @ £8,100 to Celtic Travel. Llanidloes, Powys 7/2016.
244	Y126 BPB	Re-registered: (**Y237 BAW**) 9/2013. Withdrawn 6/2016. To Charterfields (auctioneers), Sold @ £7,800
r/r	Y237BAW	to M Hayward (operator & dealer) Carmarthen, 7/2016. Exported 7/2016.
245	Y158 RLC	Re-registered: (**Y252 XHH**) 9/2013. Withdrawn 6/2016. Not auctioned.
r/r	Y252XHH	Sold to Edwards Coaches. Llantwit Fardre, Mid-Glam with part of the business 6/2016.

246	SX02WDS	Re-registered: (**CT02 NAE**) 10/2013. Withdrawn 6/2016. Not auctioned.
r/r	CT02 NAE	Sold to Edwards Coaches. Llantwit Fardre, Mid-Glam with part of the business 6/2016.
104	BN63NYD	Withdrawn 6/2016. Returned to King-Long UK (dealer) Coventry 6/2016 still there 9/2017.
48	V723GGE	Withdrawn 5/2016. To Charterfields (auctioneers) 6/2016.
		Sold as a 'non-runner' @ £260, to Richards Bros. Cardigan 7/2016.
247	YN06CFZ	Returned to dealer: After Sales, Knypersley, by 2/2015. To David Dove Travel. Newcastle, by 3/2017
248	Y124 PLT	Re-registered: (**Y139 YSO**) 3/2014. Withdrawn 6/2016. To Charterfields (auctioneers) 6/2016.
r/r	Y139 YSO	Sold @ £8,850 to McVicker, Benbecula, Outer Hebrides, Scotland 6/2016.
249	Y183 SRK	Re-registered: (**Y154 EBY**) 7/2014. Withdrawn 6/2016. Not Auctioned.
r/r	Y154 EBY	Sold to Edwards Coaches. Llantwit Fardre, Mid Glam, with part of the business 6/2016.
250	RUI 6748	Withdrawn 6/2016. To Charterfields (auctioneers) 6/2016. Sold @ £800 to: M Hayward (operator/dealer) Carmarthen; to Ammanford Metals Cross Hands for scrap 7/2016.
105	BK63 ZTB	Withdrawn 6/2016. Not auctioned.
		Sold to Edwards Coaches. Llantwit Fardre, Mid-Glam with part of the business 6/2016.
251	R114 SBD	Re-registered: (**A11 WLS**) 11/2014. Withdrawn 6/2016.
r/r	A11 WLS	Re-registered: (**R114 SBD**) by Charterfields (auctioneers) in 6/2016.
r/r	R114 SBD	Sold to Llew Jones. Llanrwst, Conwy 7/2016.
49	AE08 KTK	Returned to King-Long UK (dealer) Coventry 10/2014, to Air Parks, Birmingham 1/2015.
50	AE09 DJU	Returned to King-Long UK (dealer) Coventry 10/2014, to Tates Travel. Low Barugh, Surrey 4/2015.
51	AE09 DJV	Returned to King-Long UK (dealer) Coventry 10/2014, to Tates Travel. Low Barugh, Surrey 4/2015.
52	AE09 DJO	Returned to King-Long UK (dealer) Coventry 10/2014, to Air Parks, Birmingham 1/2015.
53	KX06 LYP	Returned to Guideissue (dealer) Knypersley 1/2015, to Crosville, Weston Super Mare 1/2015.
54	Y178 CFS	Returned to Finance Company 6/2016.
55	W793VMV	Returned to Finance Company 6/2016.
56	W794VMV	Returned to Finance Company 6/2016.
99	MX54 KYJ	Withdrawn c3/2016 @ depot 5/6/16. Returned to finance Company 6/2016.
57	MX12DYN	Withdrawn 6/2016. Returned to lessor, to Phil Anslow. Pontypool, Gwent by 10/2016.
58	MX12DZK	Withdrawn 6/2016. Returned to lessor.
59	YJ58 FFN	Operated on behalf of owners Pembrokeshire County Council. Withdrawn 6/2016 it returned to P C C, passed to Bysiau Cwm Taf (Taf Valley Cs) Whitland, Carmarthenshire, with the supported service.
-	R401FWT	Returned ex loan to D Caney. Bartley Green, Birmingham, 6/2016.
60	SN16OGV	Withdrawn 6/2016. Not auctioned. To Aston's Coaches. Worcester 7/2016.
61	SN16ORS	Withdrawn 6/2016. To GWA (auctioneers) to Stephenson. Rochford, Essex 440 (7/2016).
62	SN16ORU	Withdrawn 6/2016. To GWA (auctioneers) to Stephenson. Rochford, Essex 441 (7/2016).
-	BL14 LSO	Withdrawn 6/2016. To A P Travel. Cowbridge, Vale of Glamorgan 6/2016.
-	BL14 LSV	Withdrawn 6/2016. To A P Travel. Cowbridge, Vale of Glamorgan 6/2016.
-	BL14 LSU	Withdrawn 6/2016. To A P Travel. Cowbridge, Vale of Glamorgan 6/2016.
-	BX62 BKV	Withdrawn 6/2016. To Vale (dealer) Thruxton 6/2016.
-	BN63NYU	Withdrawn 5/2016. To A P Travel. Cowbridge, Vale of Glamorgan 5/2016.

VEHICLE PHOTOGRAPH INDEX

MUX 794	57	R531 HDE	185	UTD 291H	122	YDE 444	51
MX04 VLT	214	R708 NJH	231	UUF 111J	148	YHY 77	97
MX54 KYJ	241	R965 RCH	255	UUF 325J	145	YJ10 EXU	219
MX07 BAO	215	RC 4627	54	V229 DDE	206	YJ58 FFN	244
MX12 DYN	244	RC 4630	54	V675 FPO	194	YJ58 FFN	252
N356 MDE	191	RDE 298S	106	V723 GGE	238	YJ60 KFP	229
N952 NAP	213	RDE 659G	82	VAW 527	139 /154	YJ60 LRL	224
NDE 330	28	RDE 772S	107	VAW 527	201	YJ60 LRL	254
NDE 331	28	RDE 876M	98	VCW 1L	153	YJ60 LRN	224
NDE 332	29 / 46	RFM 457	84 / 86	VDE 873J	89	YK04 KWD	253
NDE 332	67	RIL 1476	201 / 231	VDE 874J	89	YN04 LXJ	205
NDE 616	29	RLZ 1670	221	VFM 587	84 / 85	YN06 CFZ	238
NDE 748Y	129	RUI 6748	239	VGT 330	76	YN08 NKJ	217
NDE 803M	96	RWW 985	96	VHN 897	288	YX07 AWV	214
NDE 86R	104	S103 EGK	225	W108 NDE	190	YX14 RZE	254
NDE 999R	105	S107 EGK	226	W109 NDE	190	109 CUF	119
NLJ 518M	124	S113 EGK	227	W793 VMV	243	109 CUF	138
NSV 324	181 / 213	S488 UAK	223	W794 VMV	243	109 CUF	182
OAH 751	92	S638 JGP	228	WA04 EWT	219	115 CUF	137
OCA 631P	134	S862 BHR	211	WA08 GPO	230	120 LDE	65
OCD 770G	147	SDE 400	44	WA08 JVX	217	1231 FM	116
ODE 1	50	SDE 450	31 / 32	WBX 871T	113	50 NDE	65
ODE 401	37 / 38	SDE 450	47	WCD 524K	148	519 JHU	103
ODE 402	38	SFM 8	83	WDE 343	45	538 OHU	110
ODE 600	30	SIL 6637	182	WFH 170S	131	538 OHU	114
OFM 670	88	SIL 9611	120	WHN 122	86	538 OHU	130
OHA 298	52	SIL 9612	121	WHN 411G	147	538 OHU	232
OHY 984	85	SN 08 AAJ	216	WRK 3X	149	587 NCG	139
OKY 54R	154	SN16 OGV	245	XFM 180	90	614 XDE	76
OO 9548	97	SN16 ORS	245	XHW 402	88	617 DDV	223
OTT 56	95	SN16 ORU	246	XHW 411	91	635 SDE	69
OWT 787M	98 / 126	SNG 763	92	XHW 418	87	664 WDE	77
P384 YHT	215	SPK 116M	125	XUD 367	230	702 RDE	67
P771 BJF	222	SPK 119M	125	Y154 EBY	234	734 PDE	68
P779 WDE	184	SVX 233	64	Y178 CFS	243	7793 NG	114
P901 CTO	220	SWY 334L	116	Y199 JDE	193	804 SHW	115 /117
PDE 570M	98	SX02 WDS	235	Y201 JDE	193	804 SHW	222
PRE 735	72	T142 RDE	189	Y252 XHH	234	817 FKH	132
PVO 624	75 / 135	T143 RDE	188	Y619 GFM	233	817 FKH	204
PVO 624	162	T430 KAG	221	Y619 GFM	252	842 SUO	112
R50 TGM	232	UDE 111	51 / 66	Y733 OBE	194	928 AHY	103
R114 SBD	240	URR 349	79	YBX 608V	117	9195 PU	163 /164
R414 VCC	204	UTB 550	62	YC51 HAO	208	9195 PU	184

Silcox Coaches

Registered Name: Silcox Motor Coach Co. Ltd.
Registered in England 678372
VAT Reg. No. 122 4914 93

LWS/SMC/ljk/98074

Our ref:

Your ref:

Mr

Head Office: Waterloo Garage
Pembroke Dock
Pembrokeshire
SA72 4RR
Tel: (01646) 683143
Fax: (01646) 621787

Also at: Town Wall Arcade
Tenby
Pembrokeshire
SA70 7JE
Tel: (01834) 842189

1 April 1998

Dear Mr

I was interested to read your letter regarding the bus and coach bodies which were built in our own workshops between 1947 and 1956.

It all started in late 1947 when we were being quoted two to three years delivery on new buses and coaches. At the time we had six Bristol 5LG's with Strachan Body Builders for bodying although their delivery dates were reasonable we decided we could not wait for further bodies. The first chassis we managed to buy was a new Crossley and I designed the body myself and did all the drawings. Having not long left University with an Engineering Degree it was not too difficult. although quite time consuming.

At the time we had some good craftsmen who had been employed in the local ship building industry which was slimming down. The bodies were built in our own workshops at Pembroke Dock and we continued to build bodies for about seven years including two double decks which were specially designed to go under a low bridge near Penally. These were only 12 feet 10 inches high.

We bought in seats and window units ready made otherwise everything was done in our own workshops. The Crossley did not last long mainly due to engine problems, but the others especially the Bristols did very well.

We gave up building our own bodies when we bought out Morrisons of Tenby and my father decided to semi-retire. This reduced the time I had to upgrade designs. In any case by this time body builders were now quoting much more reasonable delivery dates.

I hope you will find this information interesting and if you want to phone me for more information I still drift in to the office most mornings to keep my hand in.

Yours sincerely,
SILCOX MOTOR COACH CO LTD

L. W. Silcox

Directors
L.W.Silcox B.Sc.(Eng)   Mrs D.E.Miller   K.W.Silcox B.Sc, M.B.A., F.I.M.I.   Mrs R.Silcox   D.W.Silcox B.A.
Chairman and Managing Director   Secretary

Above: This letter written and signed by Leonard William Silcox confirms the fact that he designed and built his own bus and coach bodies with the assistance of his very skillfull staff. See pages 25-40.